THE IN-BETWEEN
VOLUME 1

Written by SHANE ROESCHLEIN

Art by DEAN KOTZ

Colors by STEFANIA SANTI

Letters by A LARGER WORLD

D1089009

INSIGHT COMICS

FOR BIROU.

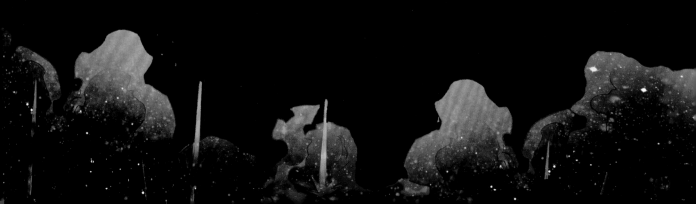

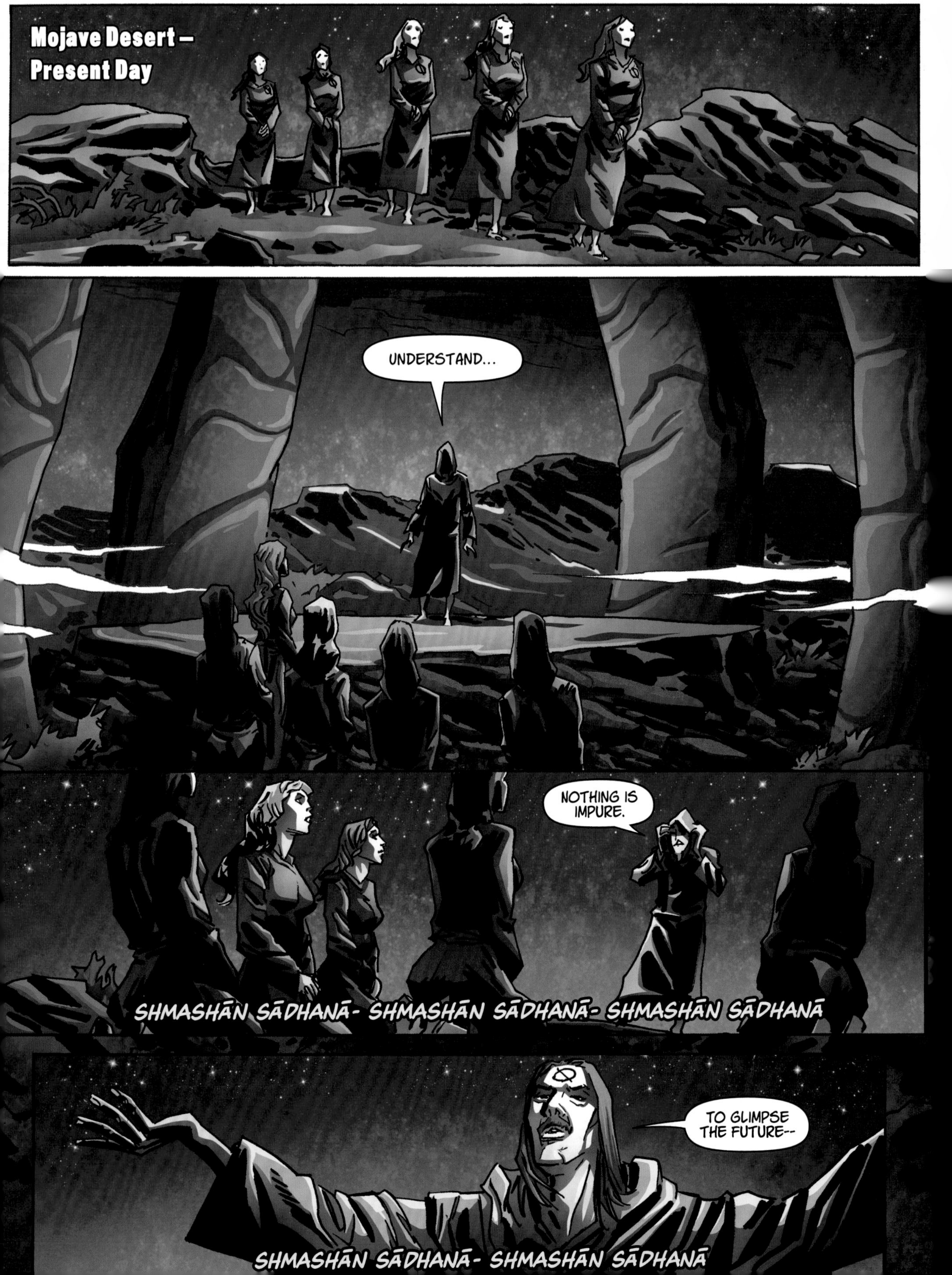
Mojave Desert – Present Day
UNDERSTAND...
NOTHING IS IMPURE.
SHMASHĀN SĀDHANĀ- SHMASHĀN SĀDHANĀ- SHMASHĀN SĀDHANĀ
TO GLIMPSE THE FUTURE--
SHMASHĀN SĀDHANĀ- SHMASHĀN SĀDHANĀ

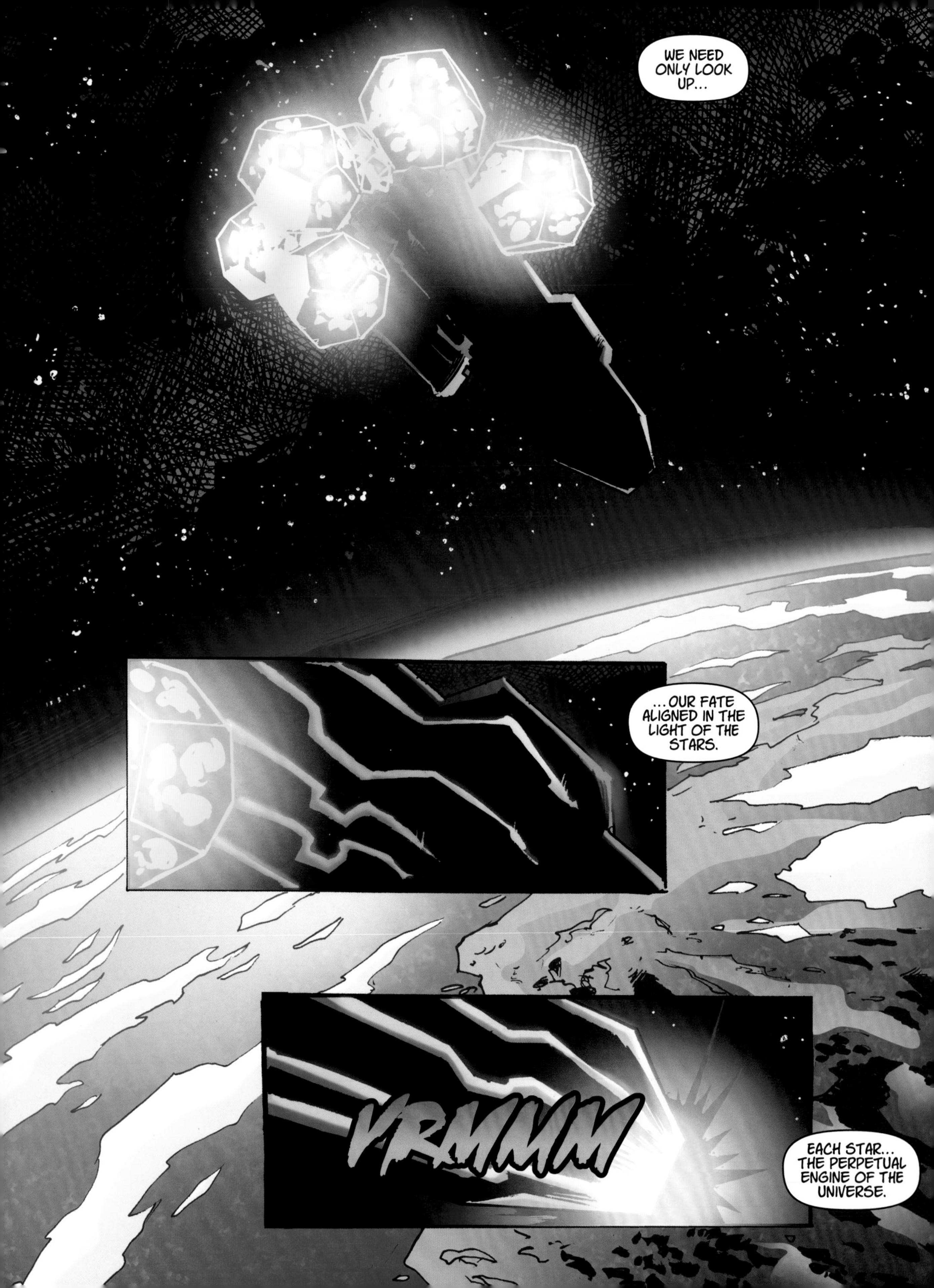
WE NEED ONLY LOOK UP...
...OUR FATE ALIGNED IN THE LIGHT OF THE STARS.
VRMMM
EACH STAR... THE PERPETUAL ENGINE OF THE UNIVERSE.

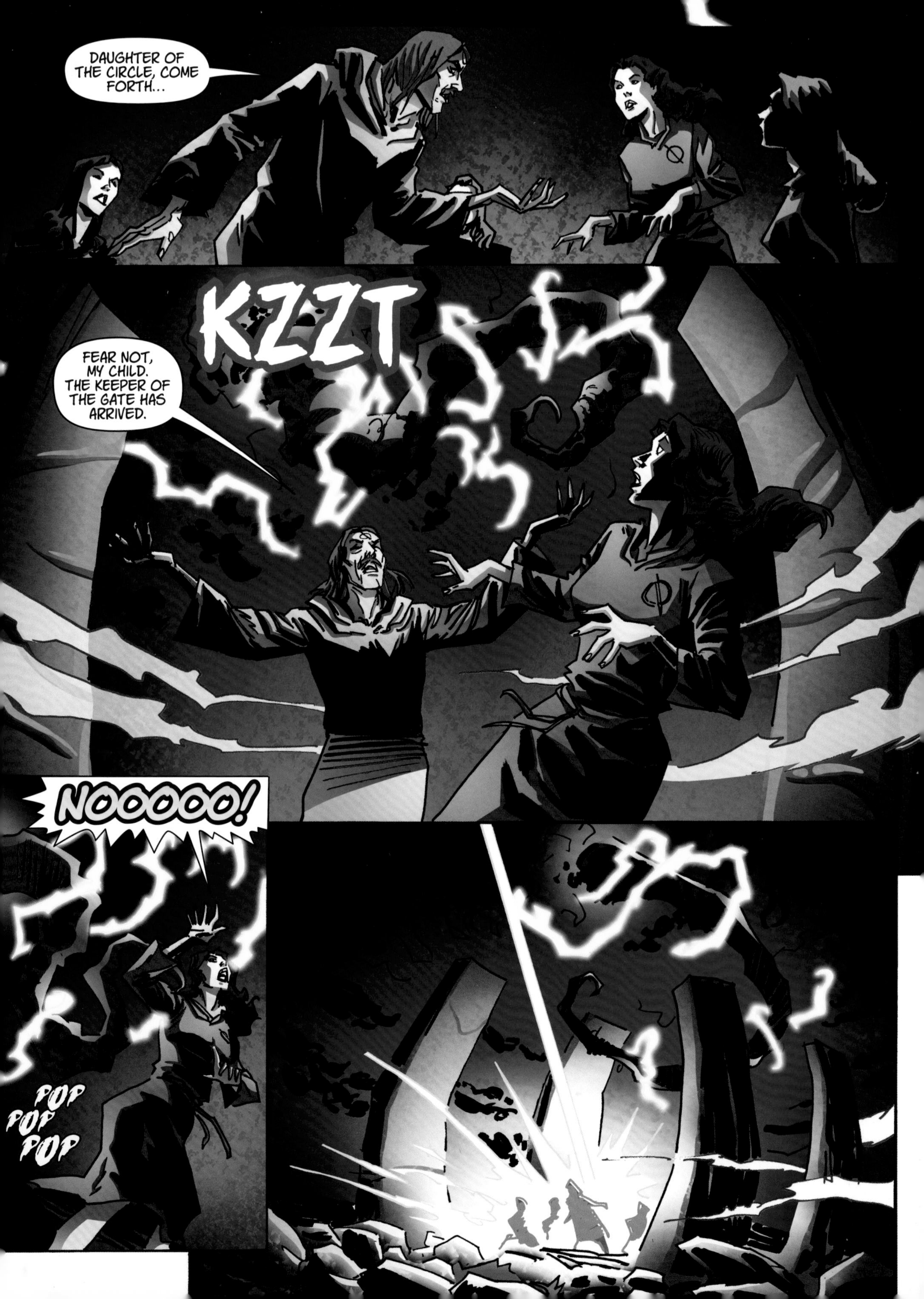
DAUGHTER OF THE CIRCLE, COME FORTH...
KZZT
FEAR NOT, MY CHILD. THE KEEPER OF THE GATE HAS ARRIVED.
NOOOOO!
POP POP POP

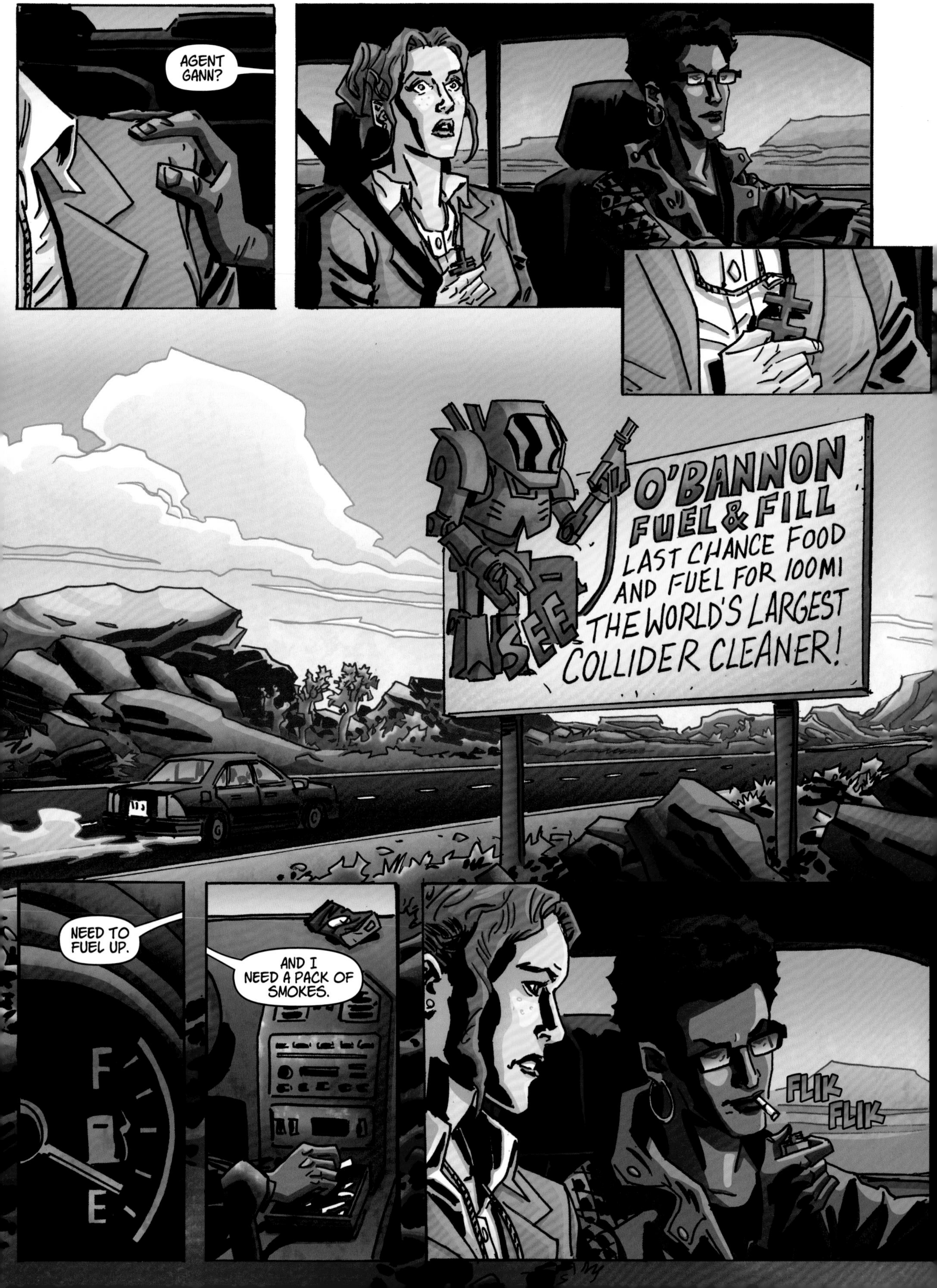
AGENT GANN?
O'BANNON
FUEL & FILL
LAST CHANCE FOOD
AND FUEL FOR 100MI
SEE
THE WORLD'S LARGEST
COLLIDER CLEANER!
NEED TO FUEL UP.
F
E
AND I NEED A PACK OF SMOKES.
FLIK
FLIK

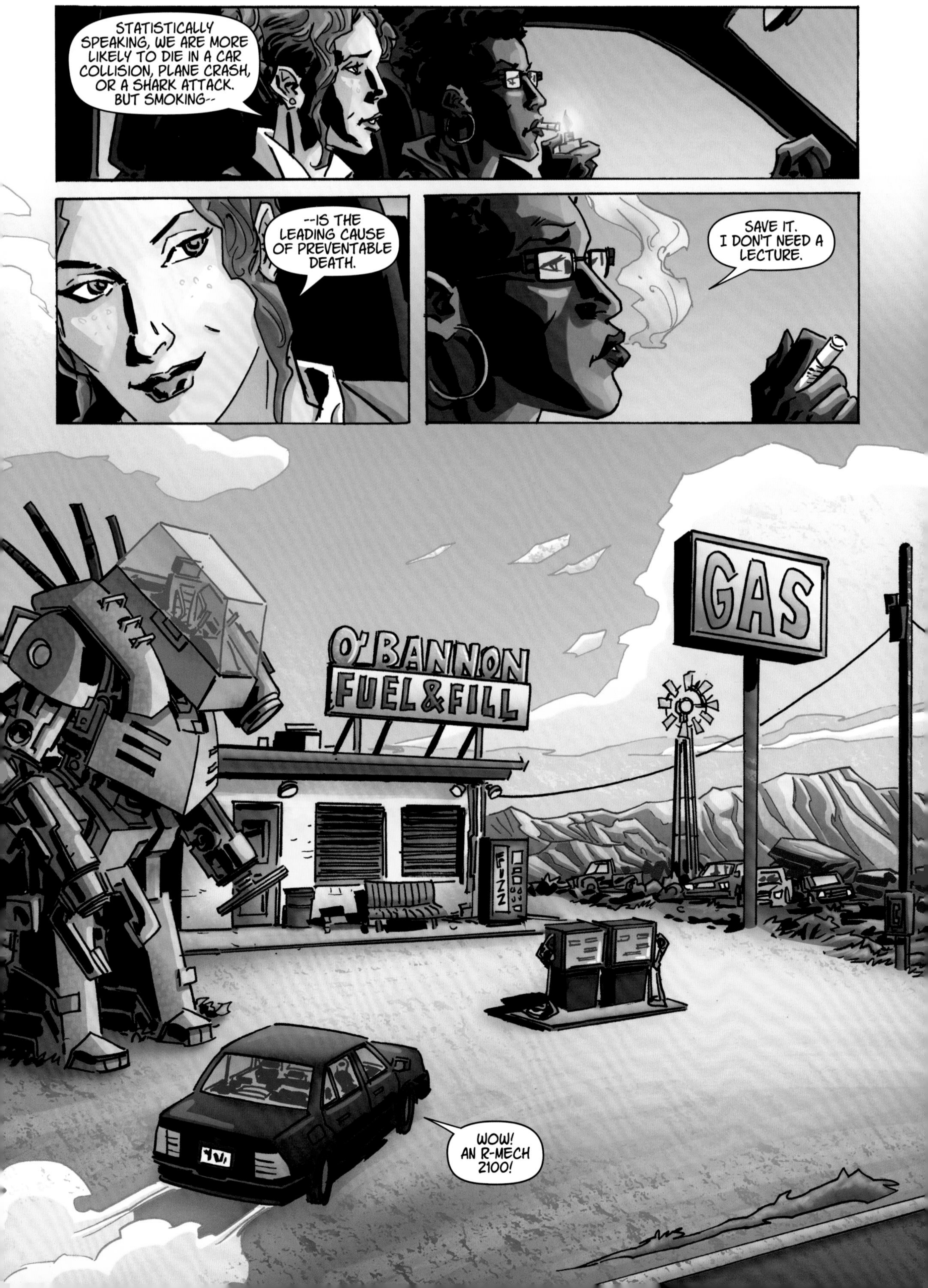
STATISTICALLY SPEAKING, WE ARE MORE LIKELY TO DIE IN A CAR COLLISION, PLANE CRASH, OR A SHARK ATTACK. BUT SMOKING--
--IS THE LEADING CAUSE OF PREVENTABLE DEATH.
SAVE IT. I DON'T NEED A LECTURE.
O'BANNON FUEL&FILL
GAS
FIZZ
WOW! AN R-MECH 2100!

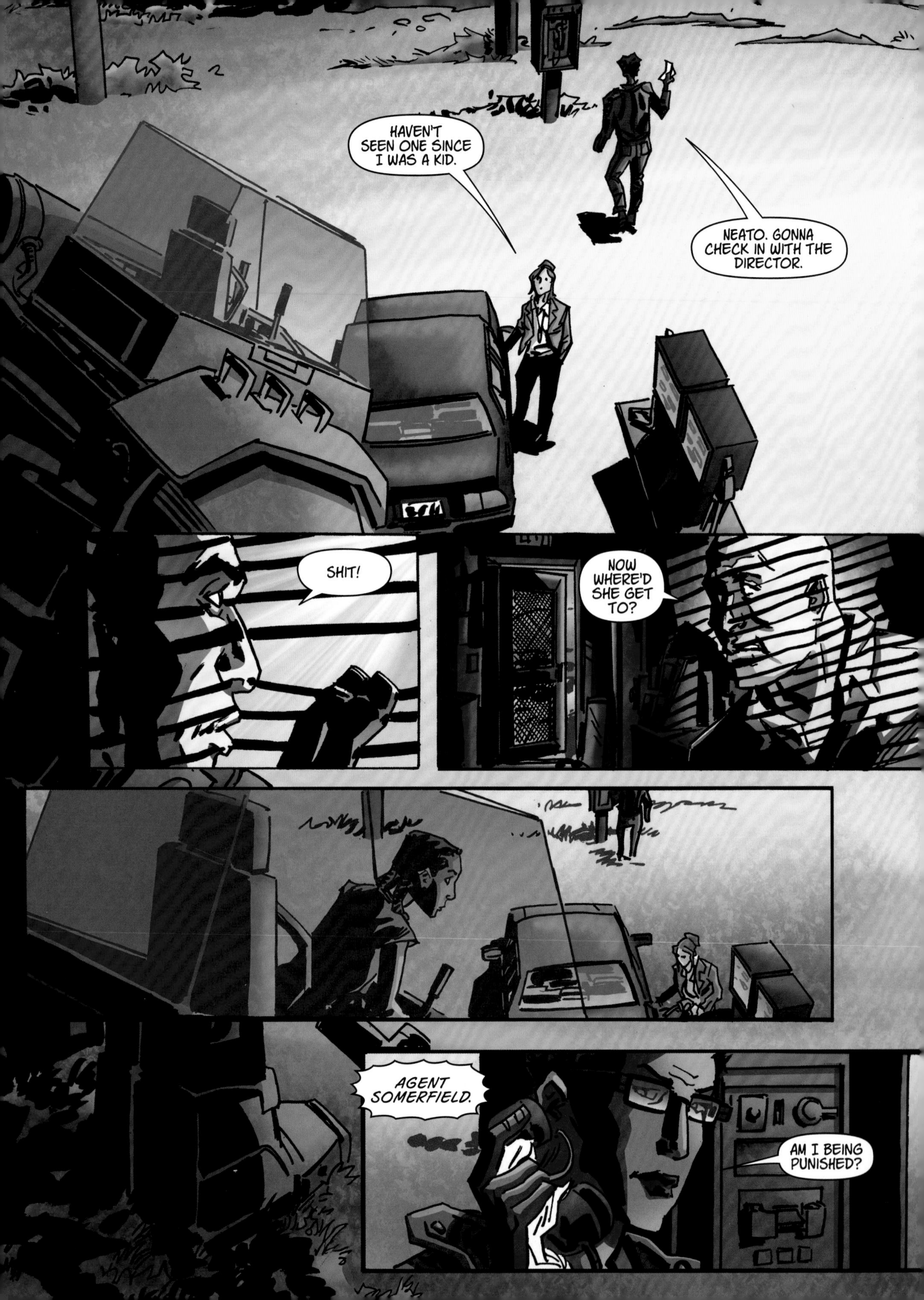
HAVEN'T SEEN ONE SINCE I WAS A KID.
NEATO. GONNA CHECK IN WITH THE DIRECTOR.
SHIT!
NOW WHERE'D SHE GET TO?
AGENT SOMERFIELD.
AM I BEING PUNISHED?

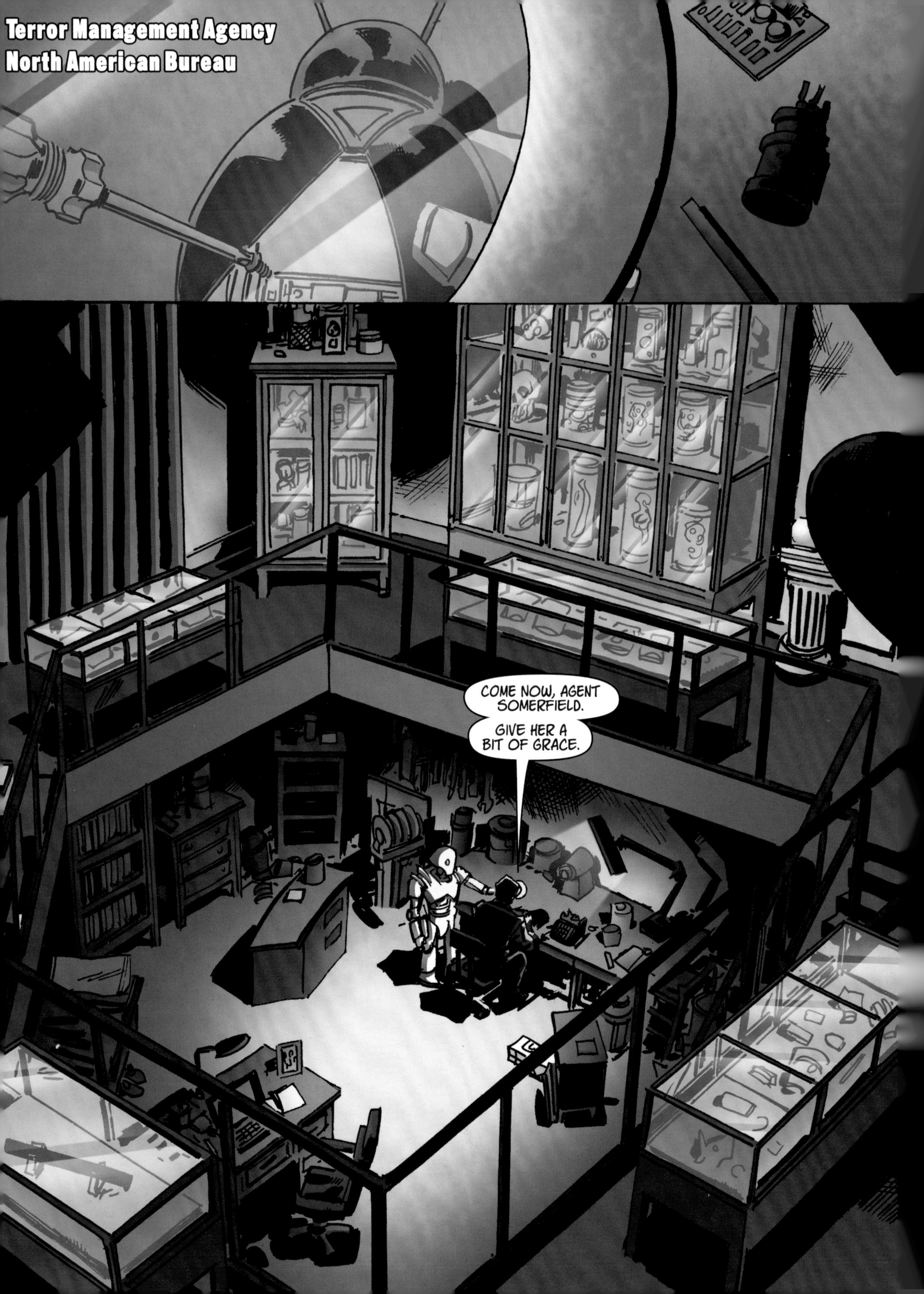
Terror Management Agency
North American Bureau
COME NOW, AGENT SOMERFIELD.
GIVE HER A BIT OF GRACE.

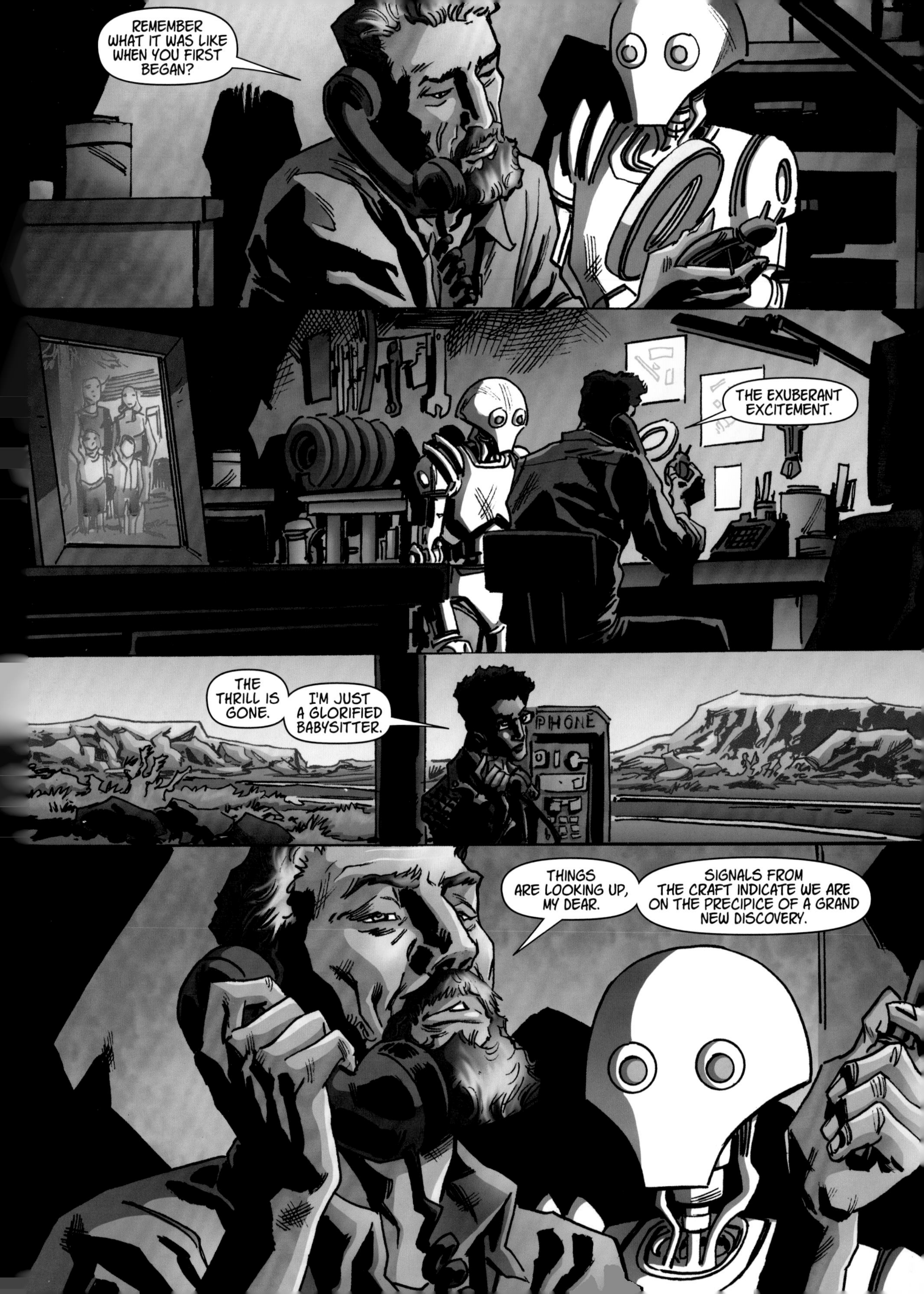
REMEMBER WHAT IT WAS LIKE WHEN YOU FIRST BEGAN?
THE EXUBERANT EXCITEMENT.
THE THRILL IS GONE.
I'M JUST A GLORIFIED BABYSITTER.
PHONE
THINGS ARE LOOKING UP, MY DEAR.
SIGNALS FROM THE CRAFT INDICATE WE ARE ON THE PRECIPICE OF A GRAND NEW DISCOVERY.

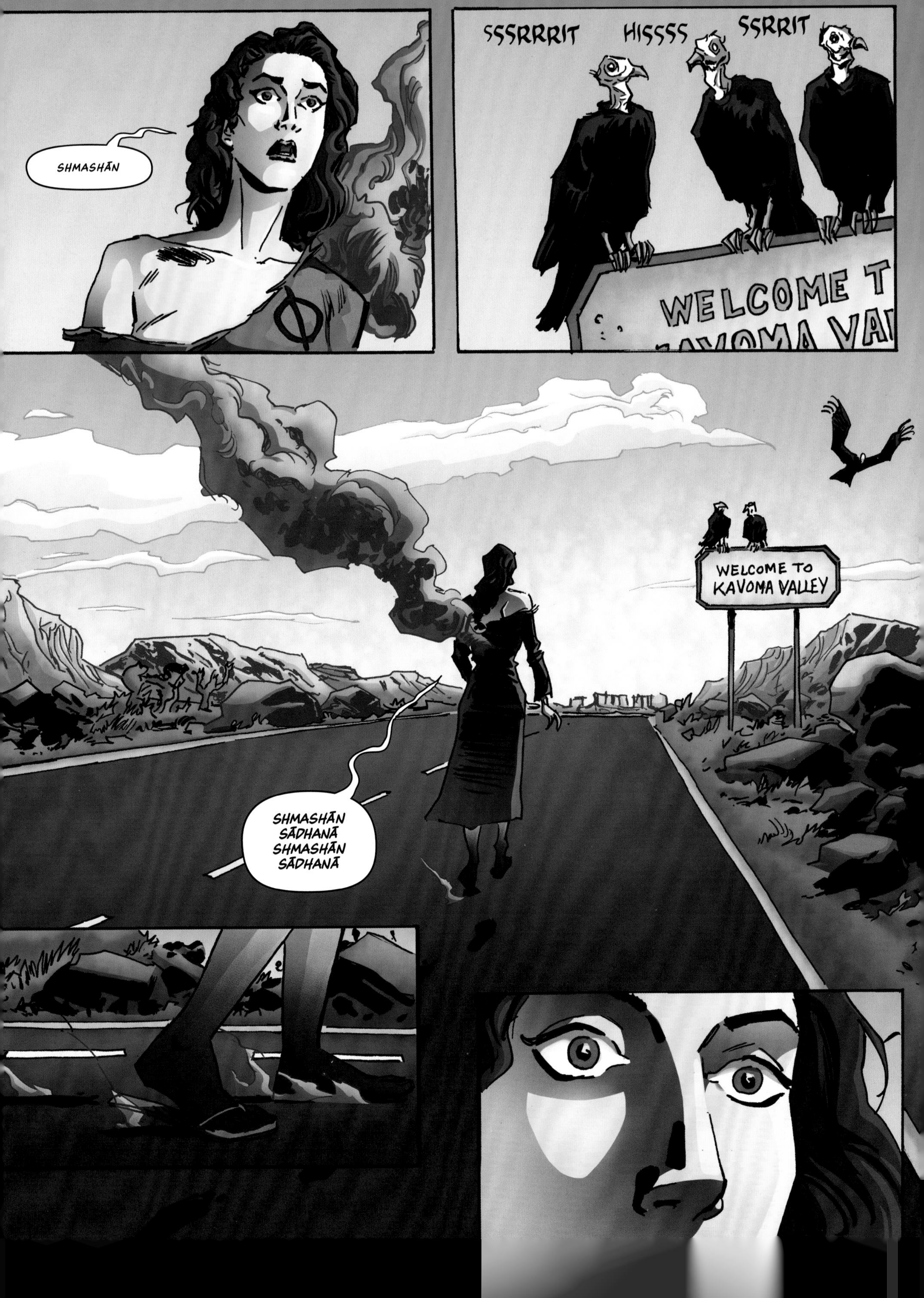
SHMASHĀN
SSSRRRIT
HISSSS
SSRRIT
WELCOME T
WELCOME TO KAVOMA VALLEY
SHMASHĀN SĀDHANĀ SHMASHĀN SĀDHANĀ

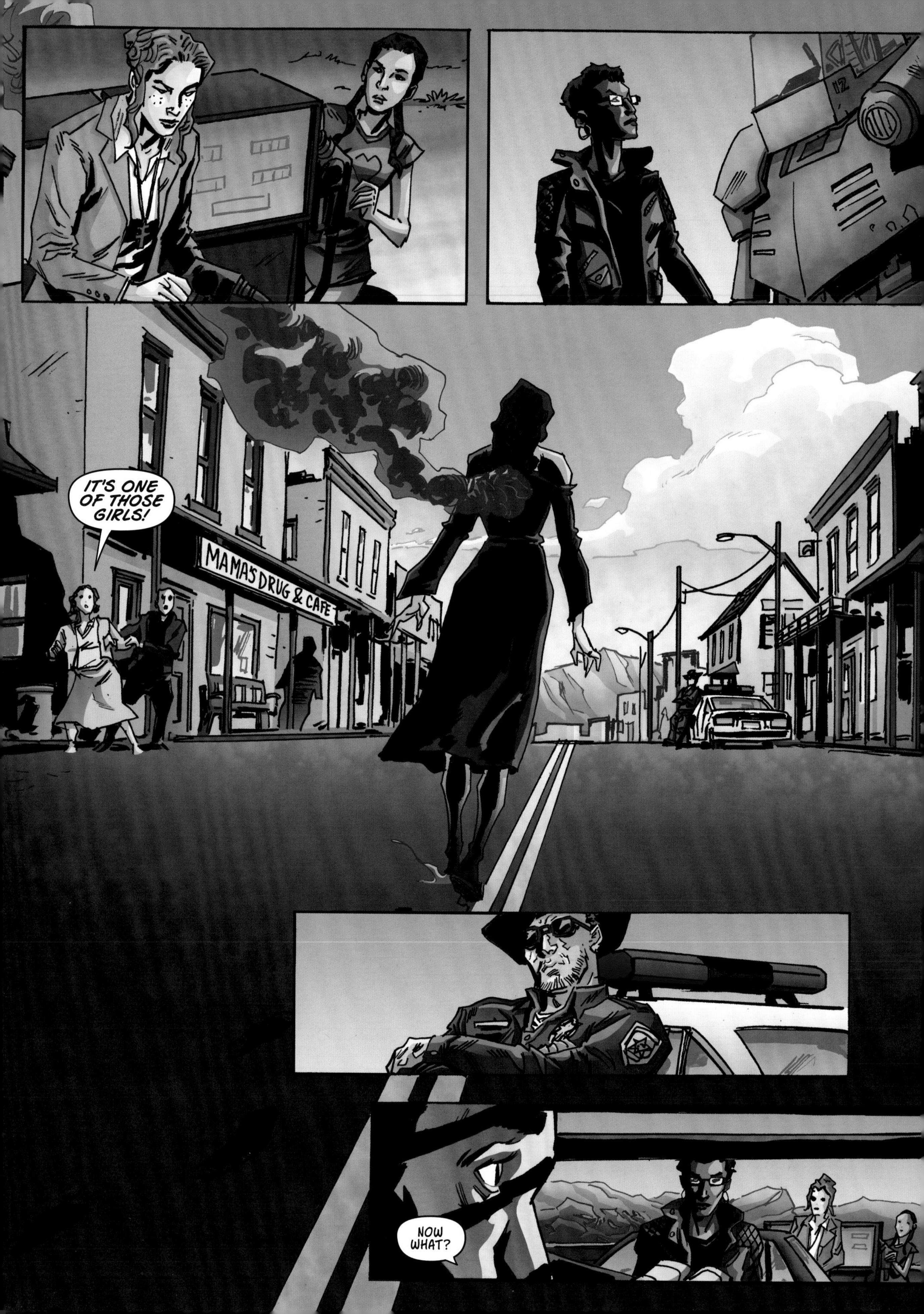
IT'S ONE OF THOSE GIRLS!
MAMA'S DRUG & CAFE
NOW WHAT?

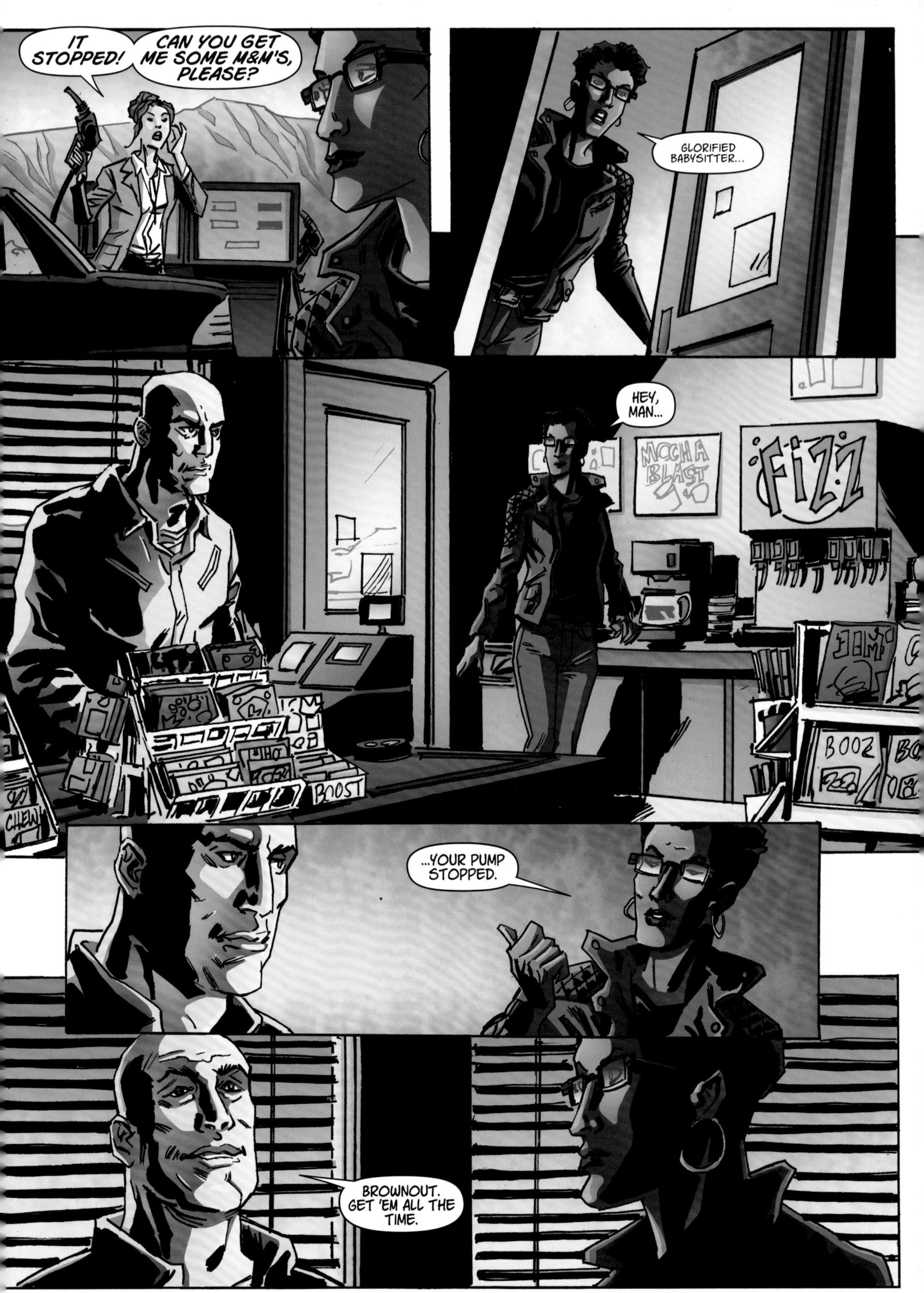
IT STOPPED!
CAN YOU GET ME SOME M&M'S, PLEASE?
GLORIFIED BABYSITTER...
HEY, MAN...
MOCHA BLAST
FIZZ
BOOST
CHEW
BOOZ
...YOUR PUMP STOPPED.
BROWNOUT. GET 'EM ALL THE TIME.

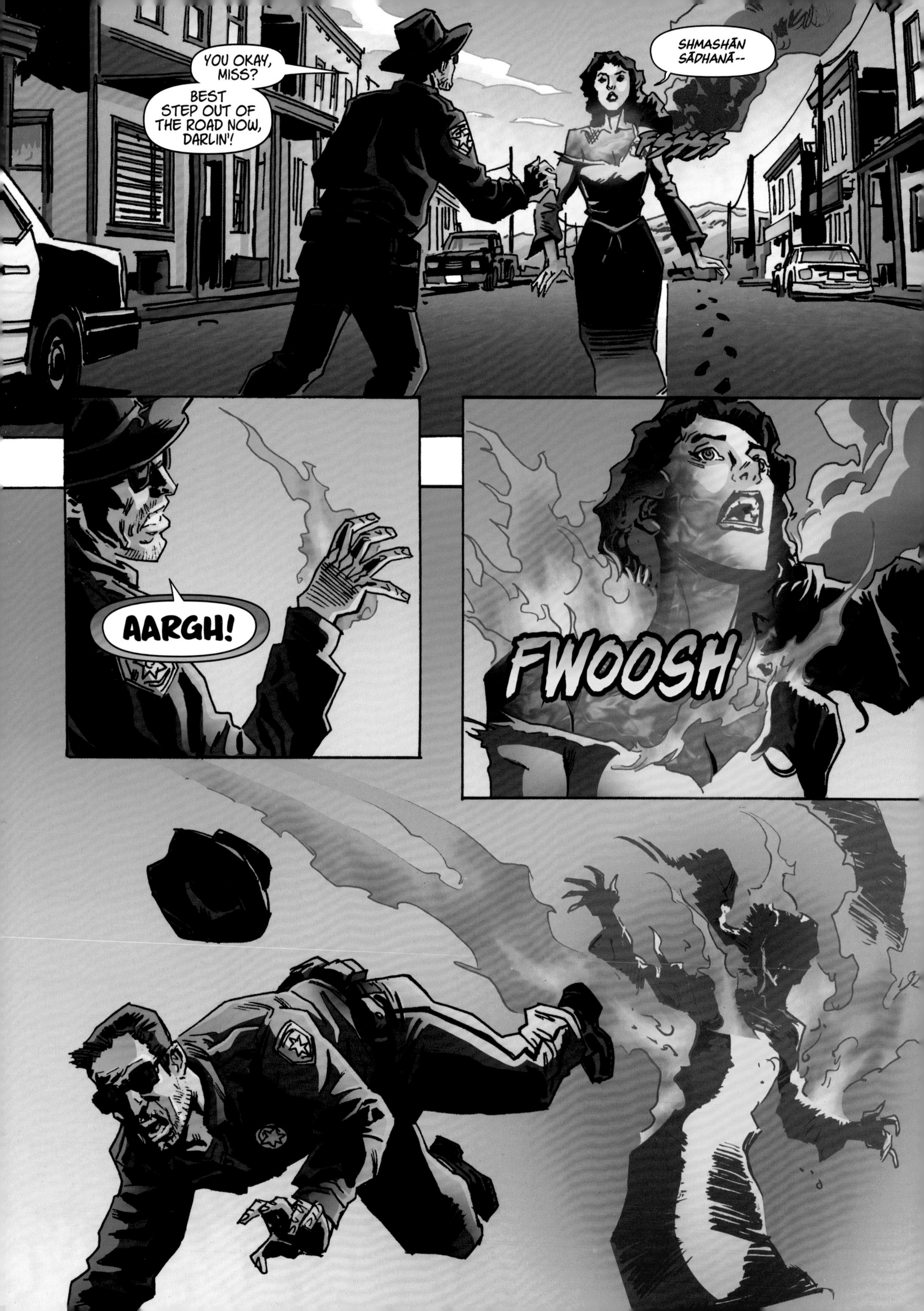
YOU OKAY, MISS?
BEST STEP OUT OF THE ROAD NOW, DARLIN'!
SHMASHĀN SĀDHANĀ--
FSSSS
AARGH!
FWOOSH

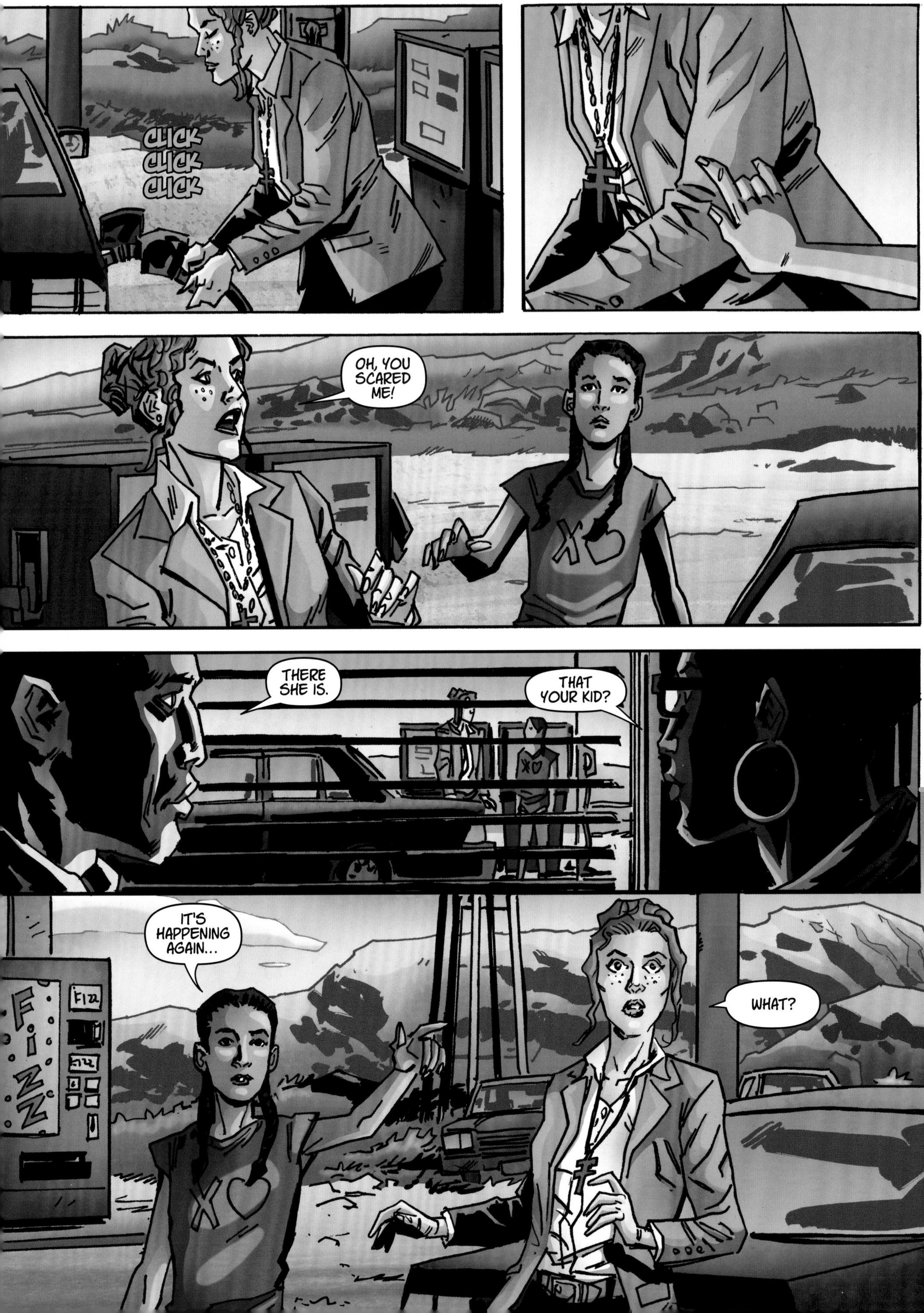
CLICK
CLICK
CLICK
OH, YOU SCARED ME!
THERE SHE IS.
THAT YOUR KID?
IT'S HAPPENING AGAIN...
WHAT?

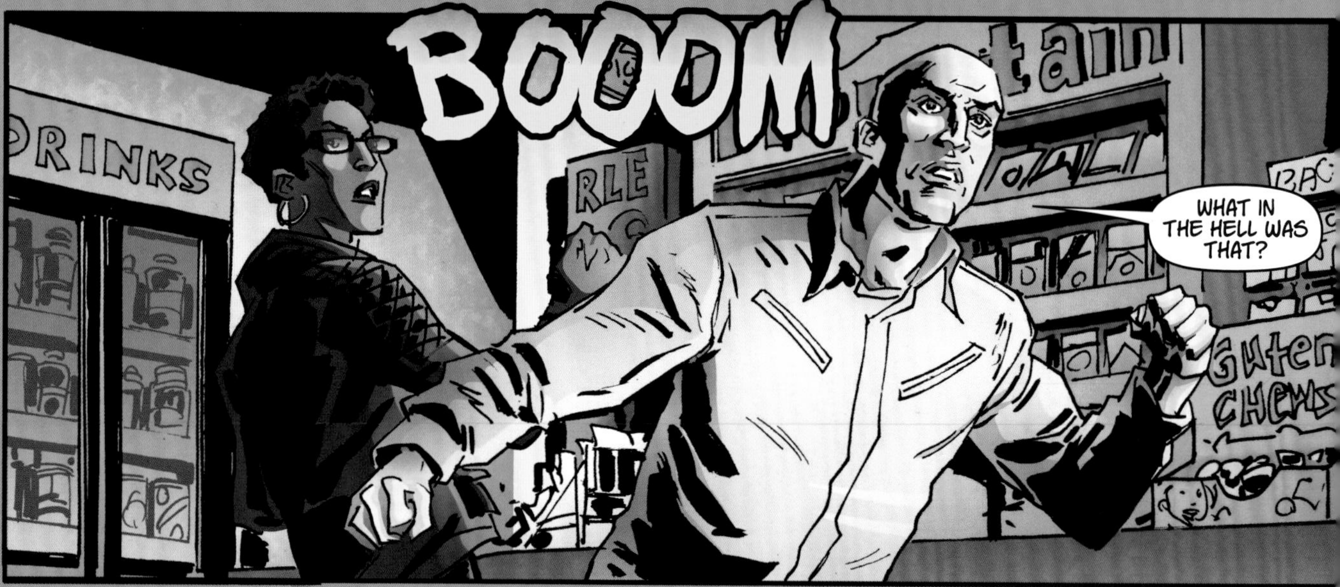
BOOOM
DRINKS
WHAT IN THE HELL WAS THAT?

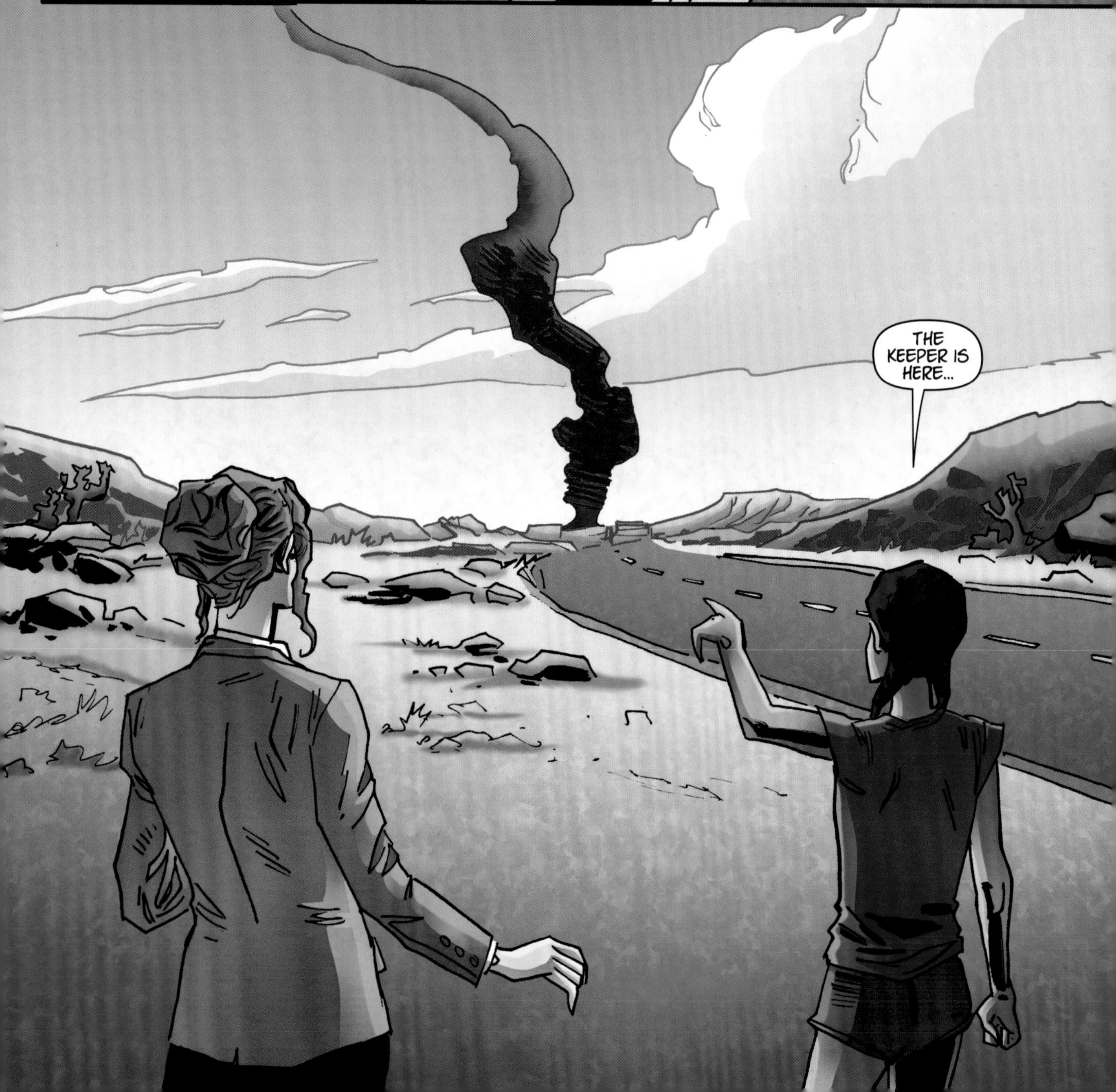
THE KEEPER IS HERE...

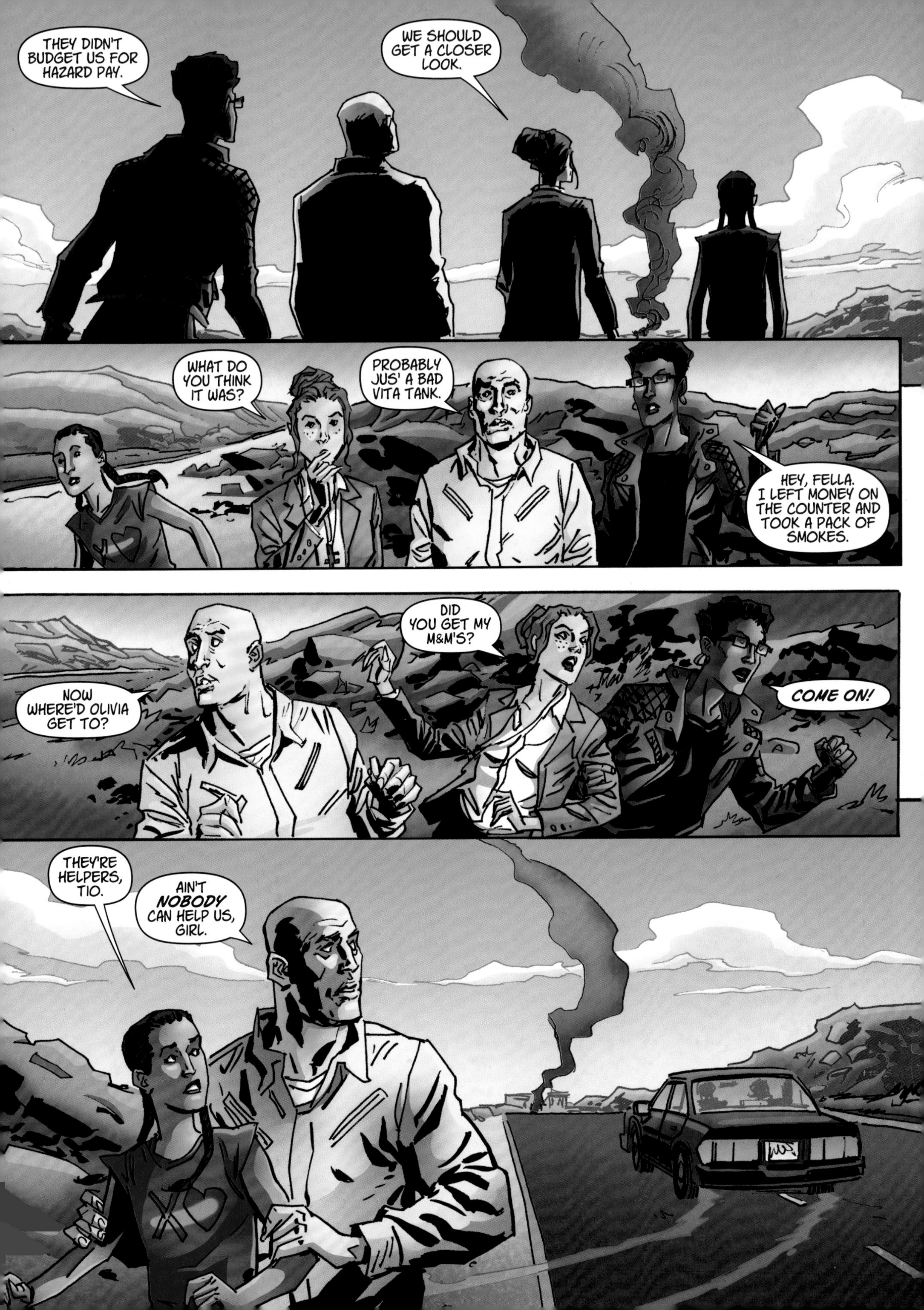
THEY DIDN'T BUDGET US FOR HAZARD PAY.
WE SHOULD GET A CLOSER LOOK.
WHAT DO YOU THINK IT WAS?
PROBABLY JUS' A BAD VITA TANK.
HEY, FELLA. I LEFT MONEY ON THE COUNTER AND TOOK A PACK OF SMOKES.
NOW WHERE'D OLIVIA GET TO?
DID YOU GET MY M&M'S?
COME ON!
THEY'RE HELPERS, TIO.
AIN'T NOBODY CAN HELP US, GIRL.

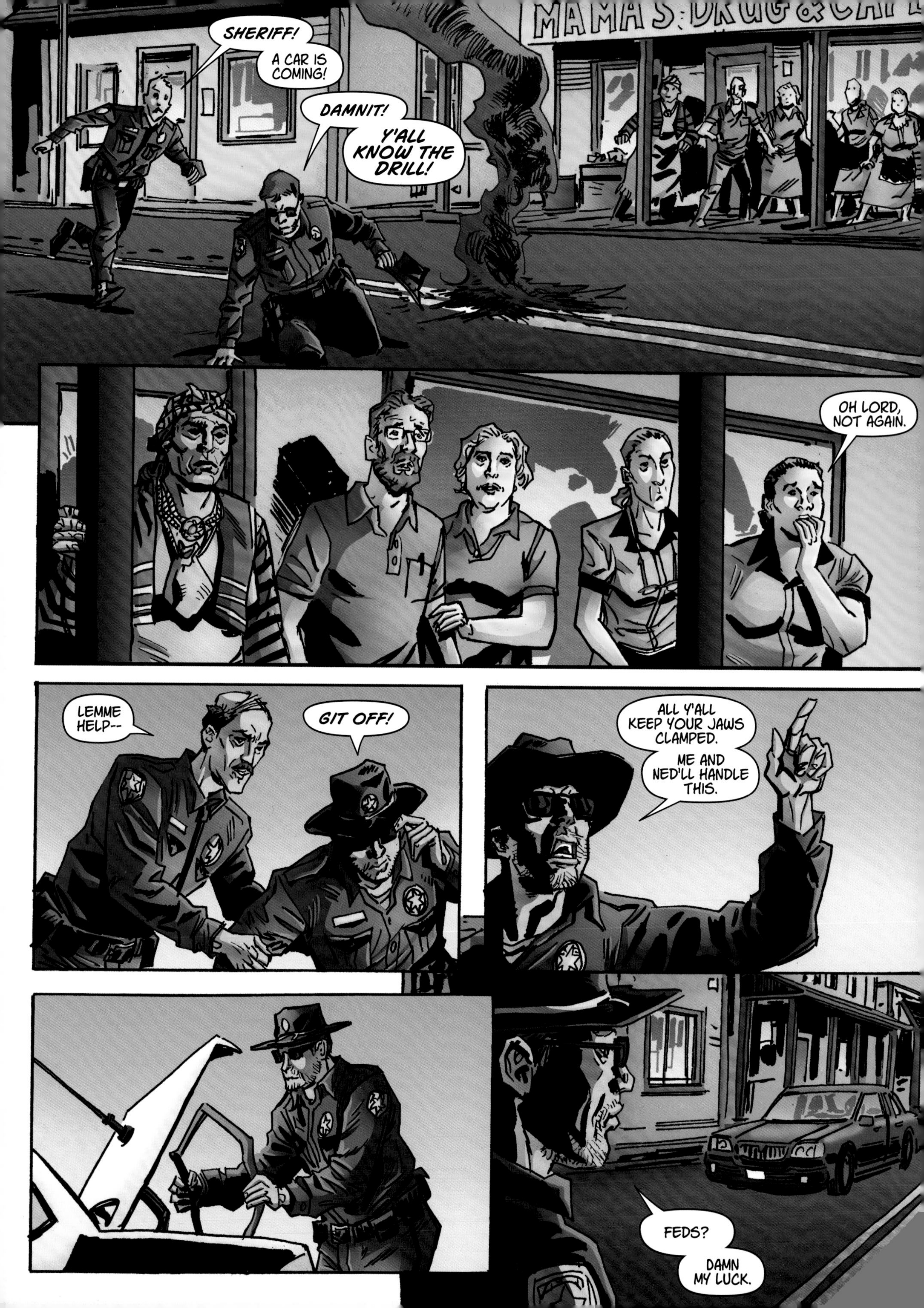
MAMA'S DRUG & CAF
SHERIFF!
A CAR IS COMING!
DAMNIT!
Y'ALL KNOW THE DRILL!
OH LORD, NOT AGAIN.
LEMME HELP--
GIT OFF!
ALL Y'ALL KEEP YOUR JAWS CLAMPED.
ME AND NED'LL HANDLE THIS.
FEDS?
DAMN MY LUCK.

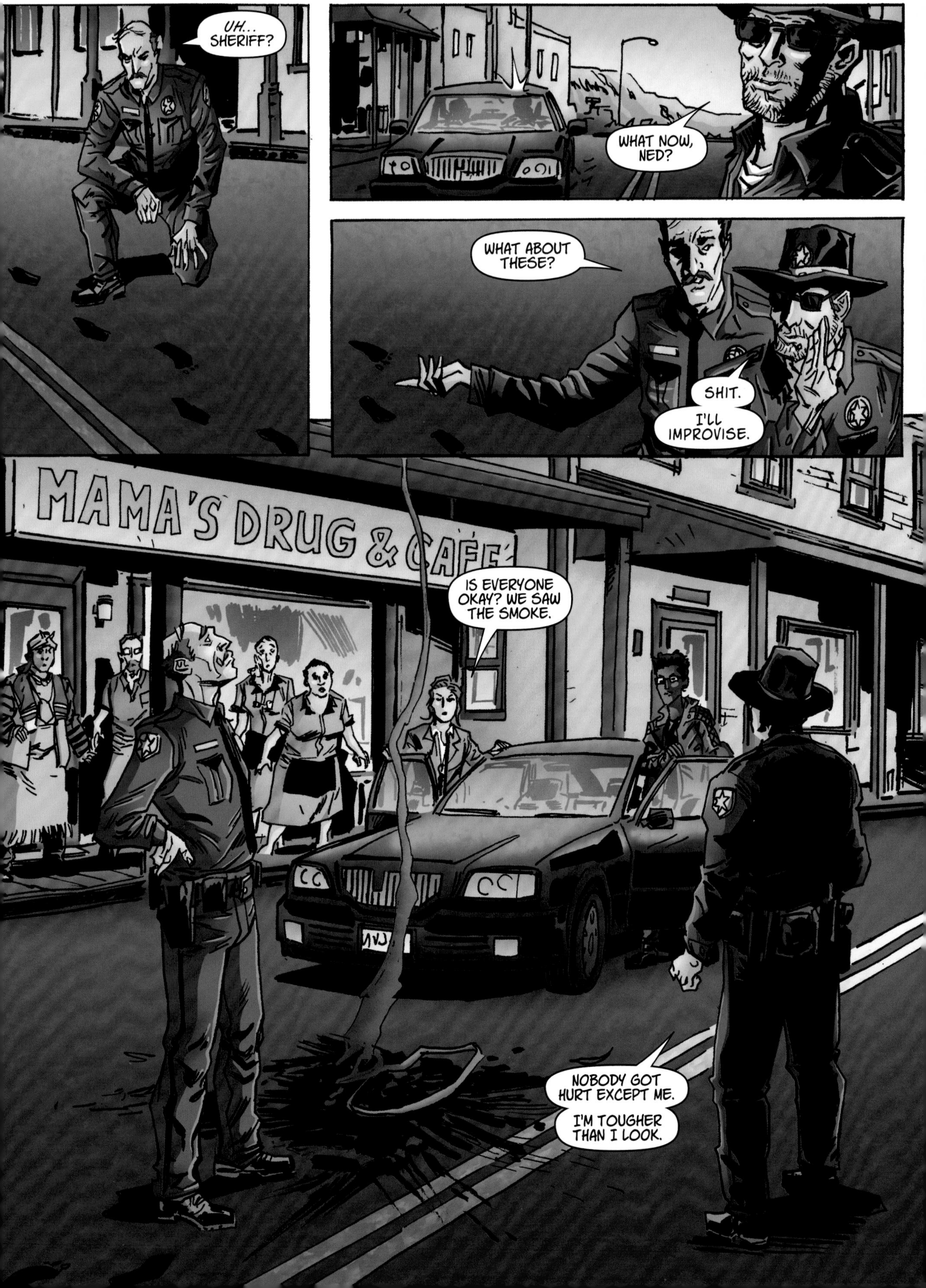
UH... SHERIFF?
WHAT NOW, NED?
WHAT ABOUT THESE?
SHIT.
I'LL IMPROVISE.
MAMA'S DRUG & CAFE
IS EVERYONE OKAY? WE SAW THE SMOKE.
NOBODY GOT HURT EXCEPT ME.
I'M TOUGHER THAN I LOOK.

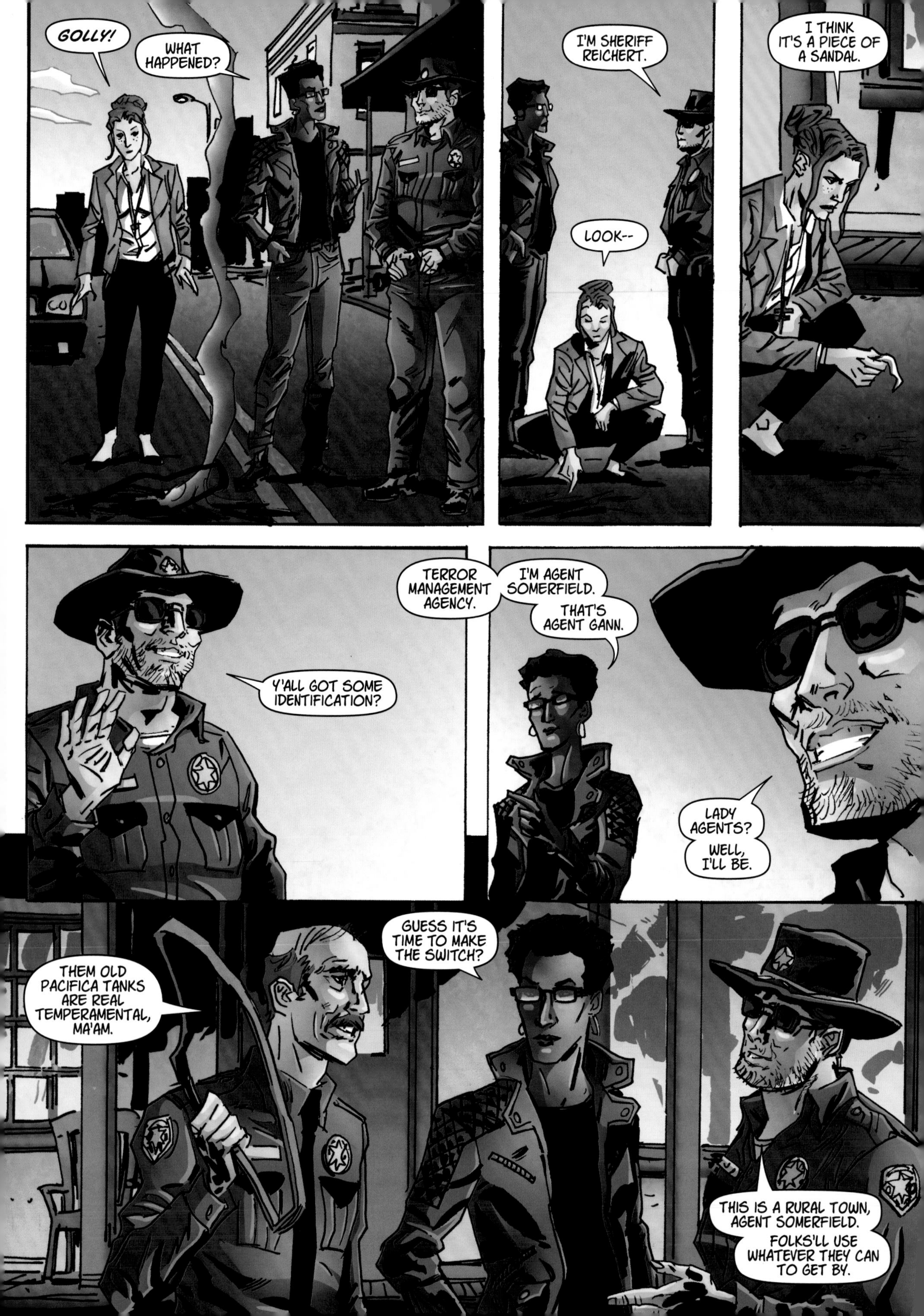
GOLLY!
WHAT HAPPENED?
I'M SHERIFF REICHERT.
LOOK--
I THINK IT'S A PIECE OF A SANDAL.
Y'ALL GOT SOME IDENTIFICATION?
TERROR MANAGEMENT AGENCY.
I'M AGENT SOMERFIELD.
THAT'S AGENT GANN.
LADY AGENTS?
WELL, I'LL BE.
THEM OLD PACIFICA TANKS ARE REAL TEMPERAMENTAL, MA'AM.
GUESS IT'S TIME TO MAKE THE SWITCH?
THIS IS A RURAL TOWN, AGENT SOMERFIELD.
FOLKS'LL USE WHATEVER THEY CAN TO GET BY.

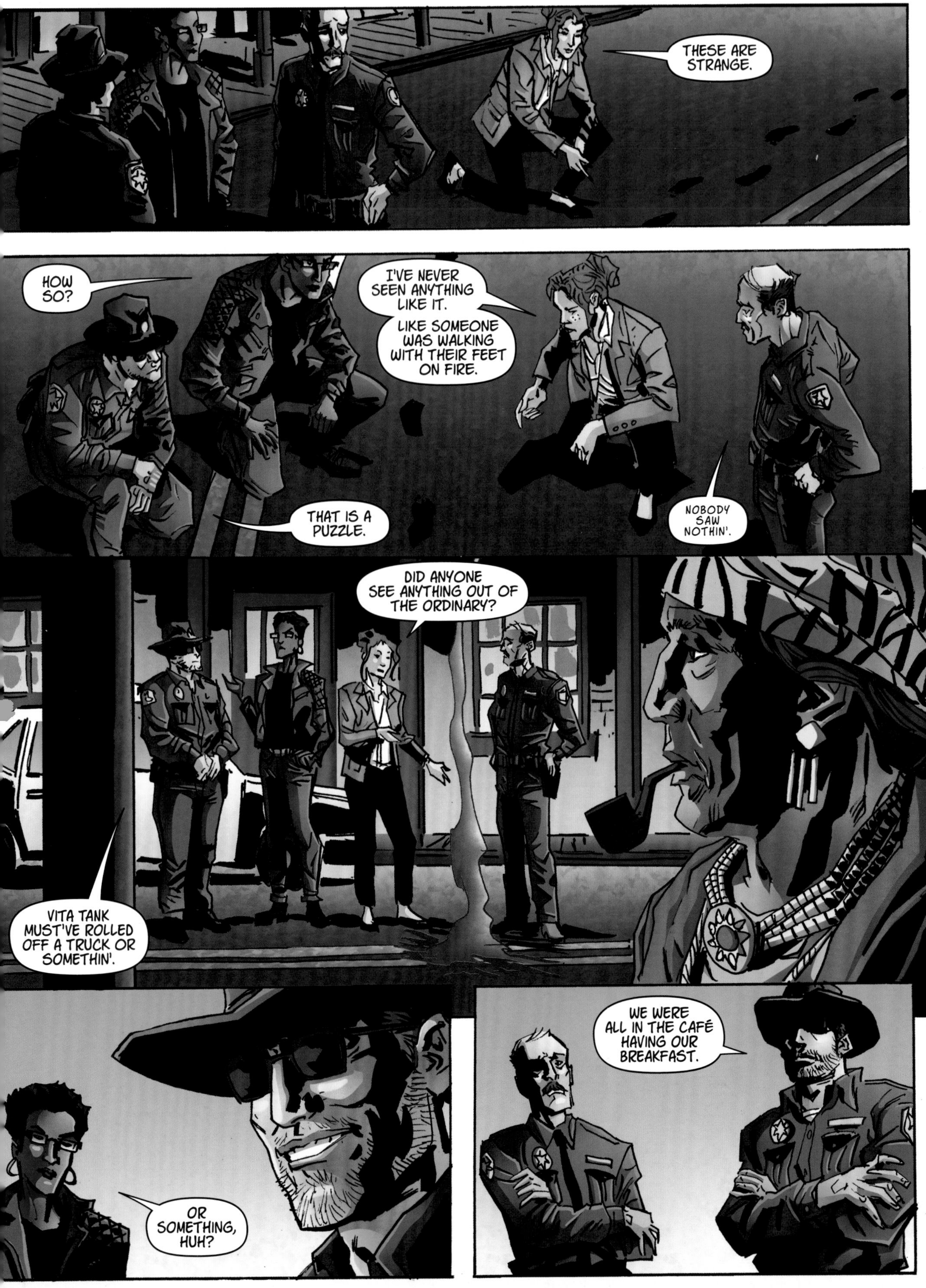
THESE ARE STRANGE.
HOW SO?
I'VE NEVER SEEN ANYTHING LIKE IT.
LIKE SOMEONE WAS WALKING WITH THEIR FEET ON FIRE.
THAT IS A PUZZLE.
NOBODY SAW NOTHIN'.
DID ANYONE SEE ANYTHING OUT OF THE ORDINARY?
VITA TANK MUST'VE ROLLED OFF A TRUCK OR SOMETHIN'.
OR SOMETHING, HUH?
WE WERE ALL IN THE CAFÉ HAVING OUR BREAKFAST.

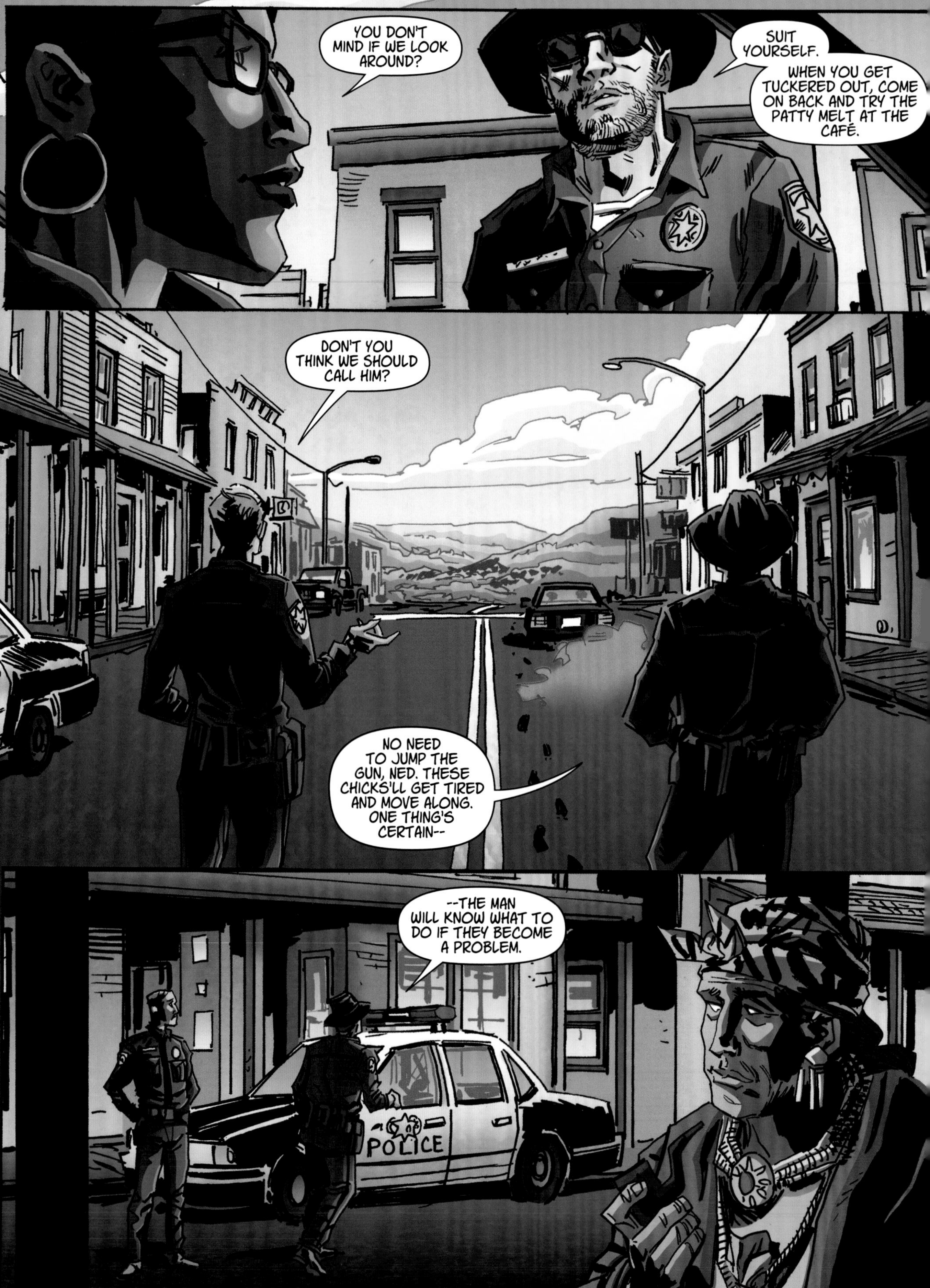
YOU DON'T MIND IF WE LOOK AROUND?
SUIT YOURSELF.
WHEN YOU GET TUCKERED OUT, COME ON BACK AND TRY THE PATTY MELT AT THE CAFÉ.
DON'T YOU THINK WE SHOULD CALL HIM?
NO NEED TO JUMP THE GUN, NED. THESE CHICKS'LL GET TIRED AND MOVE ALONG. ONE THING'S CERTAIN--
--THE MAN WILL KNOW WHAT TO DO IF THEY BECOME A PROBLEM.
POLICE

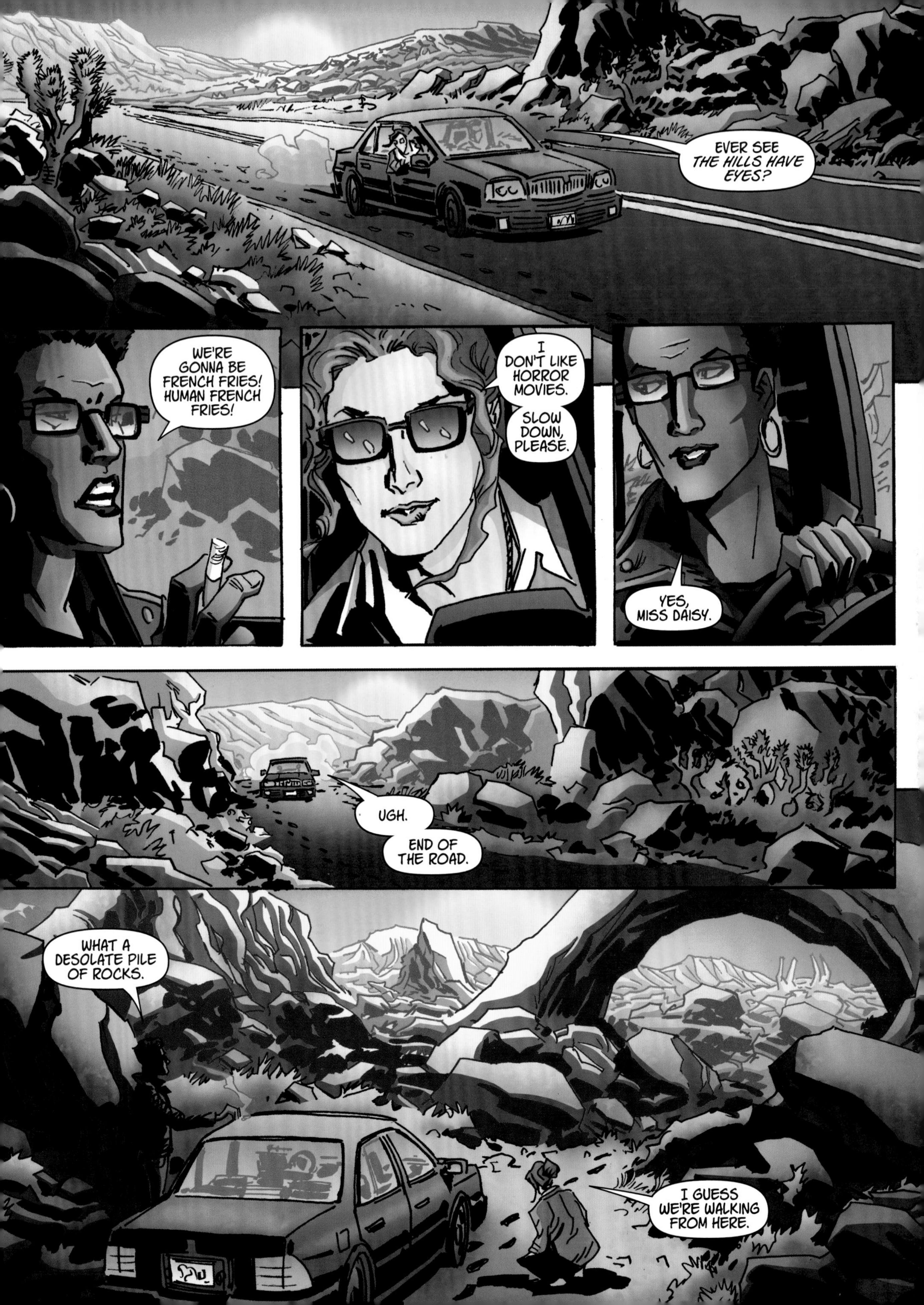
EVER SEE *THE HILLS HAVE EYES?*
WE'RE GONNA BE FRENCH FRIES! HUMAN FRENCH FRIES!
I DON'T LIKE HORROR MOVIES.
SLOW DOWN, PLEASE.
YES, MISS DAISY.
UGH.
END OF THE ROAD.
WHAT A DESOLATE PILE OF ROCKS.
I GUESS WE'RE WALKING FROM HERE.

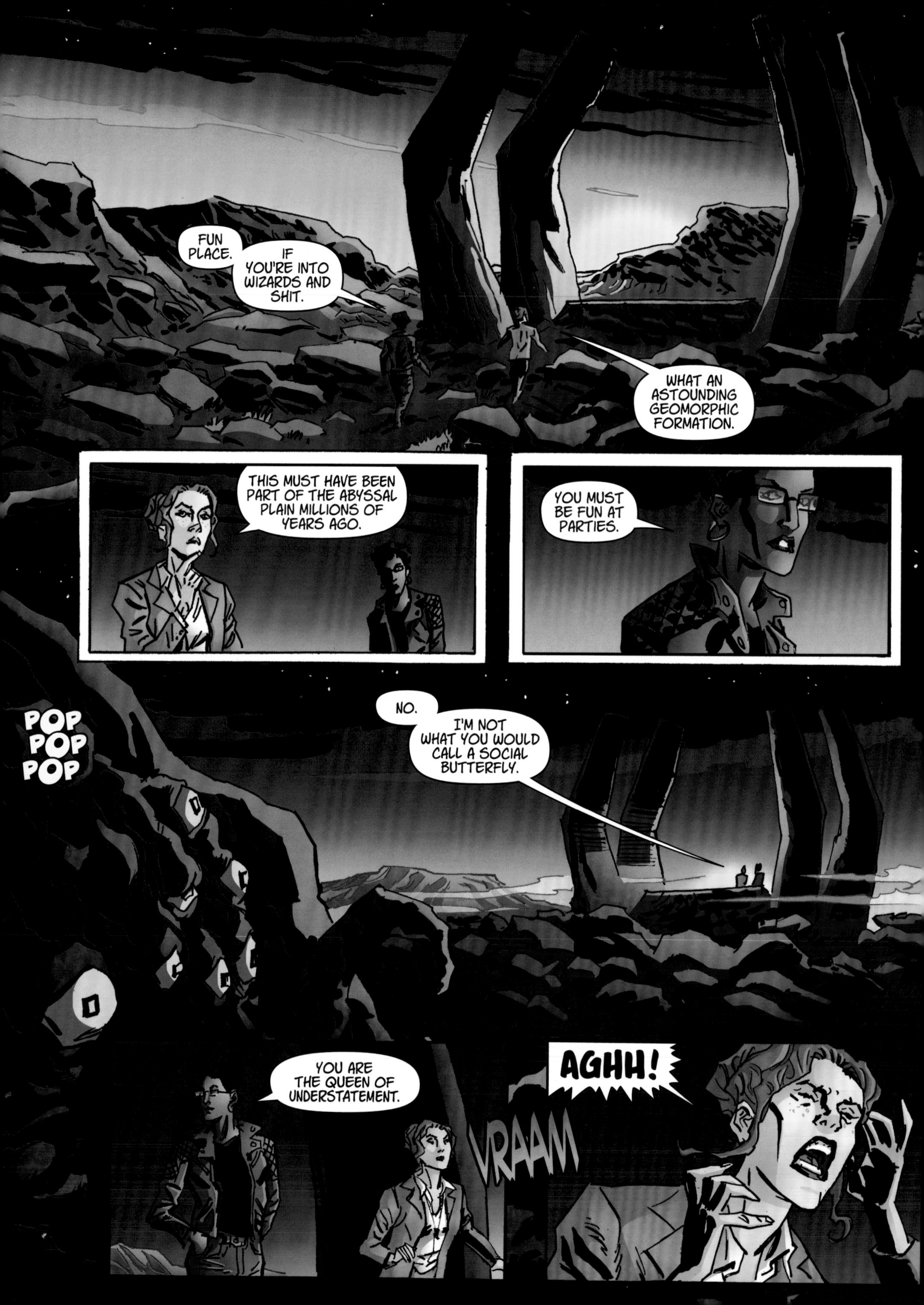
FUN PLACE.
IF YOU'RE INTO WIZARDS AND SHIT.
WHAT AN ASTOUNDING GEOMORPHIC FORMATION.
THIS MUST HAVE BEEN PART OF THE ABYSSAL PLAIN MILLIONS OF YEARS AGO.
YOU MUST BE FUN AT PARTIES.
POP POP POP
NO.
I'M NOT WHAT YOU WOULD CALL A SOCIAL BUTTERFLY.
YOU ARE THE QUEEN OF UNDERSTATEMENT.
VRAAM
AGHH!

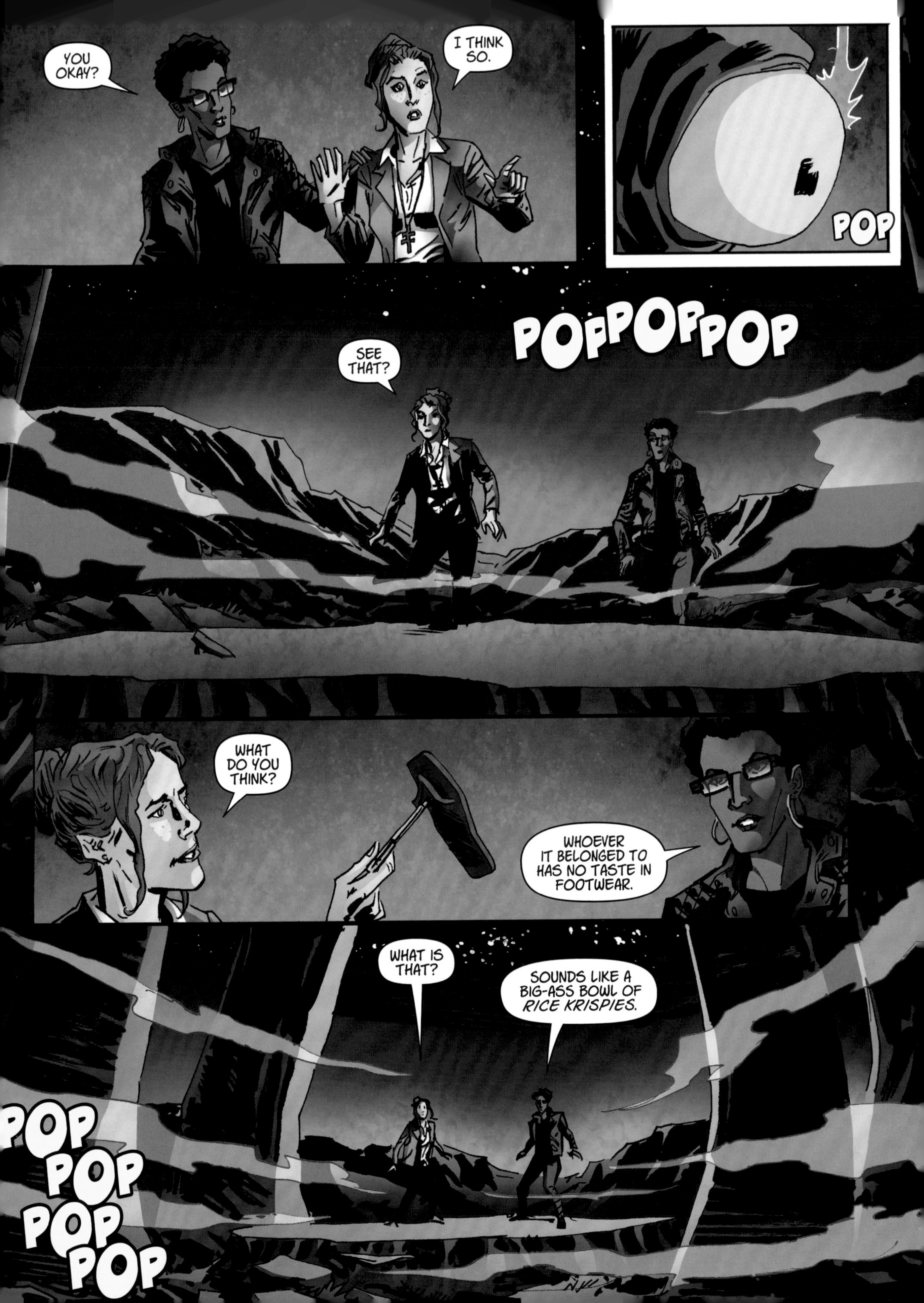
YOU OKAY?
I THINK SO.
POP
POPPOPPOP
SEE THAT?
WHAT DO YOU THINK?
WHOEVER IT BELONGED TO HAS NO TASTE IN FOOTWEAR.
WHAT IS THAT?
SOUNDS LIKE A BIG-ASS BOWL OF *RICE KRISPIES*.
POP POP POP POP

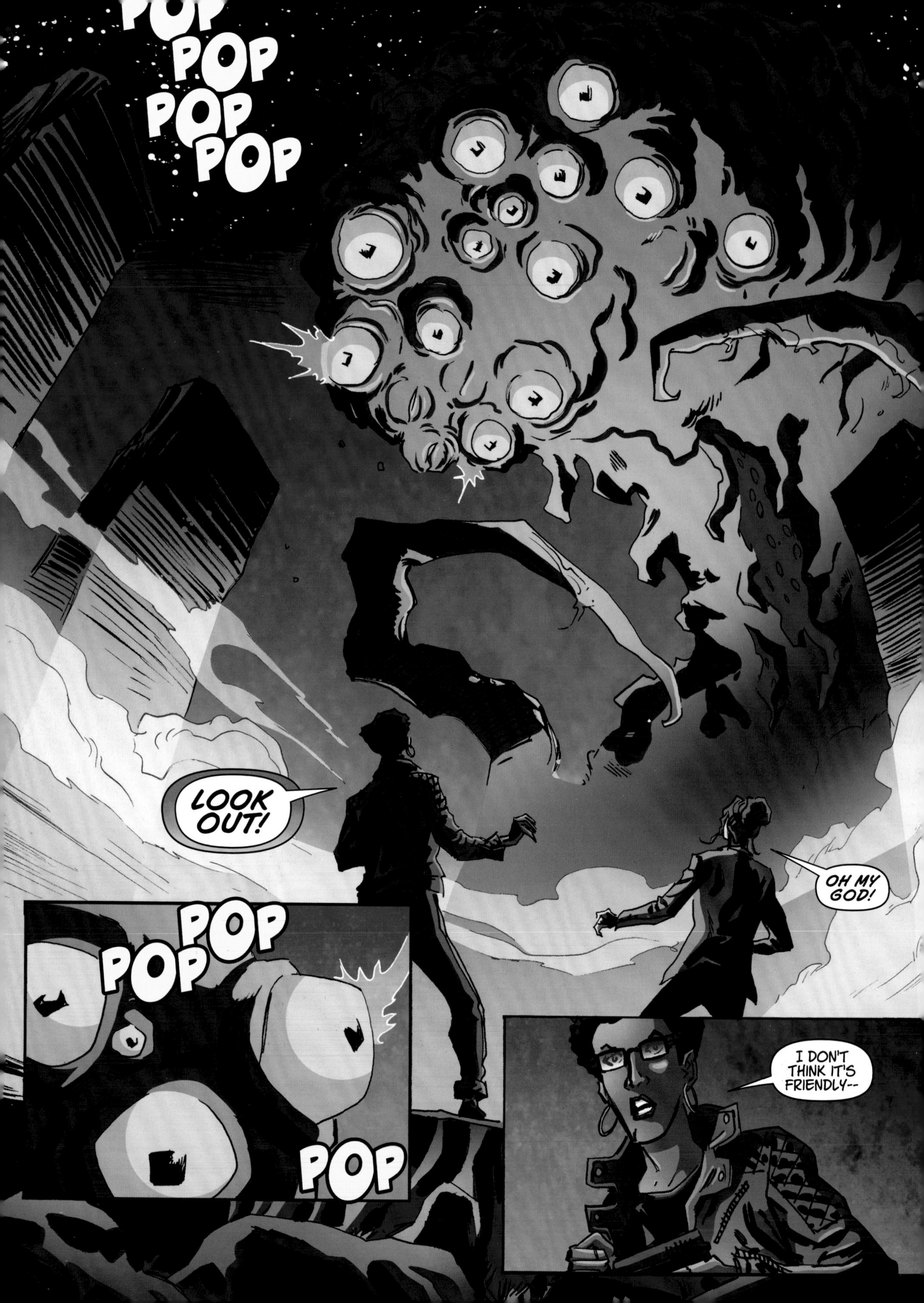
POP
POP
POP
POP
LOOK OUT!
OH MY GOD!
POP POP
POP
I DON'T THINK IT'S FRIENDLY--

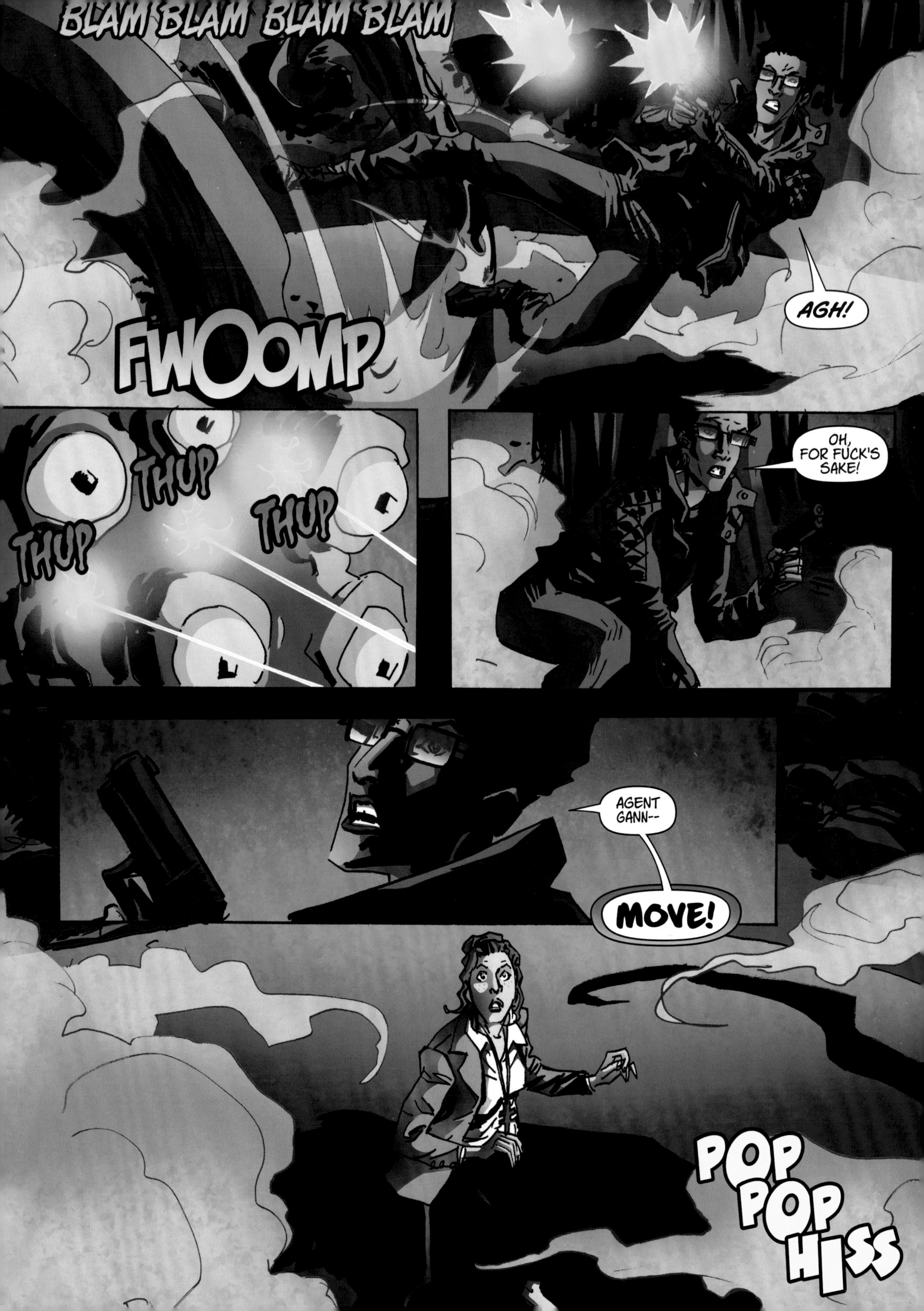
BLAM BLAM BLAM BLAM
AGH!
FWOOMP
THUP
THUP
THUP
OH, FOR FUCK'S SAKE!
AGENT GANN--
MOVE!
POP POP HISS

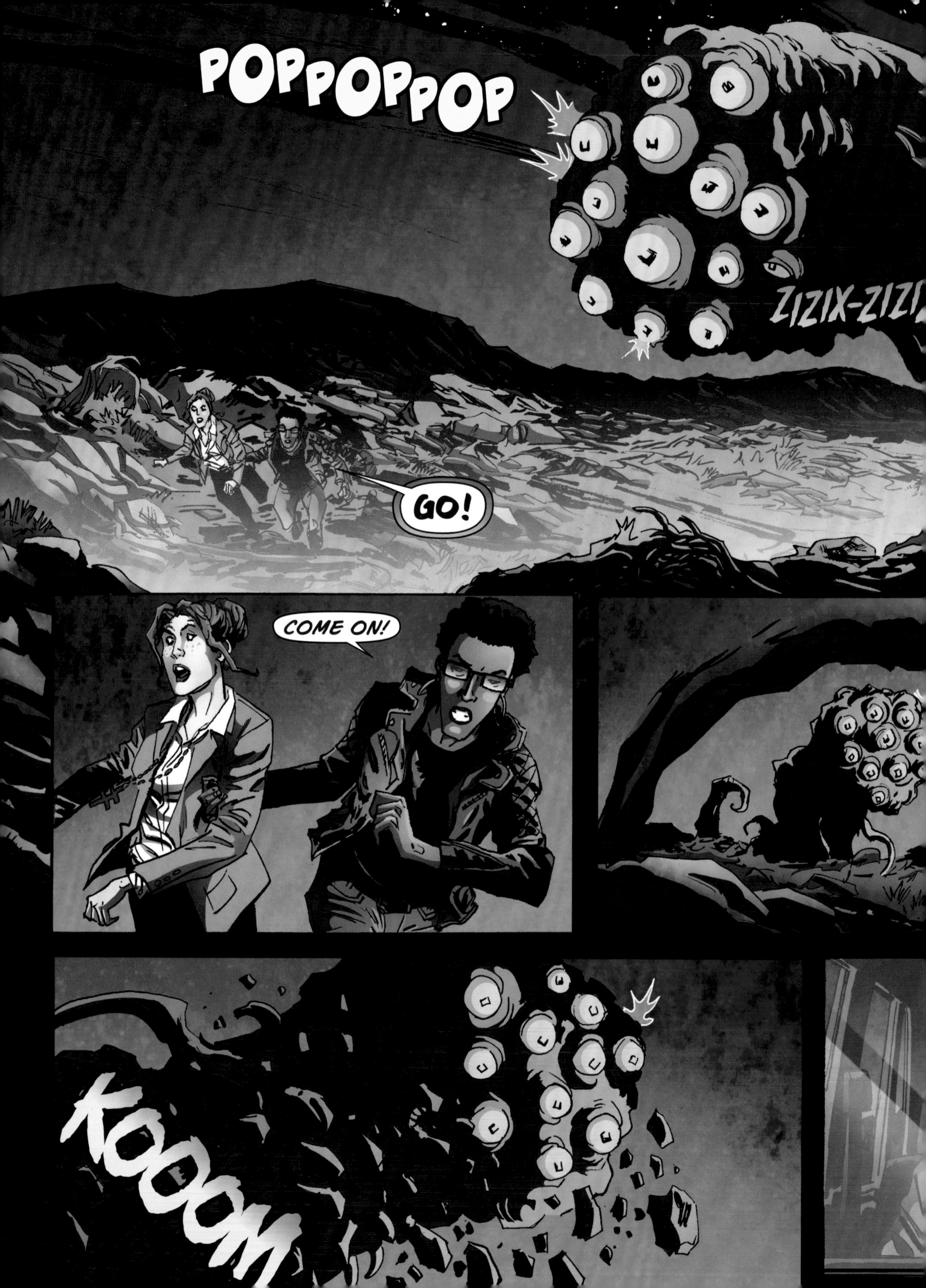
POPPOPPOP
ZIZIX-ZIZI
GO!
COME ON!
KOOOM

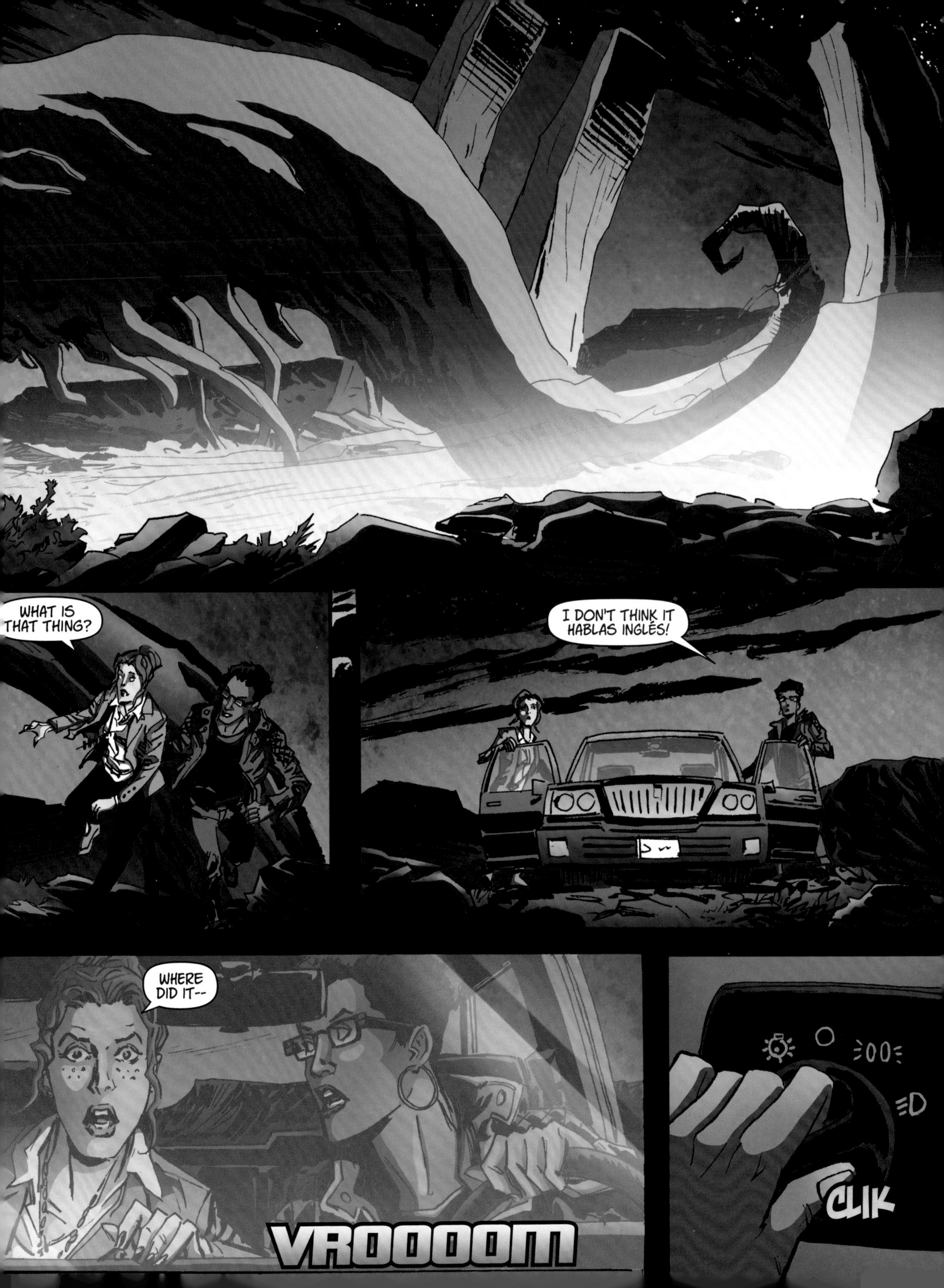
WHAT IS THAT THING?
I DON'T THINK IT HABLAS INGLÉS!
WHERE DID IT--
VROOOOOM
CLIK

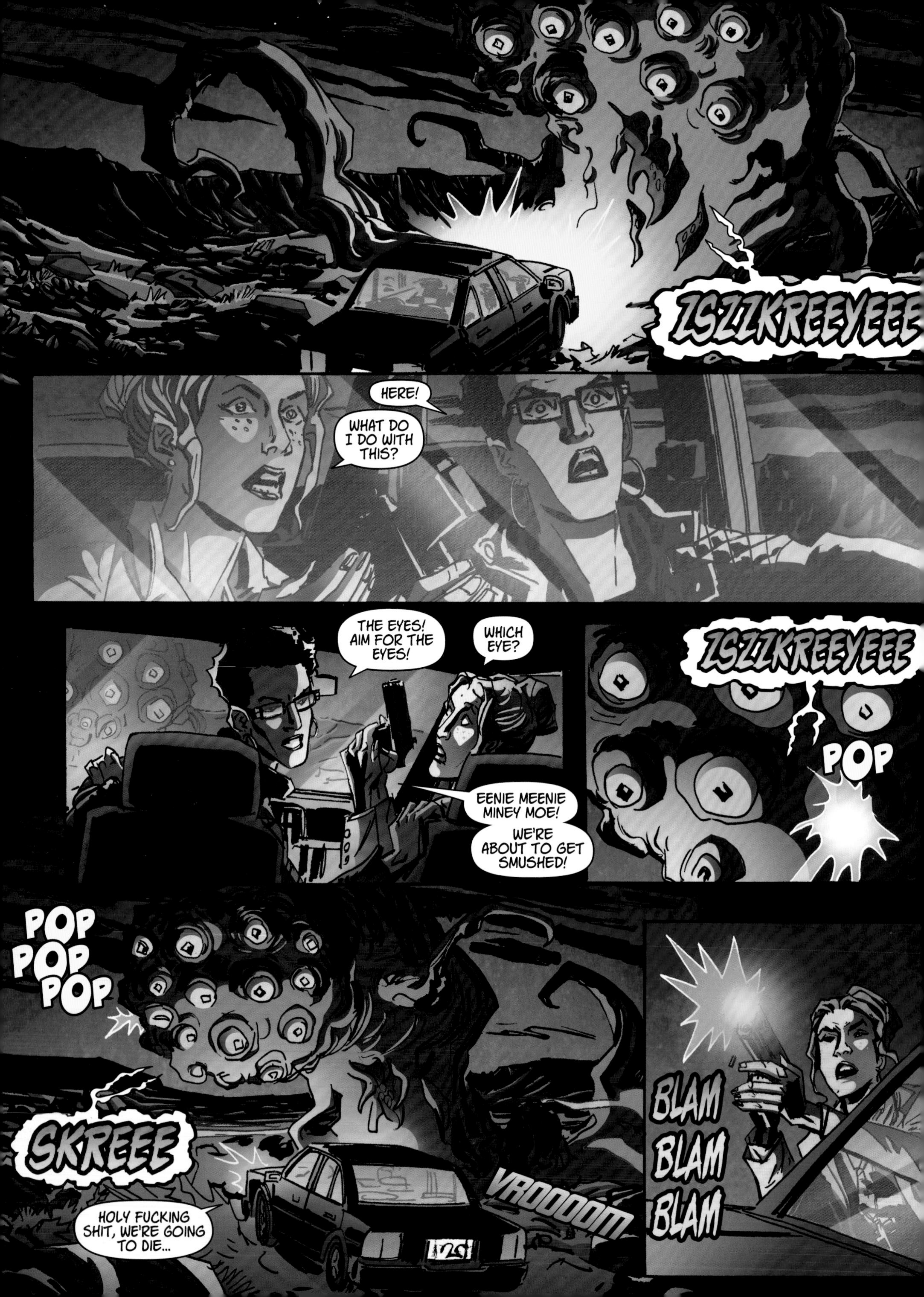
ZSZZKREEYEEE
HERE!
WHAT DO I DO WITH THIS?
THE EYES! AIM FOR THE EYES!
WHICH EYE?
EENIE MEENIE MINEY MOE!
WE'RE ABOUT TO GET SMUSHED!
ZSZZKREEYEEE
POP
POP POP POP
SKREEE
HOLY FUCKING SHIT, WE'RE GOING TO DIE...
VROOOOOM
BLAM BLAM BLAM

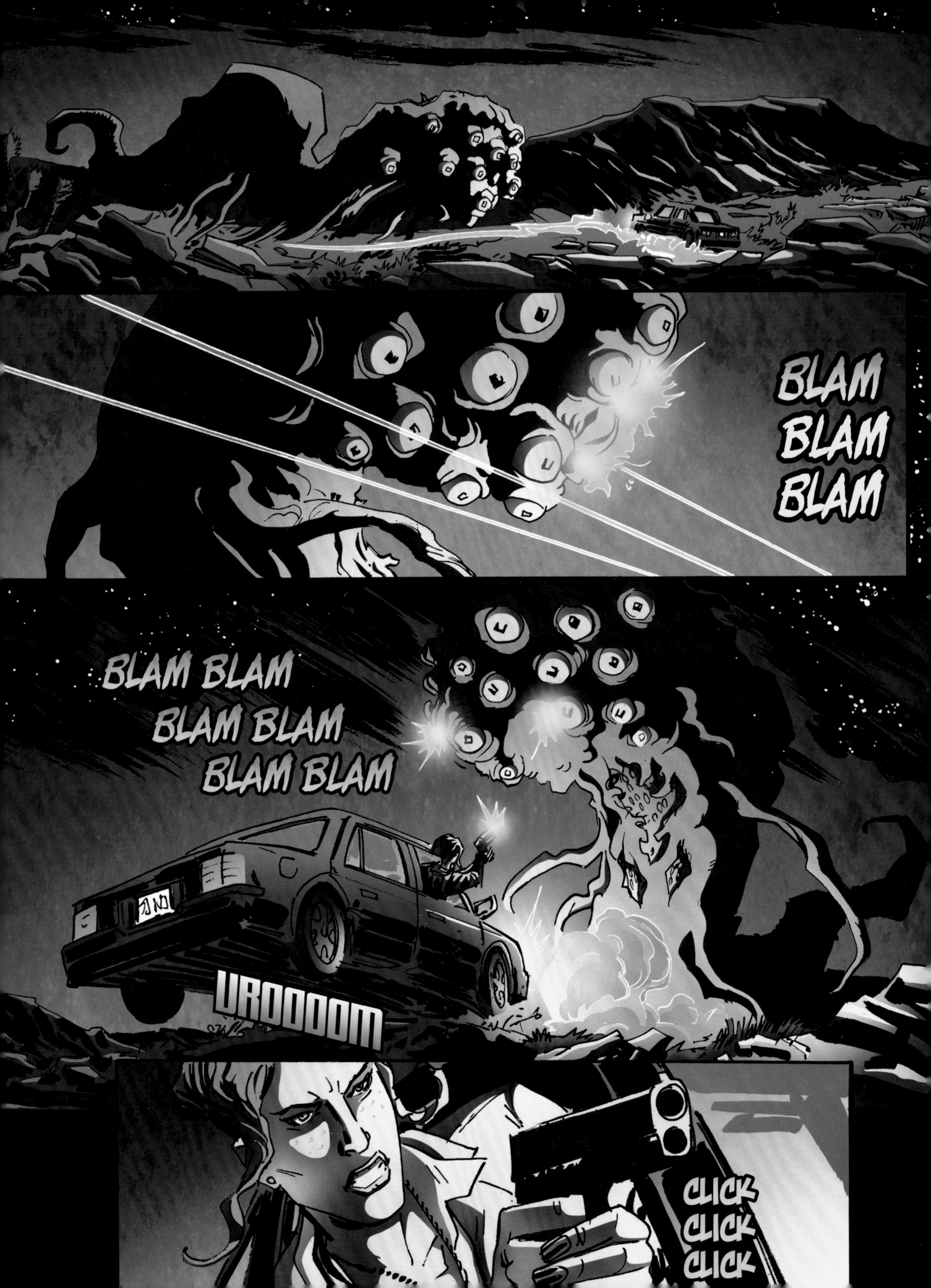
BLAM
BLAM
BLAM
BLAM BLAM
BLAM BLAM
BLAM BLAM
UROOOOM
CLICK
CLICK
CLICK

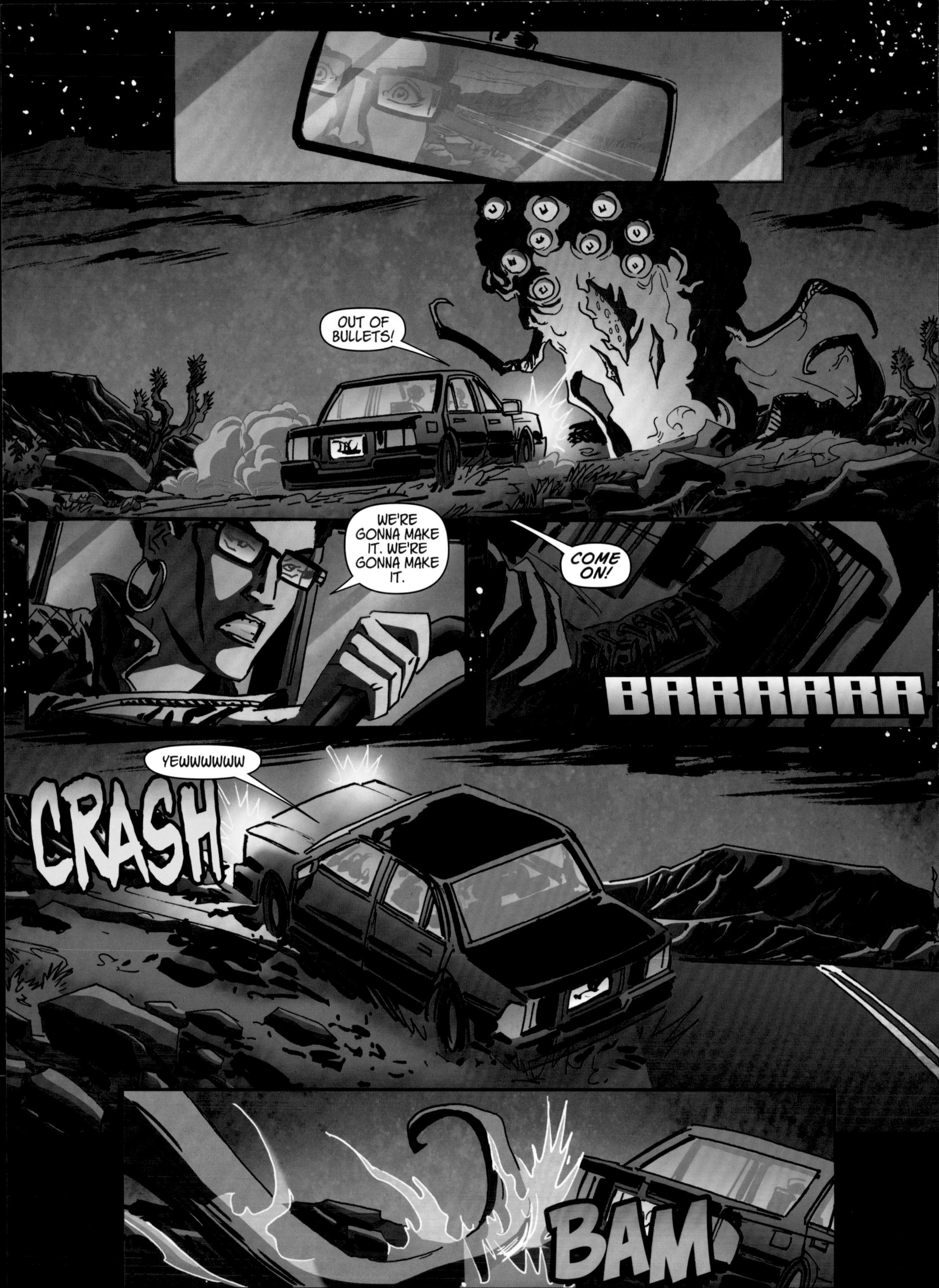
OUT OF BULLETS!
WE'RE GONNA MAKE IT. WE'RE GONNA MAKE IT.
COME ON!
BRRRRRR
YEWWWWWW
CRASH
BAM

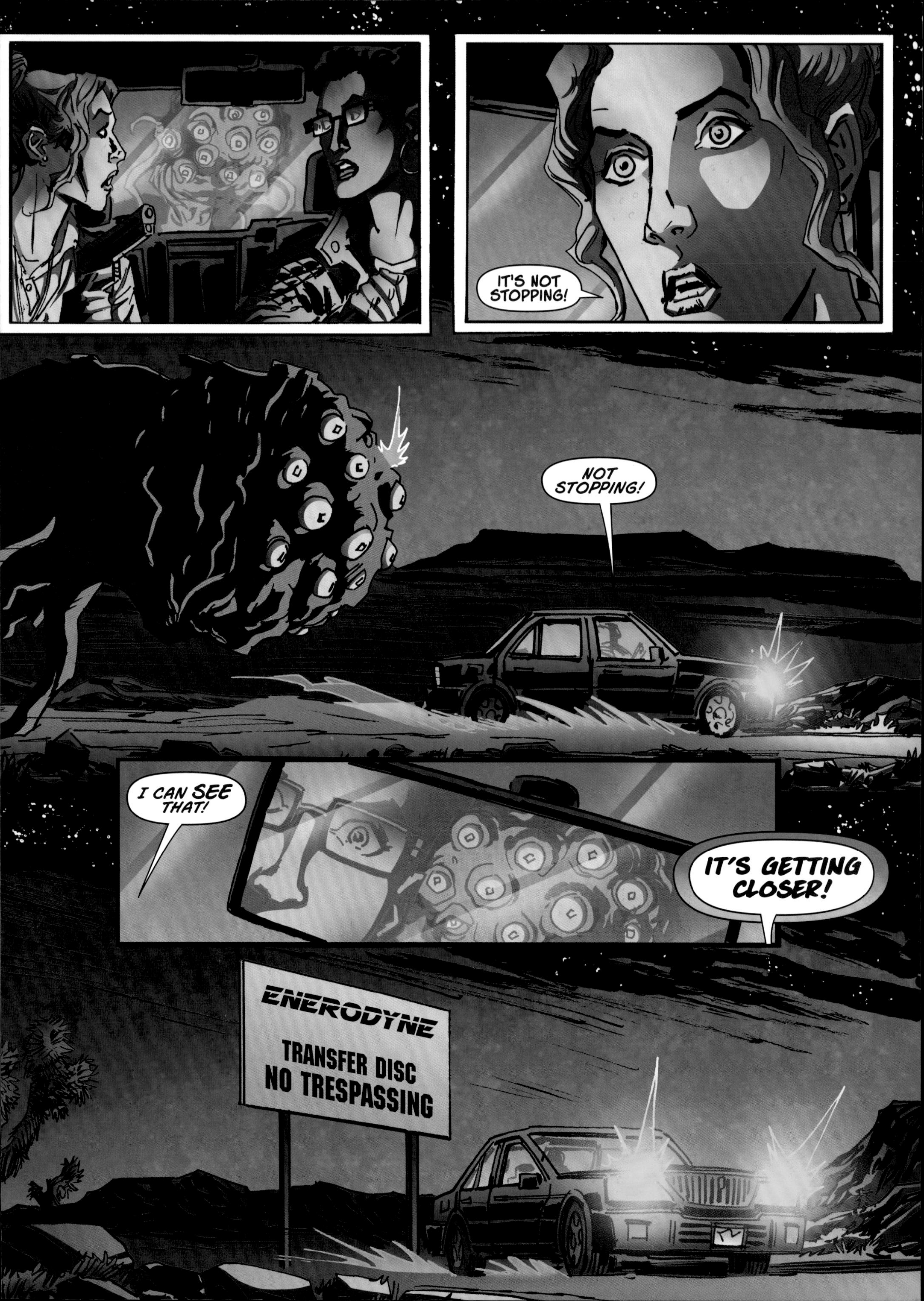
IT'S NOT STOPPING!
NOT STOPPING!
I CAN SEE THAT!
IT'S GETTING CLOSER!
ENERODYNE
TRANSFER DISC
NO TRESPASSING

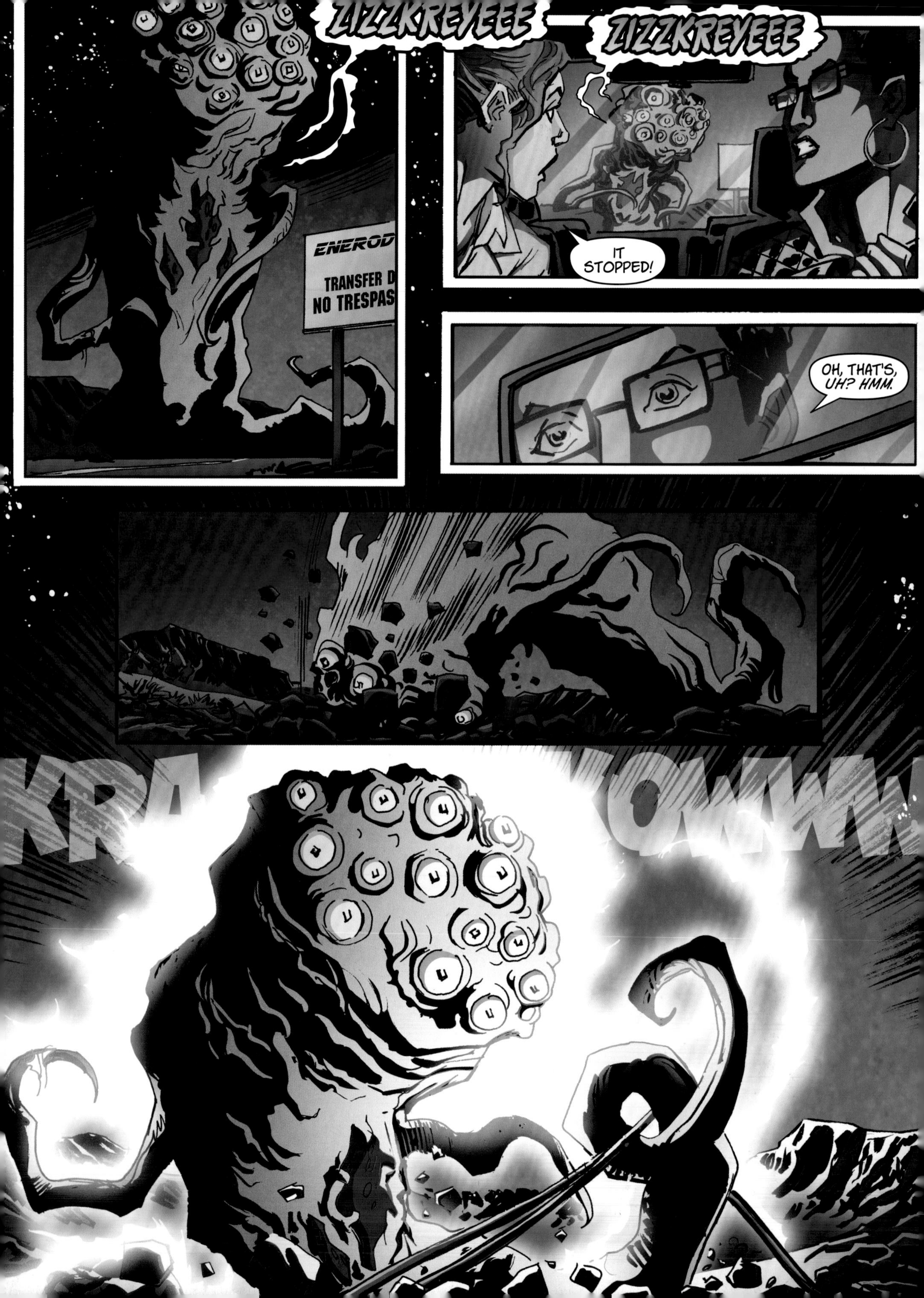
ZIZZKREYEEE
ENEROD
TRANSFER D
NO TRESPAS
ZIZZKREYEEE
IT STOPPED!
OH, THAT'S, UH? HMM.
KRA
OWWW

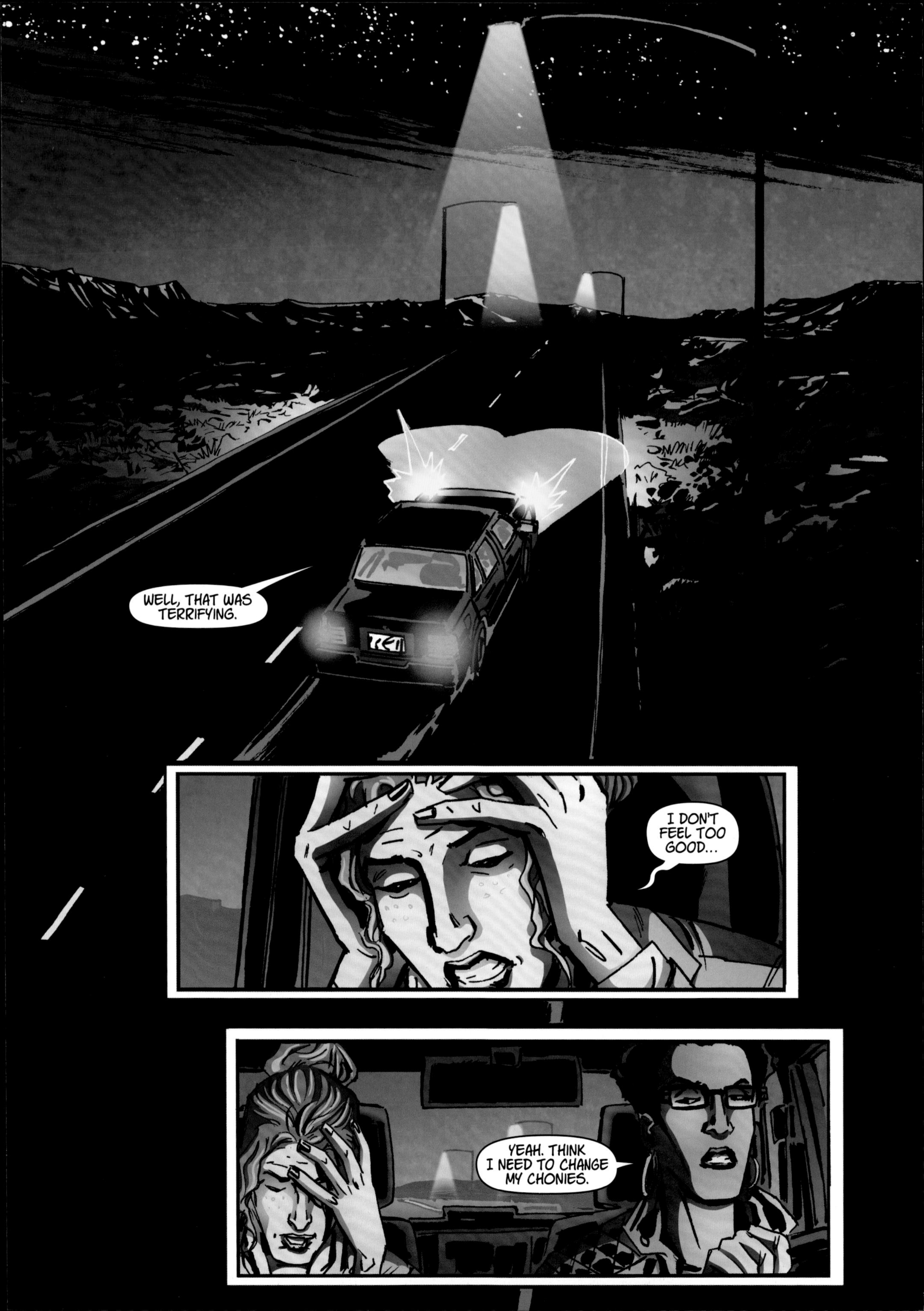
WELL, THAT WAS TERRIFYING.
I DON'T FEEL TOO GOOD...
YEAH. THINK I NEED TO CHANGE MY CHONIES.

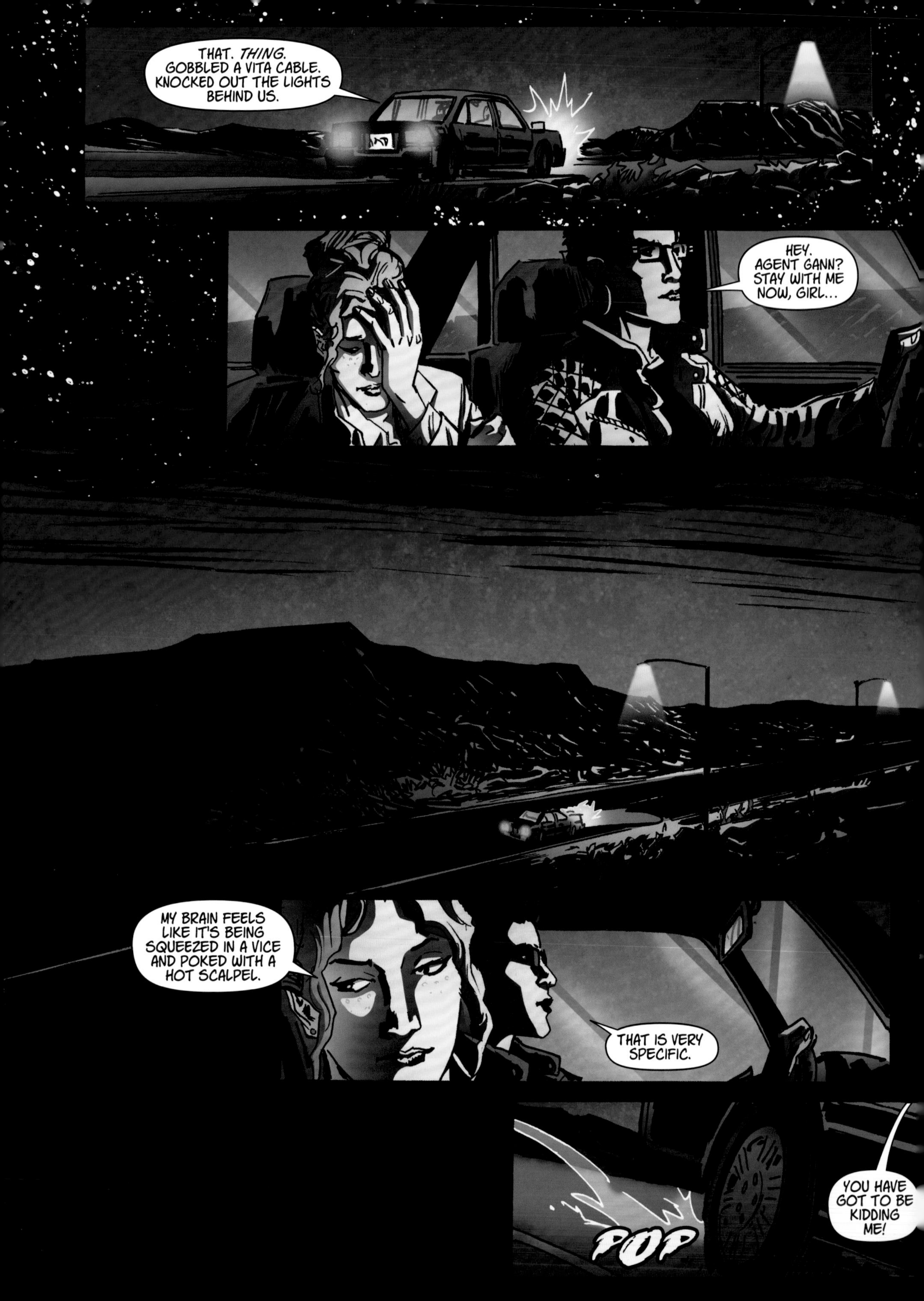
THAT. *THING.* GOBBLED A VITA CABLE. KNOCKED OUT THE LIGHTS BEHIND US.
HEY. AGENT GANN? STAY WITH ME NOW, GIRL...
MY BRAIN FEELS LIKE IT'S BEING SQUEEZED IN A VICE AND POKED WITH A HOT SCALPEL.
THAT IS VERY SPECIFIC.
POP
YOU HAVE GOT TO BE KIDDING ME!

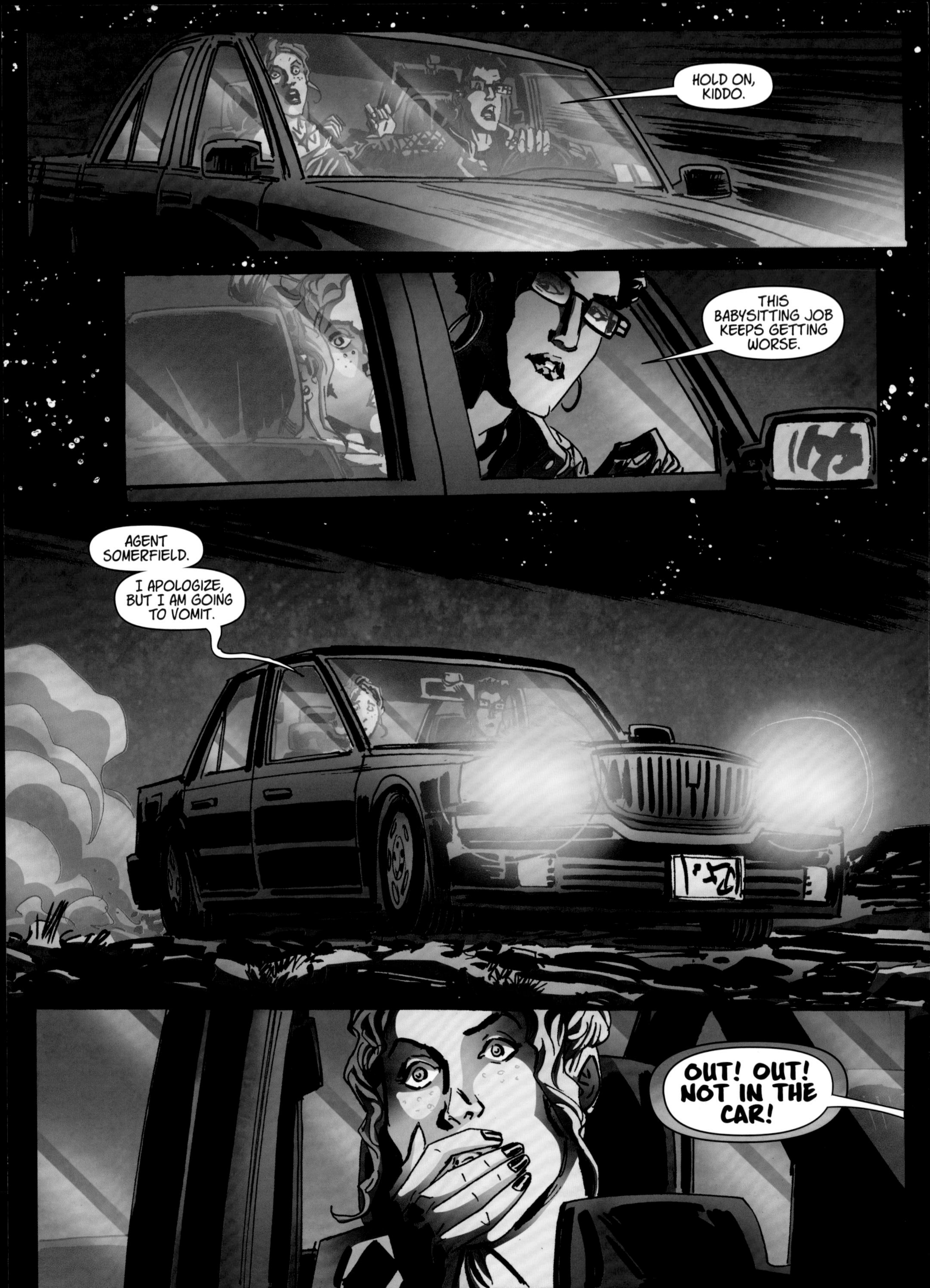
HOLD ON, KIDDO.
THIS BABYSITTING JOB KEEPS GETTING WORSE.
AGENT SOMERFIELD.
I APOLOGIZE, BUT I AM GOING TO VOMIT.
OUT! OUT! NOT IN THE CAR!

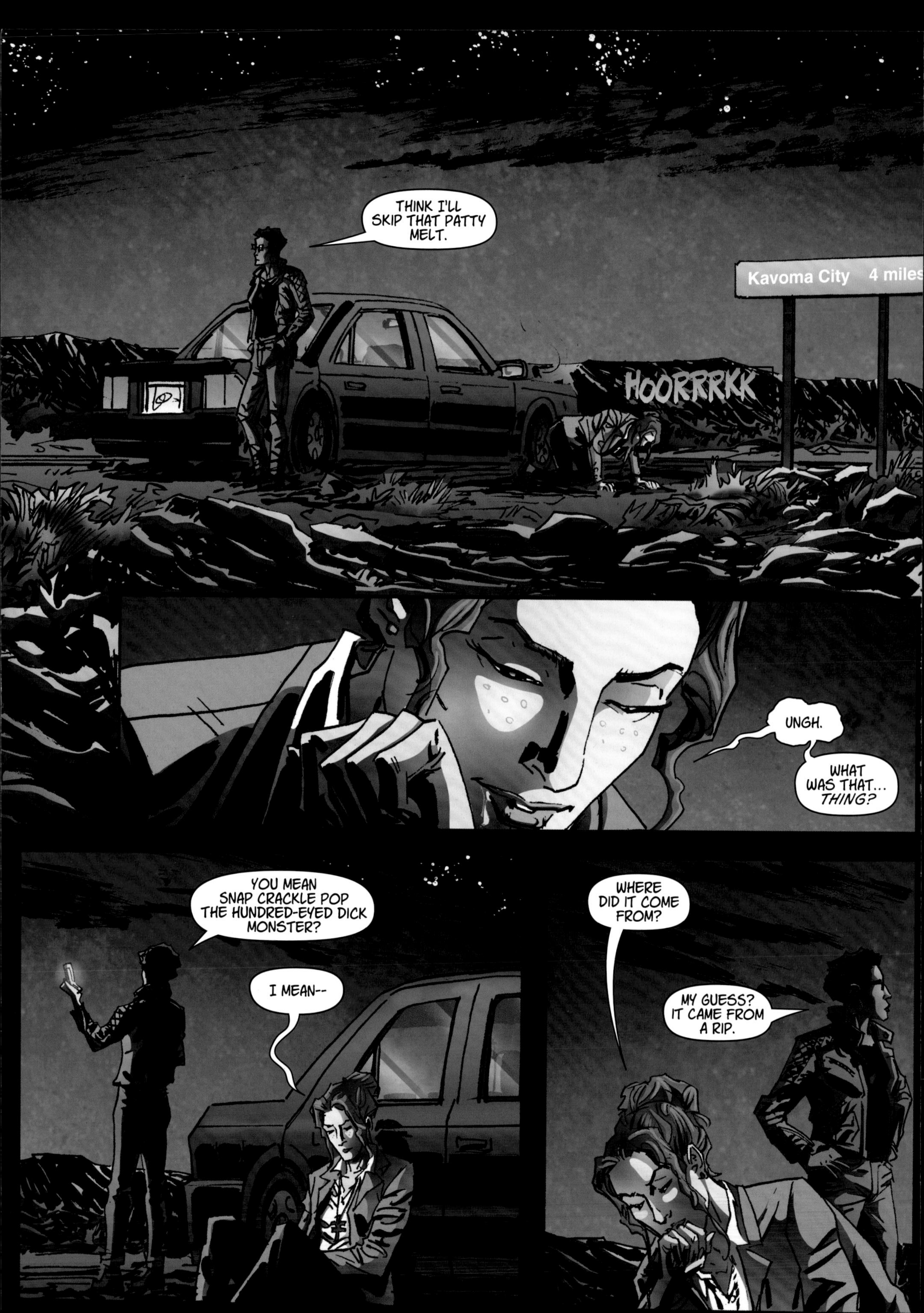
THINK I'LL SKIP THAT PATTY MELT.
Kavoma City 4 miles
HOORRRKK
UNGH.
WHAT WAS THAT... *THING?*
YOU MEAN SNAP CRACKLE POP THE HUNDRED-EYED DICK MONSTER?
I MEAN--
WHERE DID IT COME FROM?
MY GUESS? IT CAME FROM A RIP.

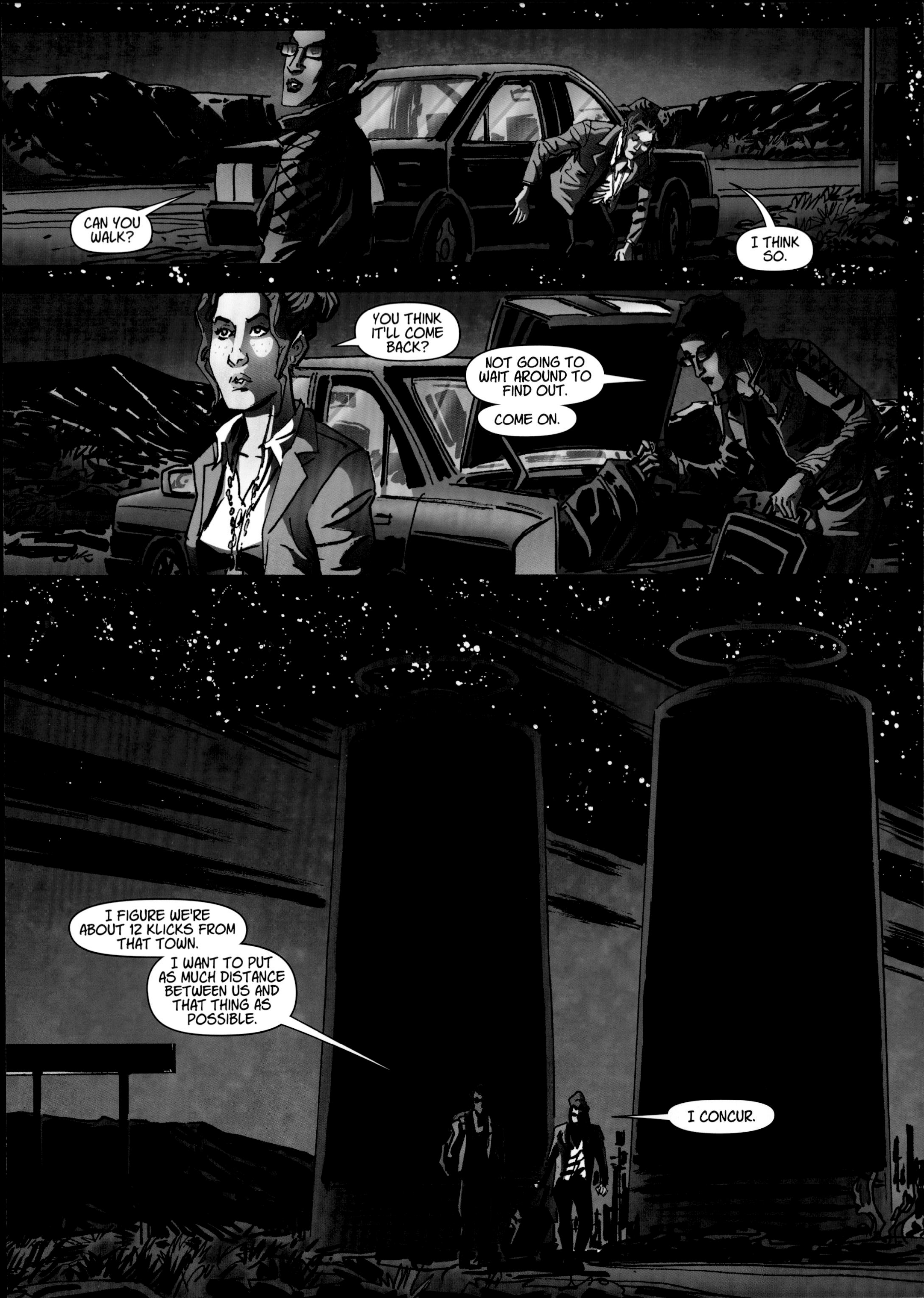
CAN YOU WALK?
I THINK SO.
YOU THINK IT'LL COME BACK?
NOT GOING TO WAIT AROUND TO FIND OUT.
COME ON.
I FIGURE WE'RE ABOUT 12 KLICKS FROM THAT TOWN.
I WANT TO PUT AS MUCH DISTANCE BETWEEN US AND THAT THING AS POSSIBLE.
I CONCUR.

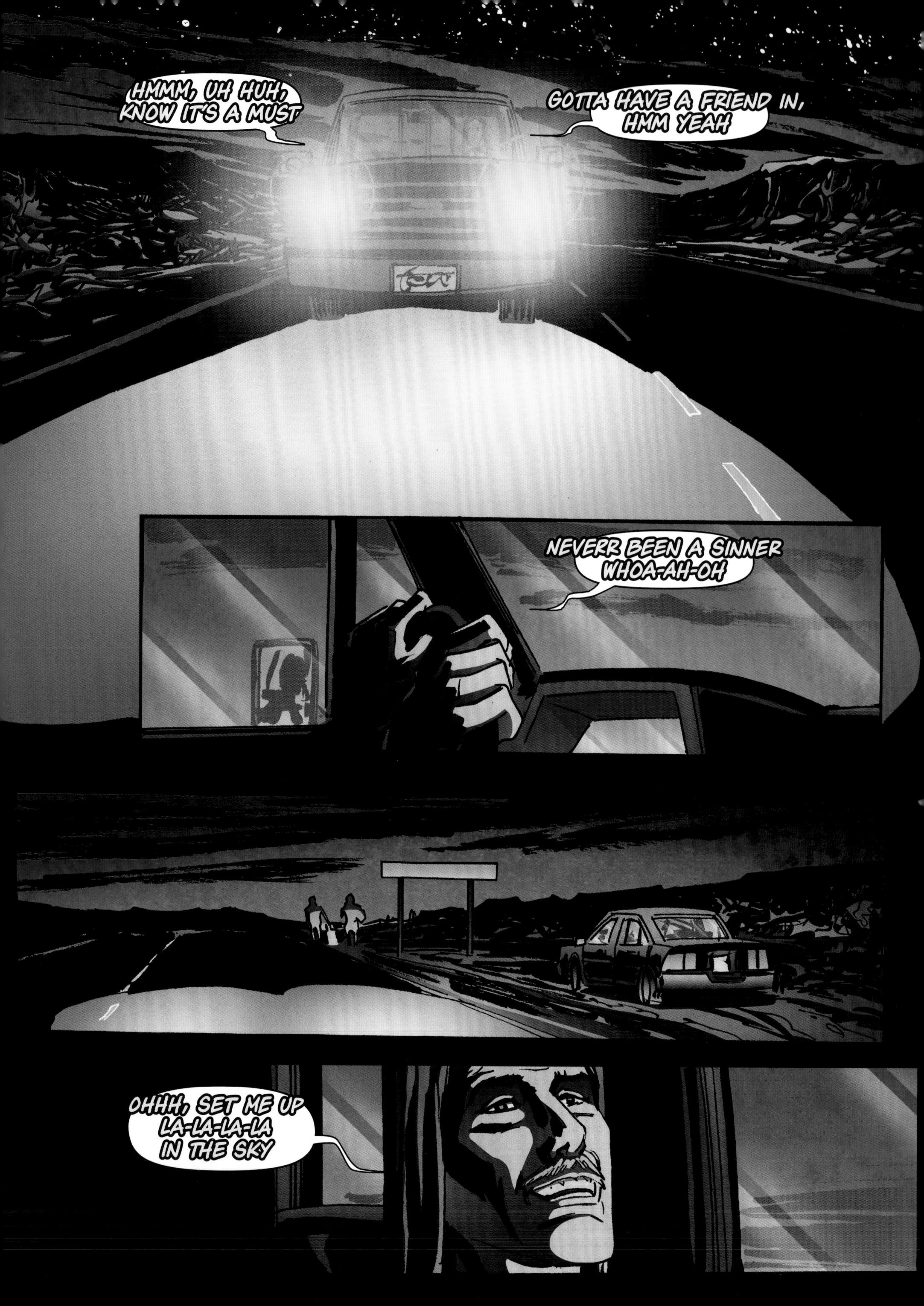
HMMM, UH HUH, KNOW IT'S A MUST
GOTTA HAVE A FRIEND IN, HMM YEAH
NEVERR BEEN A SINNER WHOA-AH-OH
OHHH, SET ME UP LA-LA-LA-LA IN THE SKY

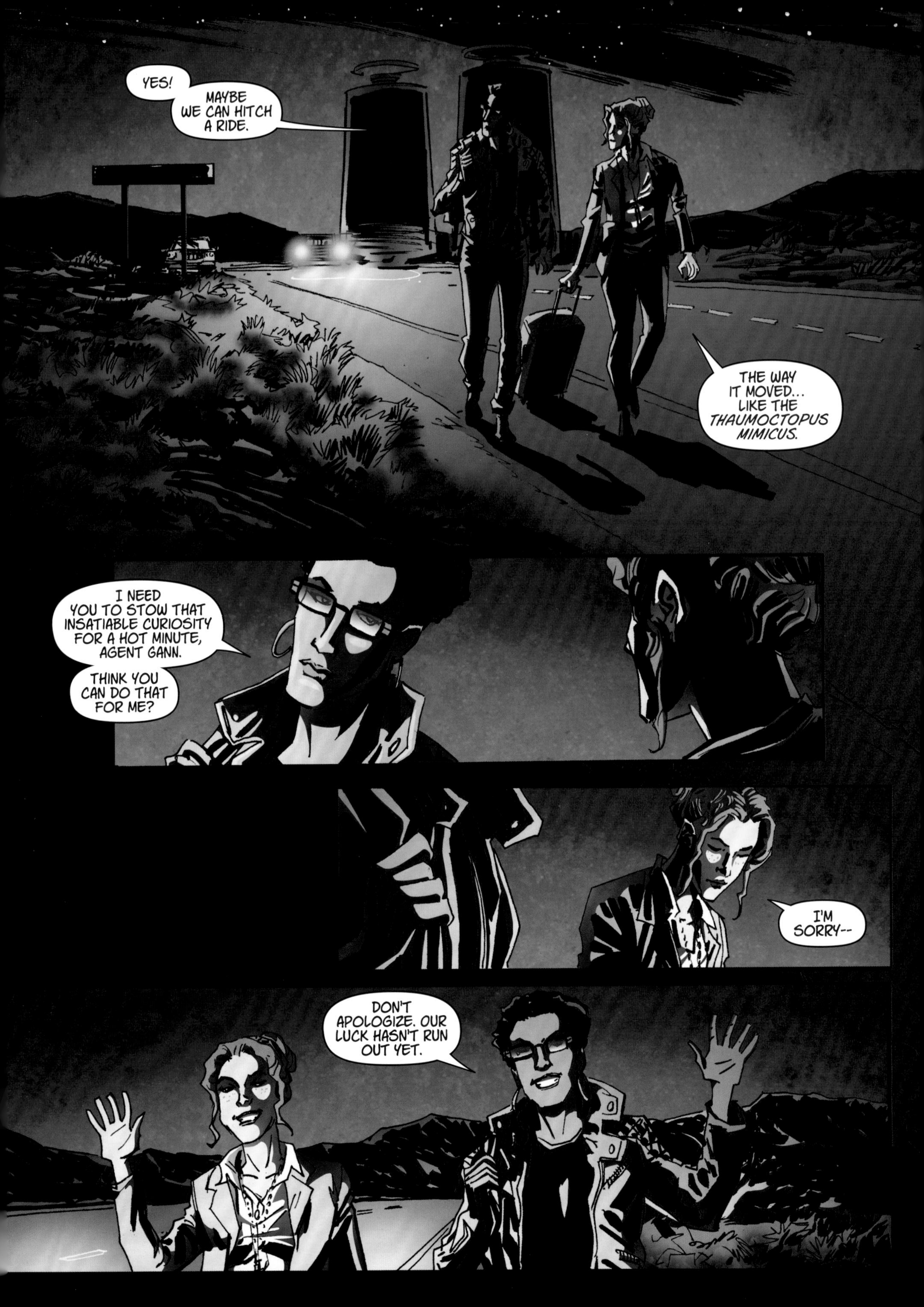
YES!
MAYBE WE CAN HITCH A RIDE.
THE WAY IT MOVED... LIKE THE *THAUMOCTOPUS MIMICUS.*
I NEED YOU TO STOW THAT INSATIABLE CURIOSITY FOR A HOT MINUTE, AGENT GANN.
THINK YOU CAN DO THAT FOR ME?
I'M SORRY--
DON'T APOLOGIZE. OUR LUCK HASN'T RUN OUT YET.

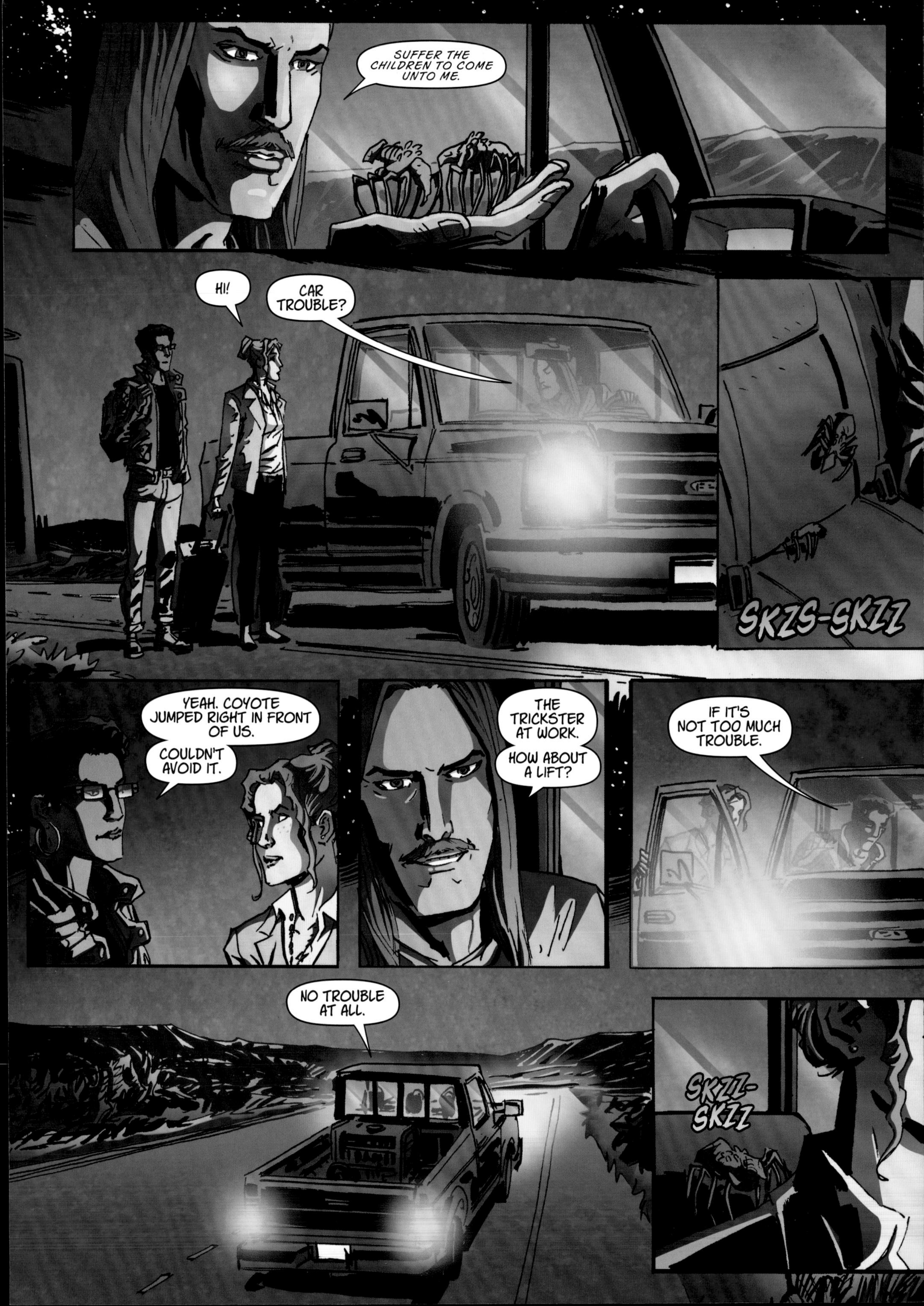
SUFFER THE CHILDREN TO COME UNTO ME.
HI!
CAR TROUBLE?
SKZS-SKZZ
YEAH. COYOTE JUMPED RIGHT IN FRONT OF US.
COULDN'T AVOID IT.
THE TRICKSTER AT WORK.
HOW ABOUT A LIFT?
IF IT'S NOT TOO MUCH TROUBLE.
NO TROUBLE AT ALL.
SKZZ-SKZZ

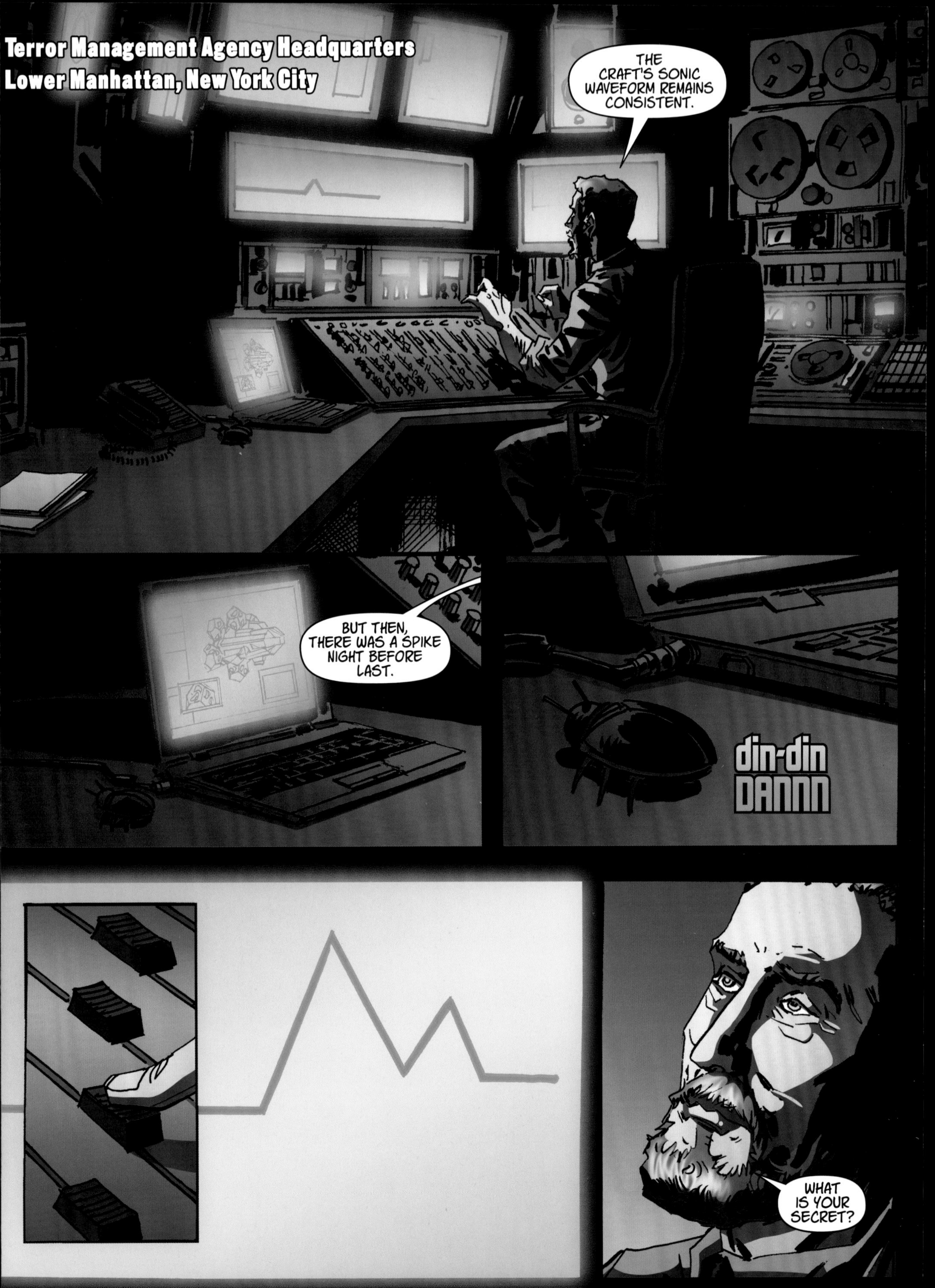
Terror Management Agency Headquarters
Lower Manhattan, New York City
THE CRAFT'S SONIC WAVEFORM REMAINS CONSISTENT.
BUT THEN, THERE WAS A SPIKE NIGHT BEFORE LAST.
din-din DANNN
WHAT IS YOUR SECRET?

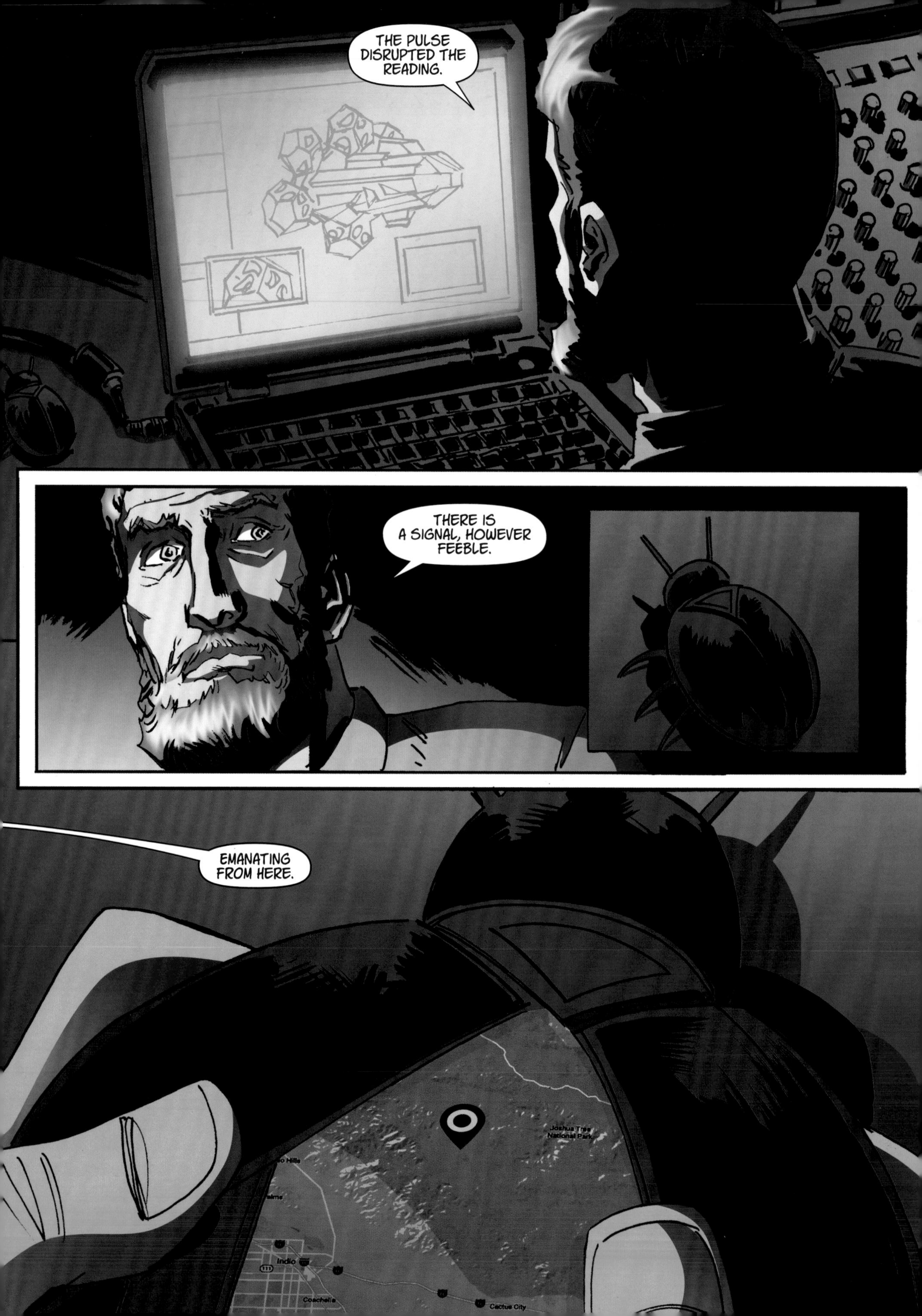
THE PULSE DISRUPTED THE READING.
THERE IS A SIGNAL, HOWEVER FEEBLE.
EMANATING FROM HERE.
Joshua Tree National Park
Indio
Coachella
Cactus City

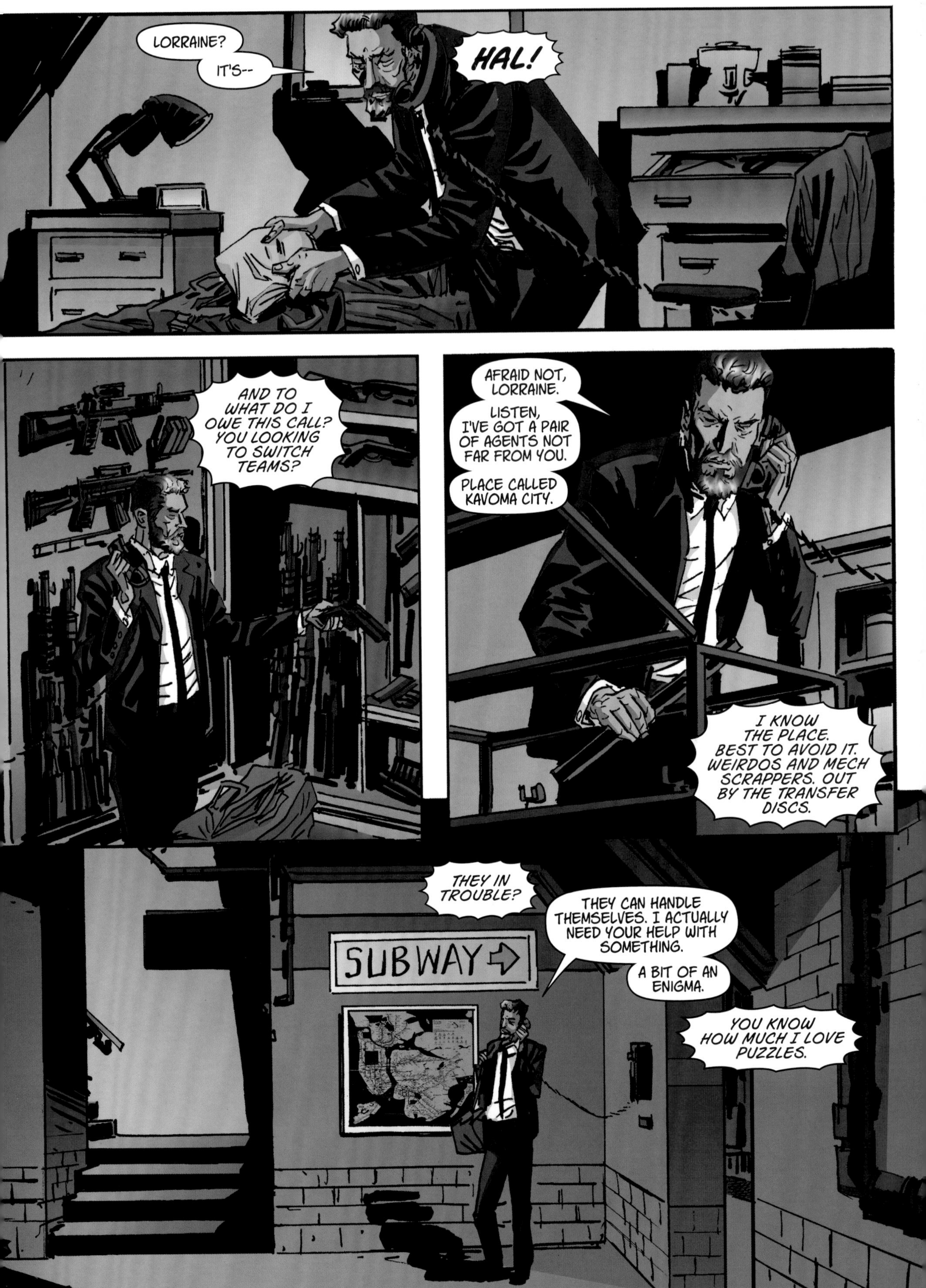
LORRAINE?
IT'S--
HAL!
AND TO WHAT DO I OWE THIS CALL? YOU LOOKING TO SWITCH TEAMS?
AFRAID NOT, LORRAINE.
LISTEN, I'VE GOT A PAIR OF AGENTS NOT FAR FROM YOU.
PLACE CALLED KAVOMA CITY.
I KNOW THE PLACE. BEST TO AVOID IT. WEIRDOS AND MECH SCRAPPERS. OUT BY THE TRANSFER DISCS.
SUBWAY
THEY IN TROUBLE?
THEY CAN HANDLE THEMSELVES. I ACTUALLY NEED YOUR HELP WITH SOMETHING.
A BIT OF AN ENIGMA.
YOU KNOW HOW MUCH I LOVE PUZZLES.

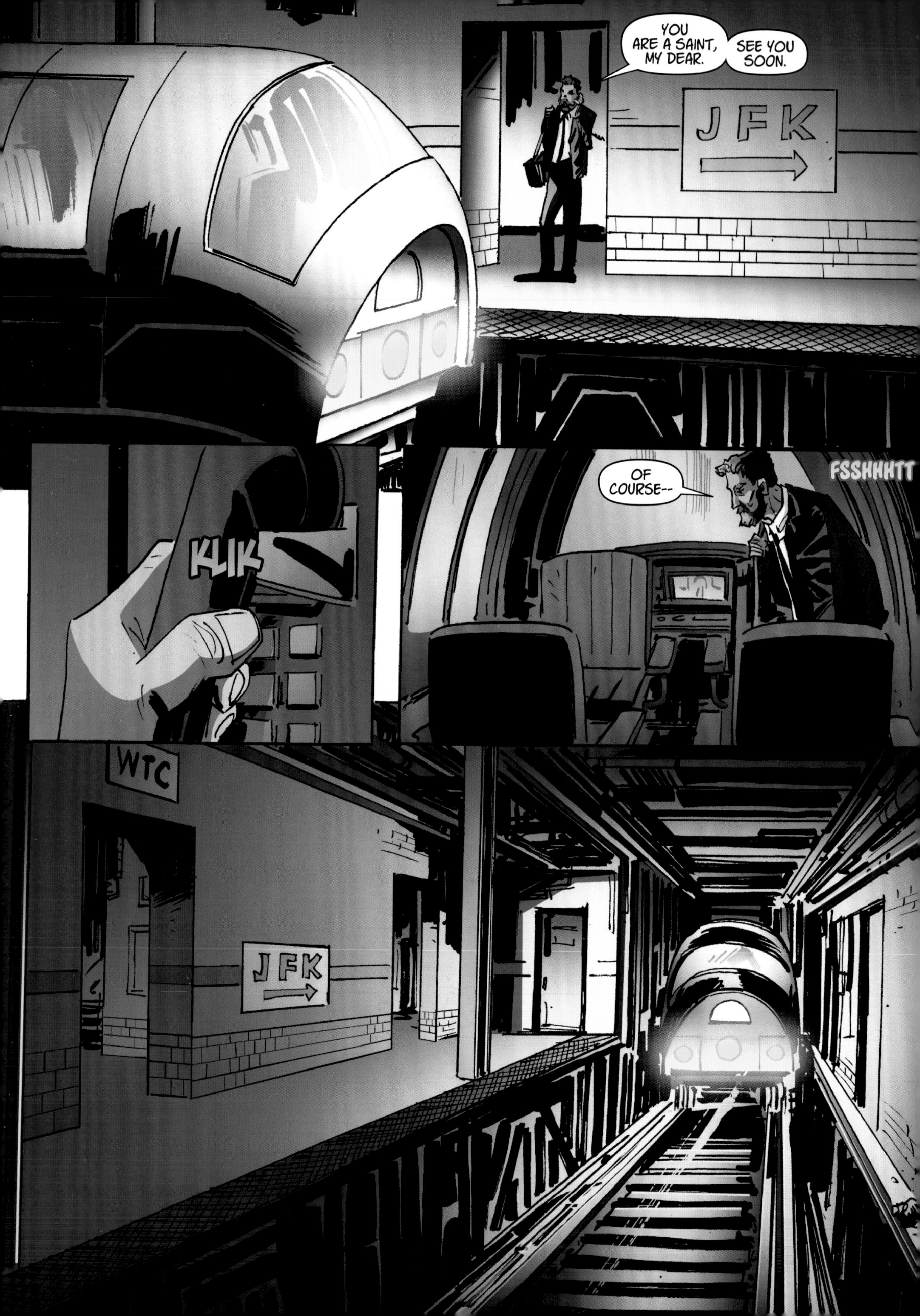
YOU ARE A SAINT, MY DEAR.
SEE YOU SOON.
JFK
KLIK
OF COURSE--
FSSHHHTT
WTC
JFK

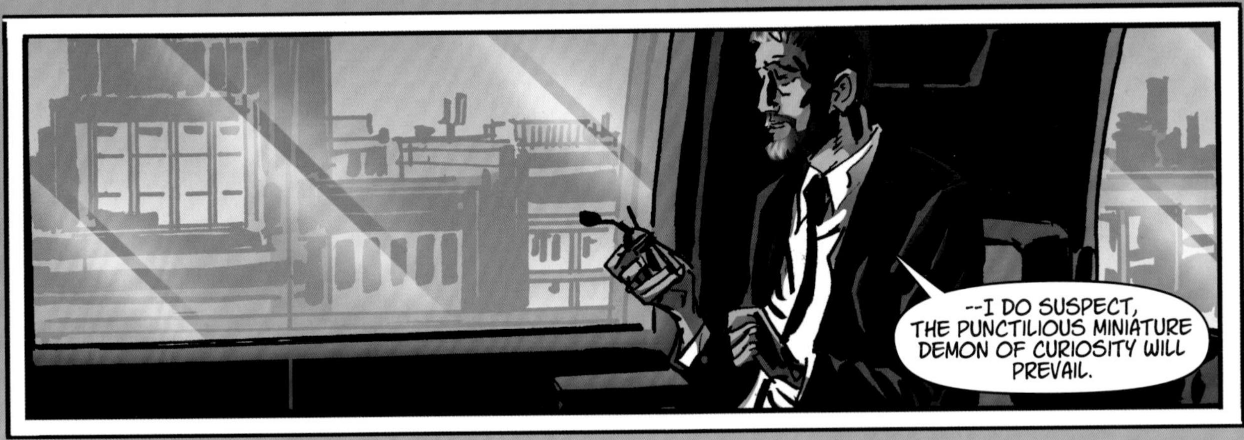
--I DO SUSPECT, THE PUNCTILIOUS MINIATURE DEMON OF CURIOSITY WILL PREVAIL.

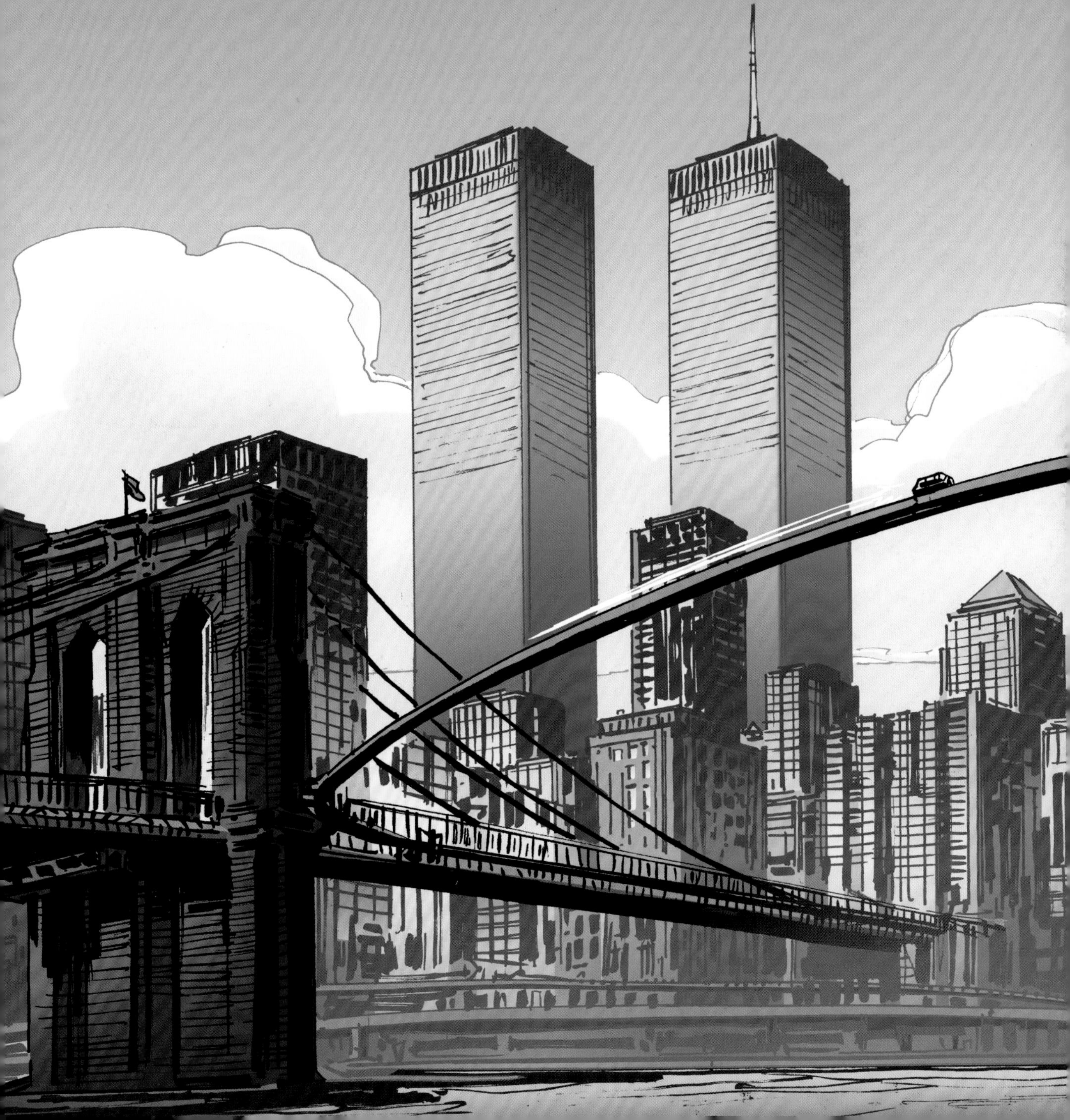

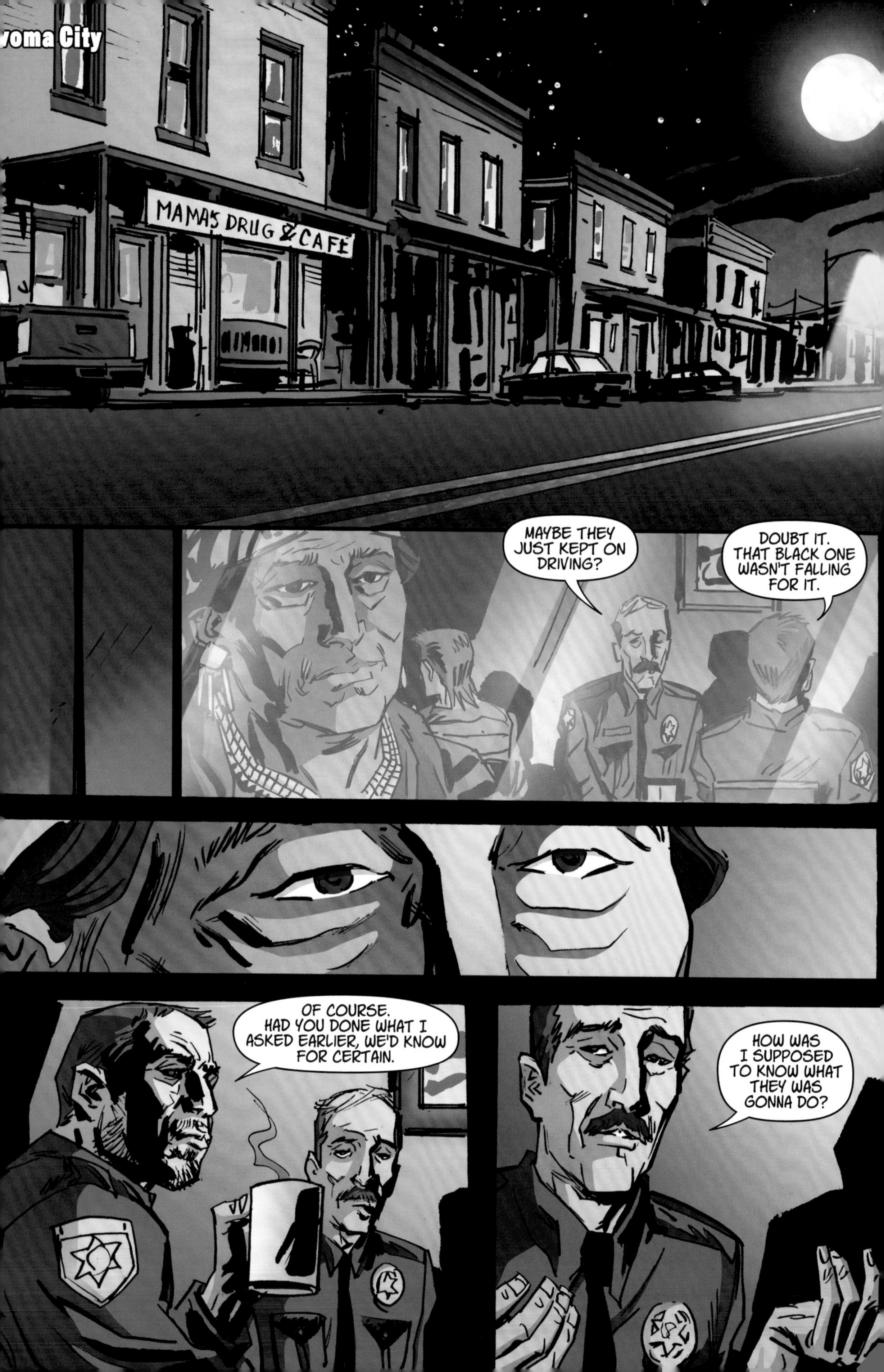

...voma City
MAMA'S DRUG & CAFE
MAYBE THEY JUST KEPT ON DRIVING?
DOUBT IT. THAT BLACK ONE WASN'T FALLING FOR IT.
OF COURSE. HAD YOU DONE WHAT I ASKED EARLIER, WE'D KNOW FOR CERTAIN.
HOW WAS I SUPPOSED TO KNOW WHAT THEY WAS GONNA DO?

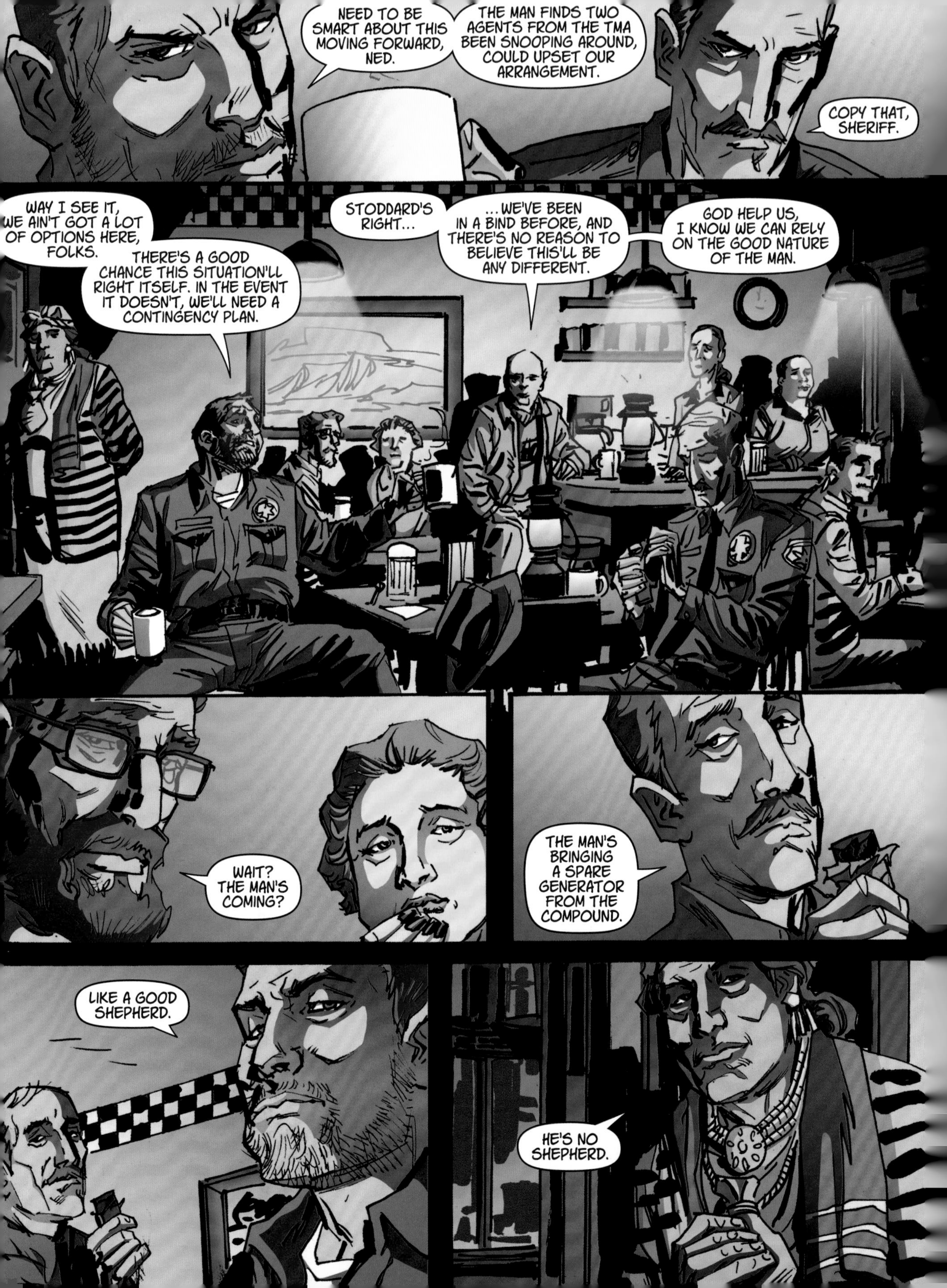
NEED TO BE SMART ABOUT THIS MOVING FORWARD, NED.
THE MAN FINDS TWO AGENTS FROM THE TMA BEEN SNOOPING AROUND, COULD UPSET OUR ARRANGEMENT.
COPY THAT, SHERIFF.
WAY I SEE IT, WE AIN'T GOT A LOT OF OPTIONS HERE, FOLKS.
THERE'S A GOOD CHANCE THIS SITUATION'LL RIGHT ITSELF. IN THE EVENT IT DOESN'T, WE'LL NEED A CONTINGENCY PLAN.
STODDARD'S RIGHT...
...WE'VE BEEN IN A BIND BEFORE, AND THERE'S NO REASON TO BELIEVE THIS'LL BE ANY DIFFERENT.
GOD HELP US, I KNOW WE CAN RELY ON THE GOOD NATURE OF THE MAN.
WAIT? THE MAN'S COMING?
THE MAN'S BRINGING A SPARE GENERATOR FROM THE COMPOUND.
LIKE A GOOD SHEPHERD.
HE'S NO SHEPHERD.

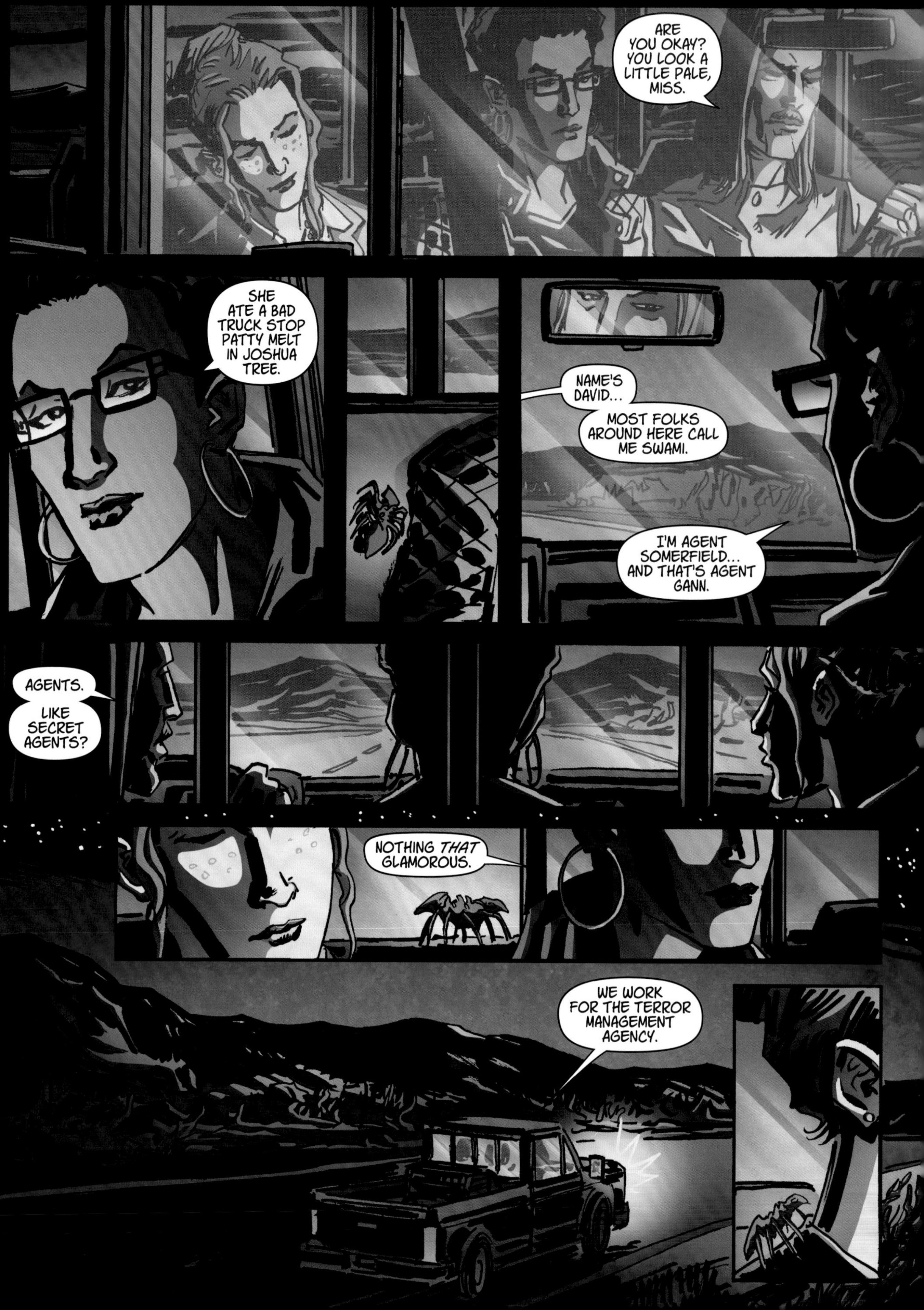
ARE YOU OKAY? YOU LOOK A LITTLE PALE, MISS.
SHE ATE A BAD TRUCK STOP PATTY MELT IN JOSHUA TREE.
NAME'S DAVID...
MOST FOLKS AROUND HERE CALL ME SWAMI.
I'M AGENT SOMERFIELD... AND THAT'S AGENT GANN.
AGENTS.
LIKE SECRET AGENTS?
NOTHING *THAT* GLAMOROUS.
WE WORK FOR THE TERROR MANAGEMENT AGENCY.

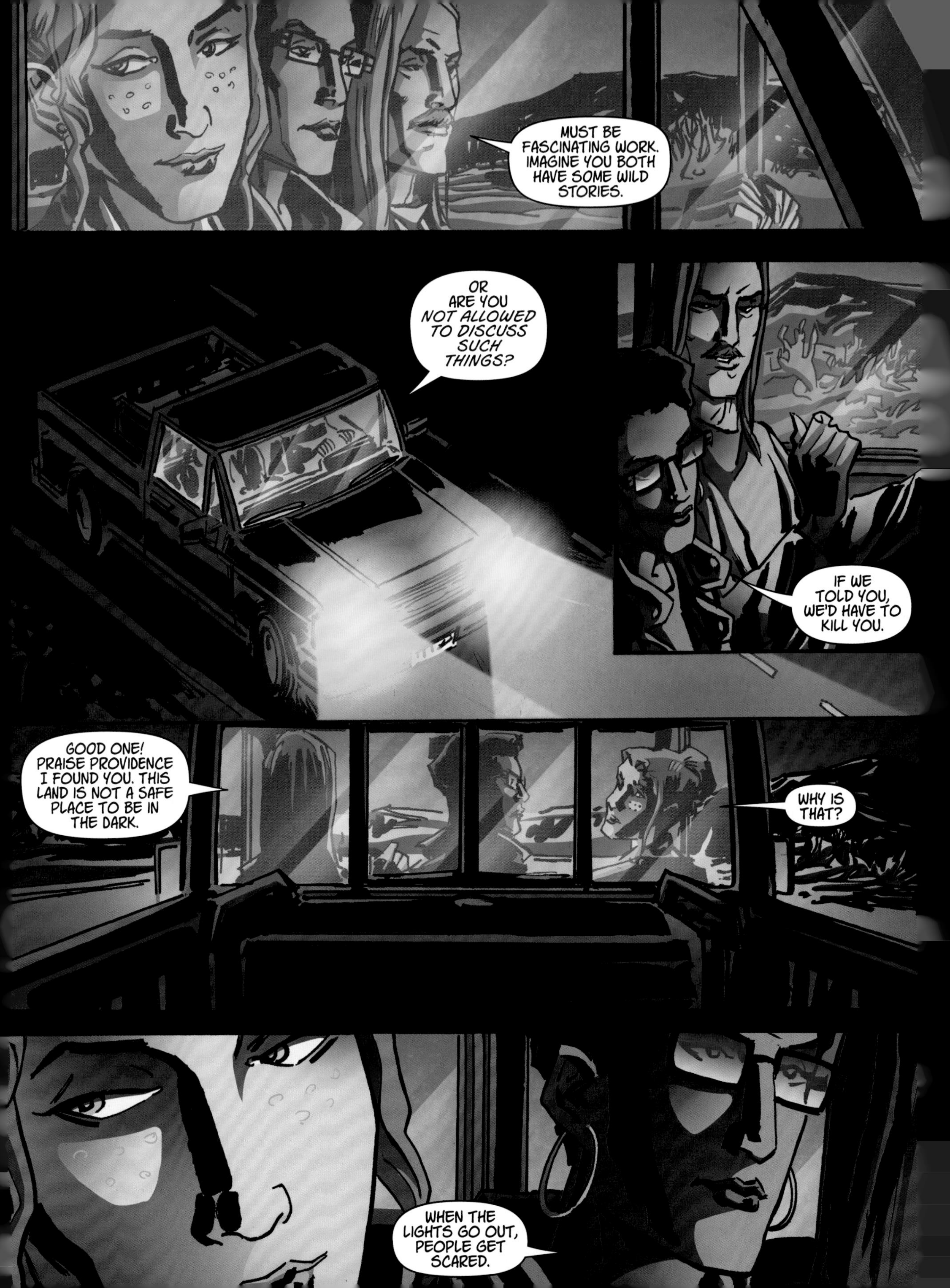
MUST BE FASCINATING WORK. IMAGINE YOU BOTH HAVE SOME WILD STORIES.
OR ARE YOU *NOT ALLOWED* TO DISCUSS SUCH THINGS?
IF WE TOLD YOU, WE'D HAVE TO KILL YOU.
GOOD ONE! PRAISE PROVIDENCE I FOUND YOU. THIS LAND IS NOT A SAFE PLACE TO BE IN THE DARK.
WHY IS THAT?
WHEN THE LIGHTS GO OUT, PEOPLE GET SCARED.

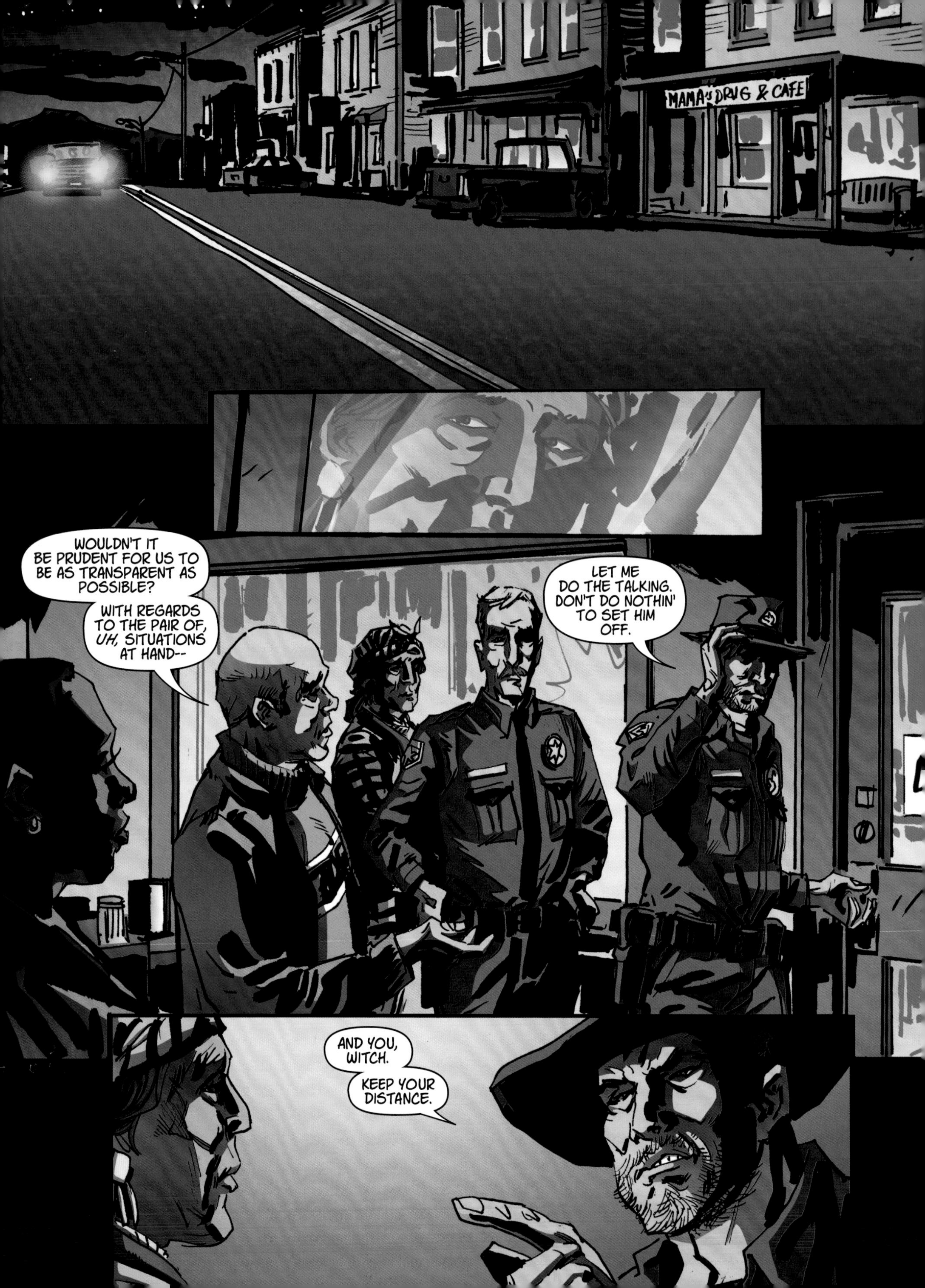
MAMA's DRUG & CAFE
WOULDN'T IT BE PRUDENT FOR US TO BE AS TRANSPARENT AS POSSIBLE?
WITH REGARDS TO THE PAIR OF, UH, SITUATIONS AT HAND--
LET ME DO THE TALKING. DON'T DO NOTHIN' TO SET HIM OFF.
AND YOU, WITCH.
KEEP YOUR DISTANCE.

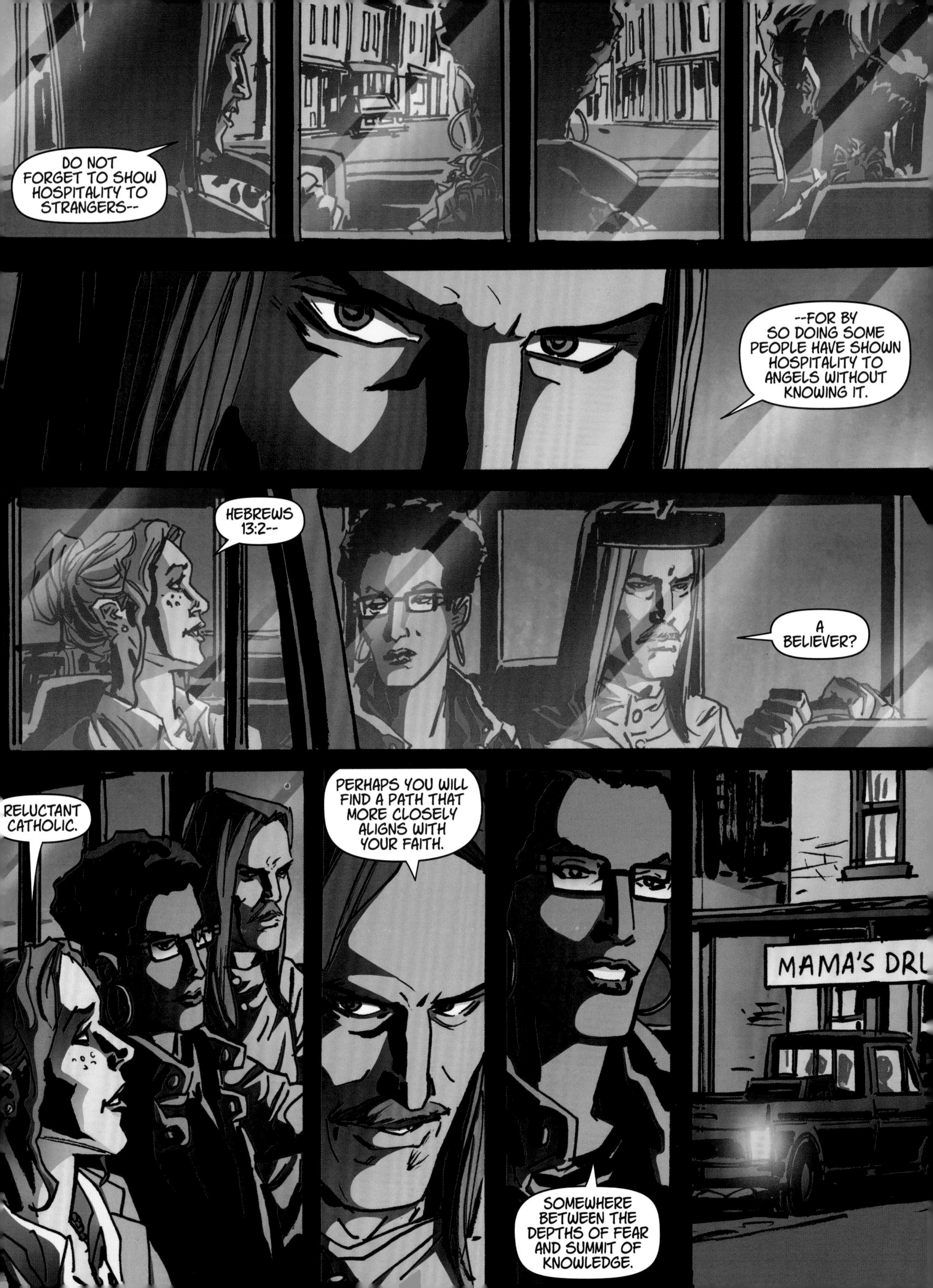
DO NOT FORGET TO SHOW HOSPITALITY TO STRANGERS--
--FOR BY SO DOING SOME PEOPLE HAVE SHOWN HOSPITALITY TO ANGELS WITHOUT KNOWING IT.
HEBREWS 13:2--
A BELIEVER?
RELUCTANT CATHOLIC.
PERHAPS YOU WILL FIND A PATH THAT MORE CLOSELY ALIGNS WITH YOUR FAITH.
SOMEWHERE BETWEEN THE DEPTHS OF FEAR AND SUMMIT OF KNOWLEDGE.
MAMA'S DRU

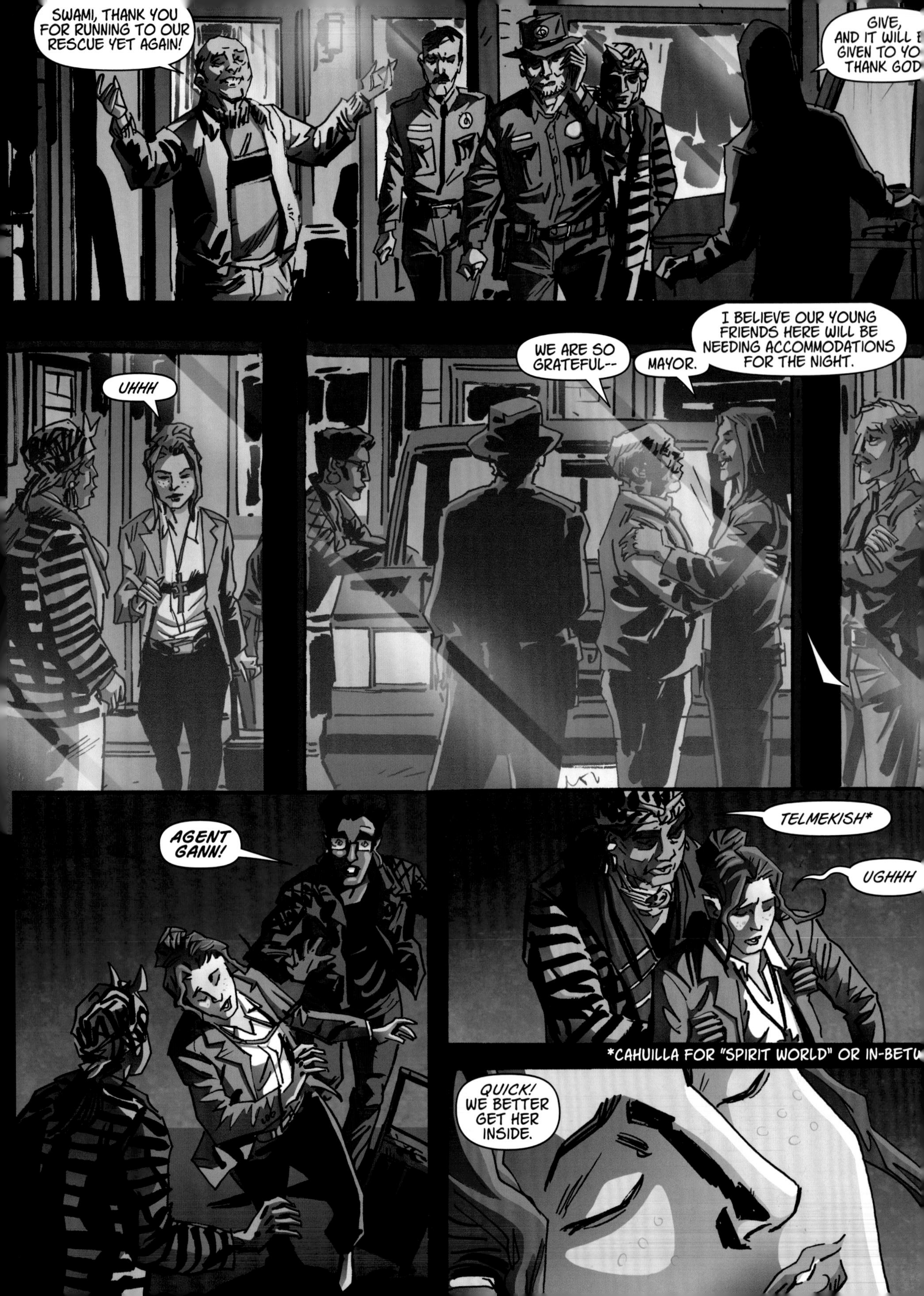
SWAMI, THANK YOU FOR RUNNING TO OUR RESCUE YET AGAIN!
GIVE, AND IT WILL B GIVEN TO YO THANK GOD
UHHH
WE ARE SO GRATEFUL--
MAYOR.
I BELIEVE OUR YOUNG FRIENDS HERE WILL BE NEEDING ACCOMMODATIONS FOR THE NIGHT.
AGENT GANN!
TELMEKISH*
UGHHH
*CAHUILLA FOR "SPIRIT WORLD" OR IN-BETU
QUICK! WE BETTER GET HER INSIDE.

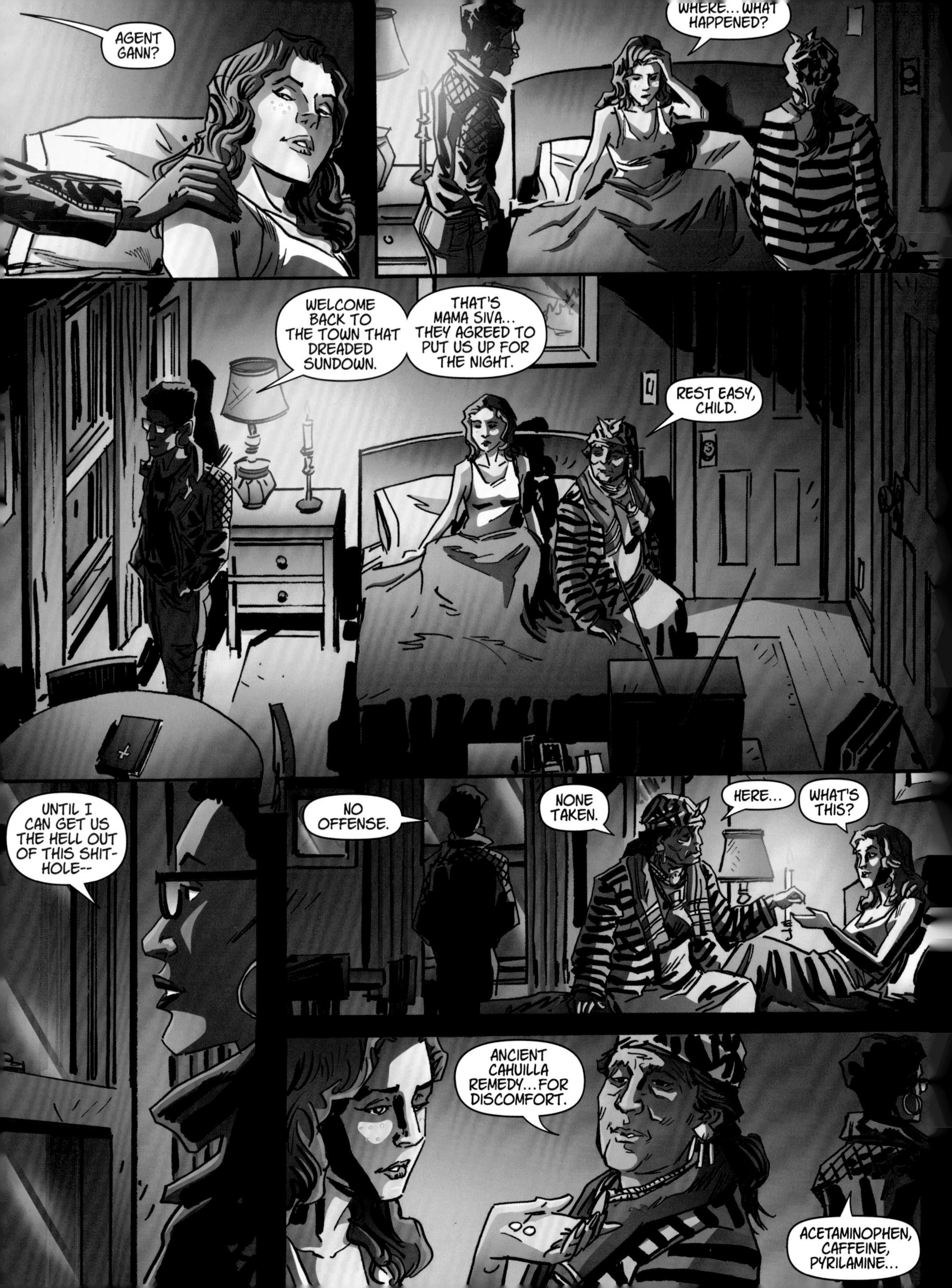
AGENT GANN?
WHERE... WHAT HAPPENED?
WELCOME BACK TO THE TOWN THAT DREADED SUNDOWN.
THAT'S MAMA SIVA... THEY AGREED TO PUT US UP FOR THE NIGHT.
REST EASY, CHILD.
UNTIL I CAN GET US THE HELL OUT OF THIS SHIT-HOLE--
NO OFFENSE.
NONE TAKEN.
HERE...
WHAT'S THIS?
ANCIENT CAHUILLA REMEDY...FOR DISCOMFORT.
ACETAMINOPHEN, CAFFEINE, PYRILAMINE...

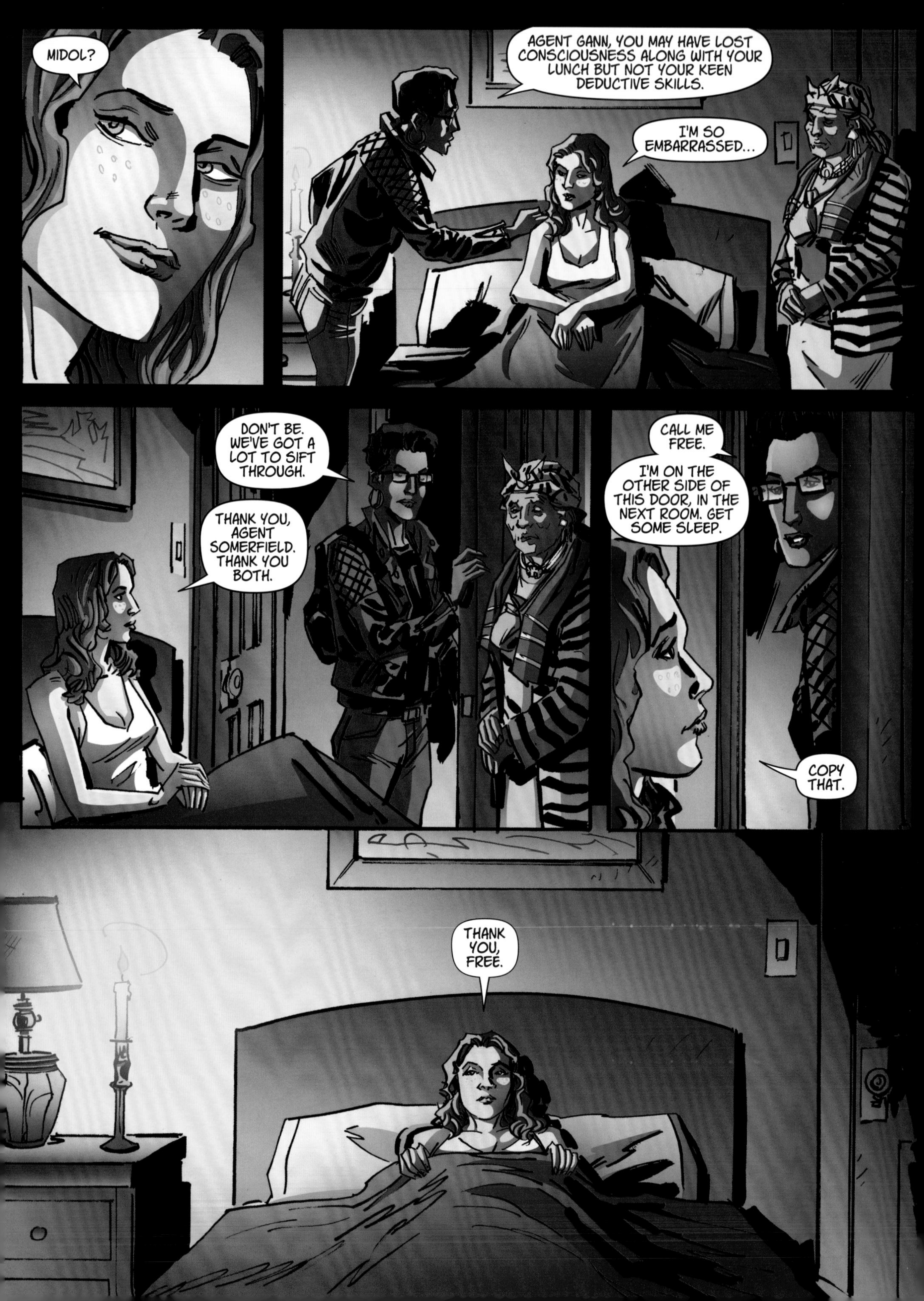
MIDOL?
AGENT GANN, YOU MAY HAVE LOST CONSCIOUSNESS ALONG WITH YOUR LUNCH BUT NOT YOUR KEEN DEDUCTIVE SKILLS.
I'M SO EMBARRASSED...
DON'T BE. WE'VE GOT A LOT TO SIFT THROUGH.
THANK YOU, AGENT SOMERFIELD. THANK YOU BOTH.
CALL ME FREE.
I'M ON THE OTHER SIDE OF THIS DOOR, IN THE NEXT ROOM. GET SOME SLEEP.
COPY THAT.
THANK YOU, FREE.

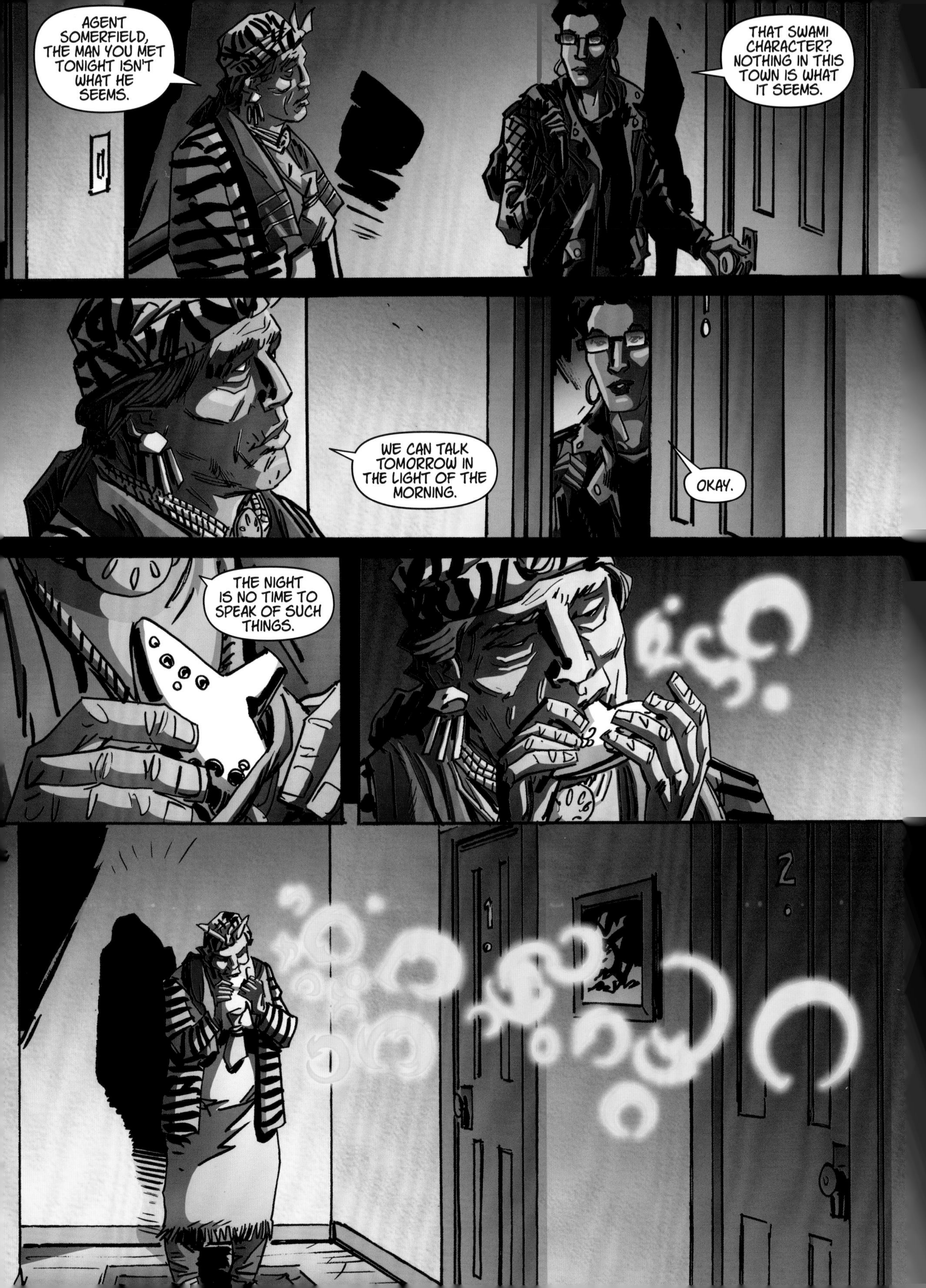
AGENT SOMERFIELD, THE MAN YOU MET TONIGHT ISN'T WHAT HE SEEMS.
THAT SWAMI CHARACTER? NOTHING IN THIS TOWN IS WHAT IT SEEMS.
WE CAN TALK TOMORROW IN THE LIGHT OF THE MORNING.
OKAY.
THE NIGHT IS NO TIME TO SPEAK OF SUCH THINGS.
1
2

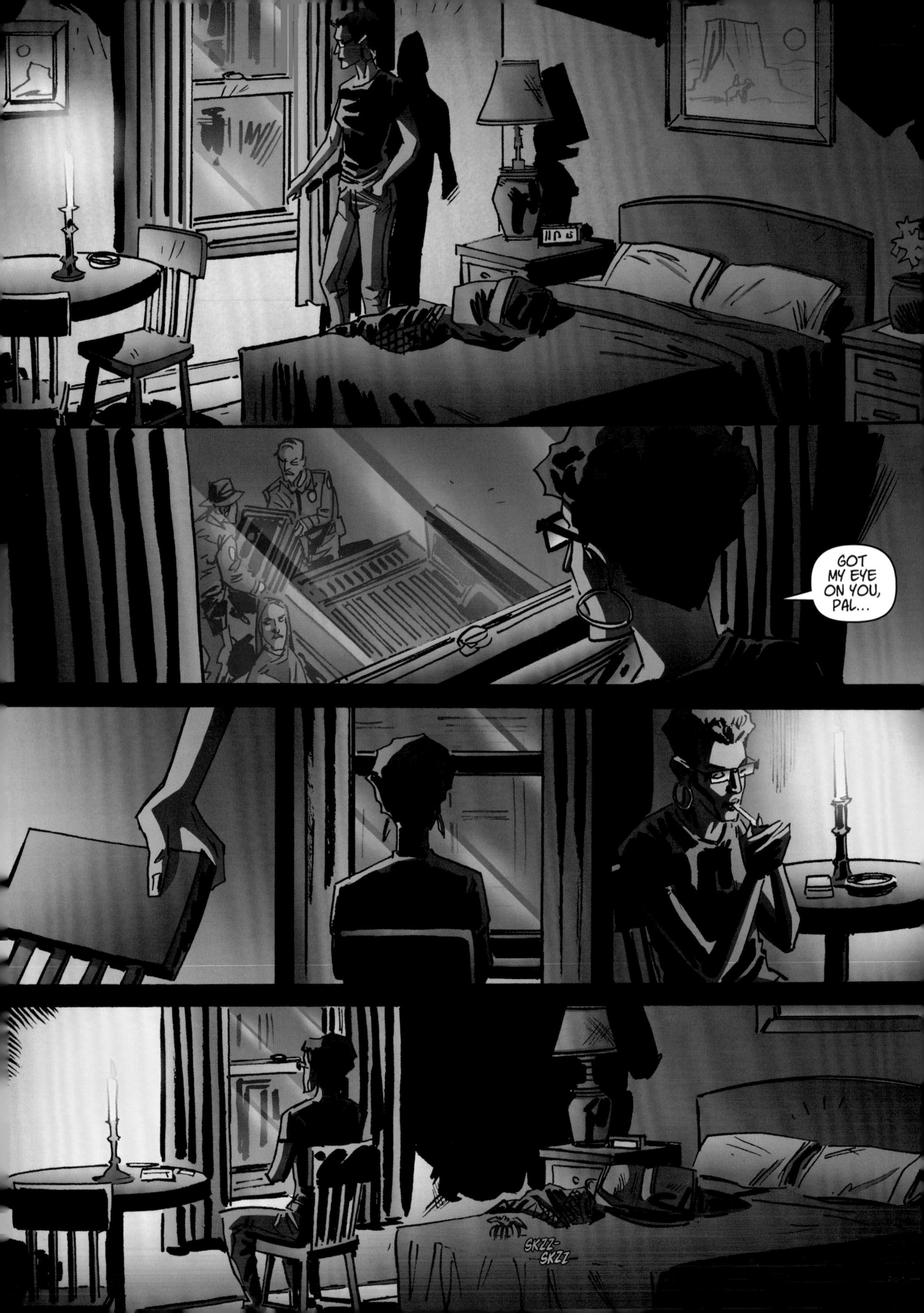
GOT MY EYE ON YOU, PAL...
SKZZ-SKZZ

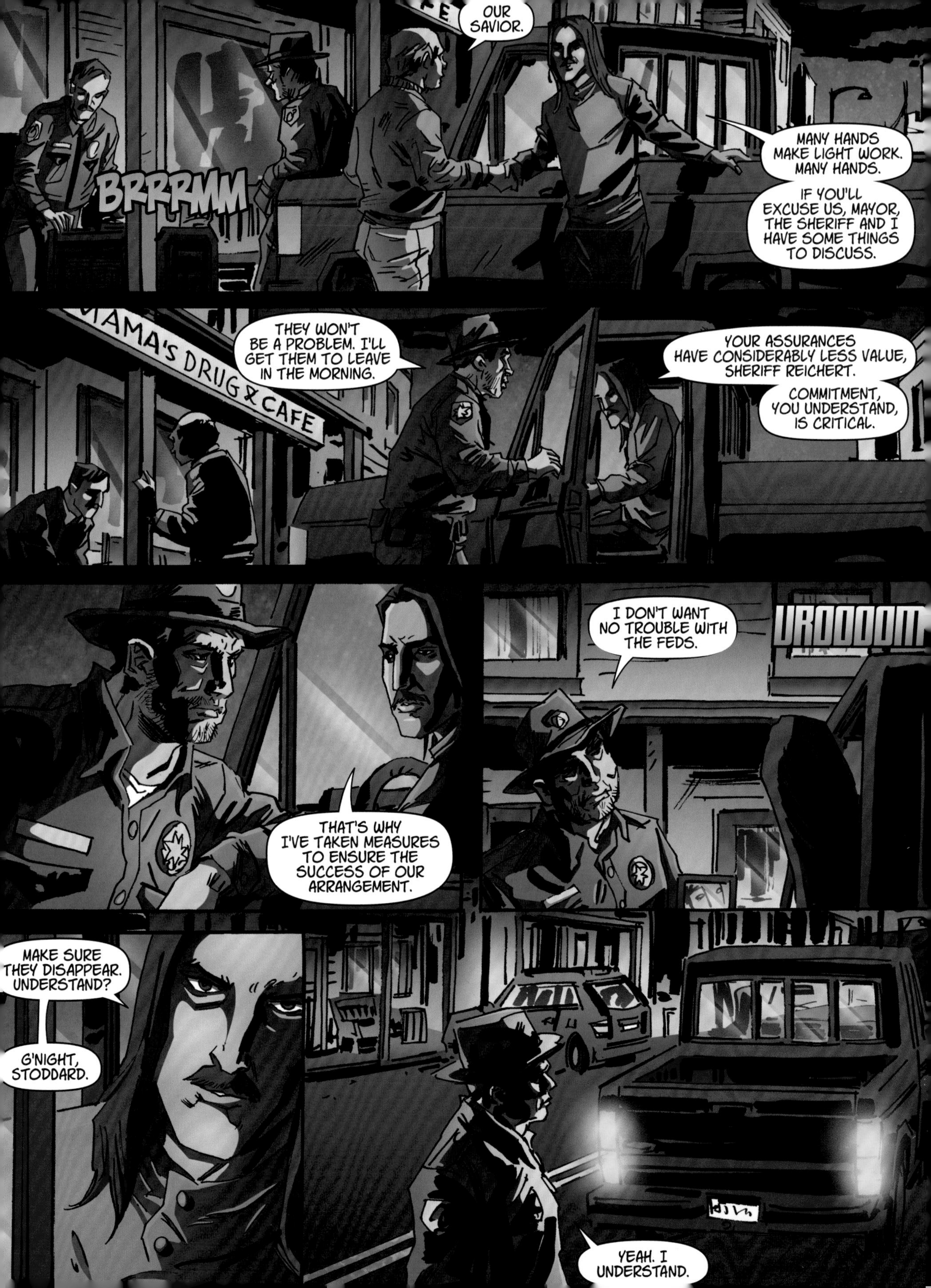
OUR SAVIOR.
BRRRMM
MANY HANDS MAKE LIGHT WORK. MANY HANDS.
IF YOU'LL EXCUSE US, MAYOR, THE SHERIFF AND I HAVE SOME THINGS TO DISCUSS.
MAMA'S DRUG & CAFE
THEY WON'T BE A PROBLEM. I'LL GET THEM TO LEAVE IN THE MORNING.
YOUR ASSURANCES HAVE CONSIDERABLY LESS VALUE, SHERIFF REICHERT.
COMMITMENT, YOU UNDERSTAND, IS CRITICAL.
THAT'S WHY I'VE TAKEN MEASURES TO ENSURE THE SUCCESS OF OUR ARRANGEMENT.
I DON'T WANT NO TROUBLE WITH THE FEDS.
UROOOOM
MAKE SURE THEY DISAPPEAR. UNDERSTAND?
G'NIGHT, STODDARD.
YEAH. I UNDERSTAND.

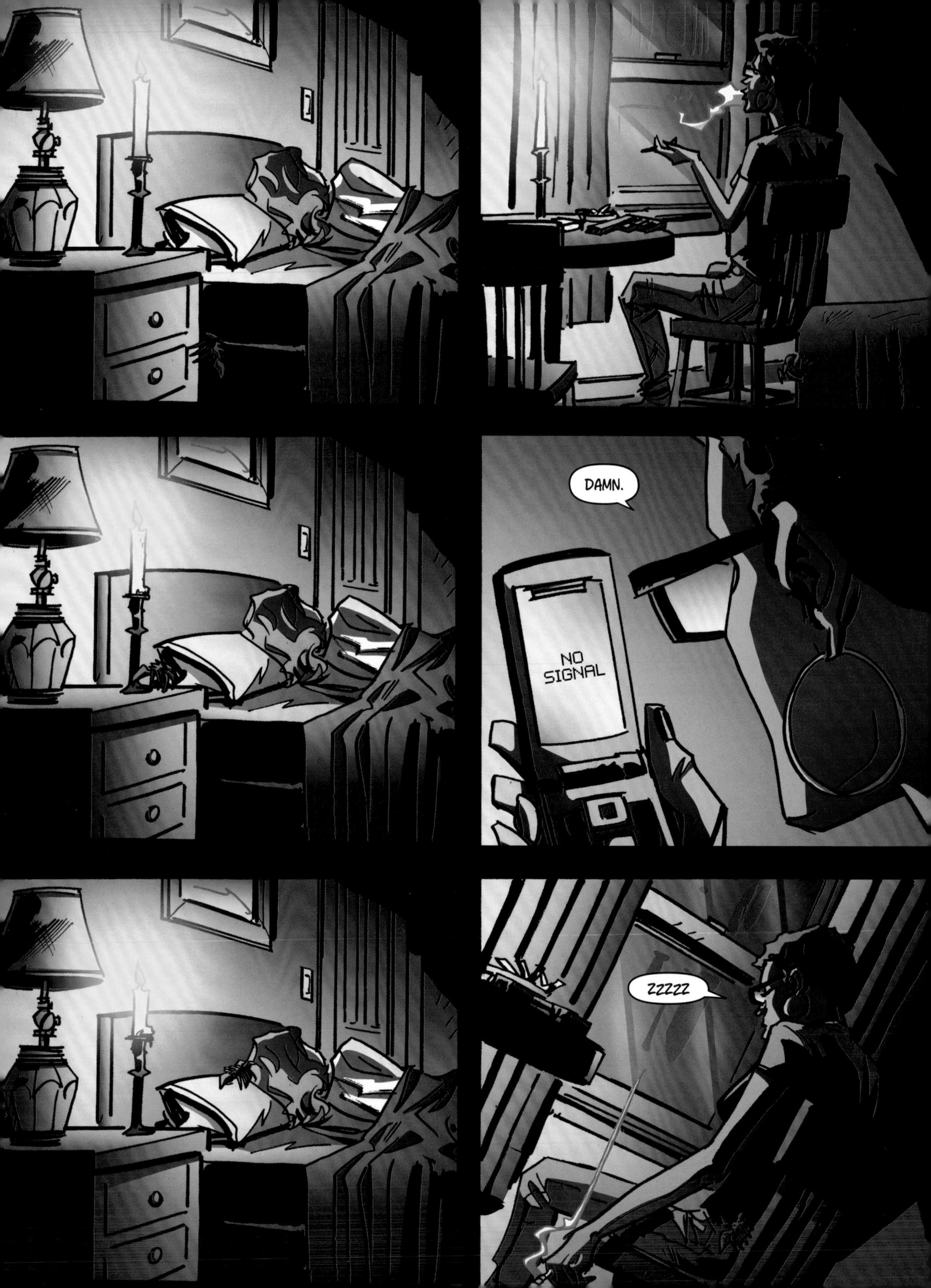
DAMN.
NO SIGNAL
ZZZZZ

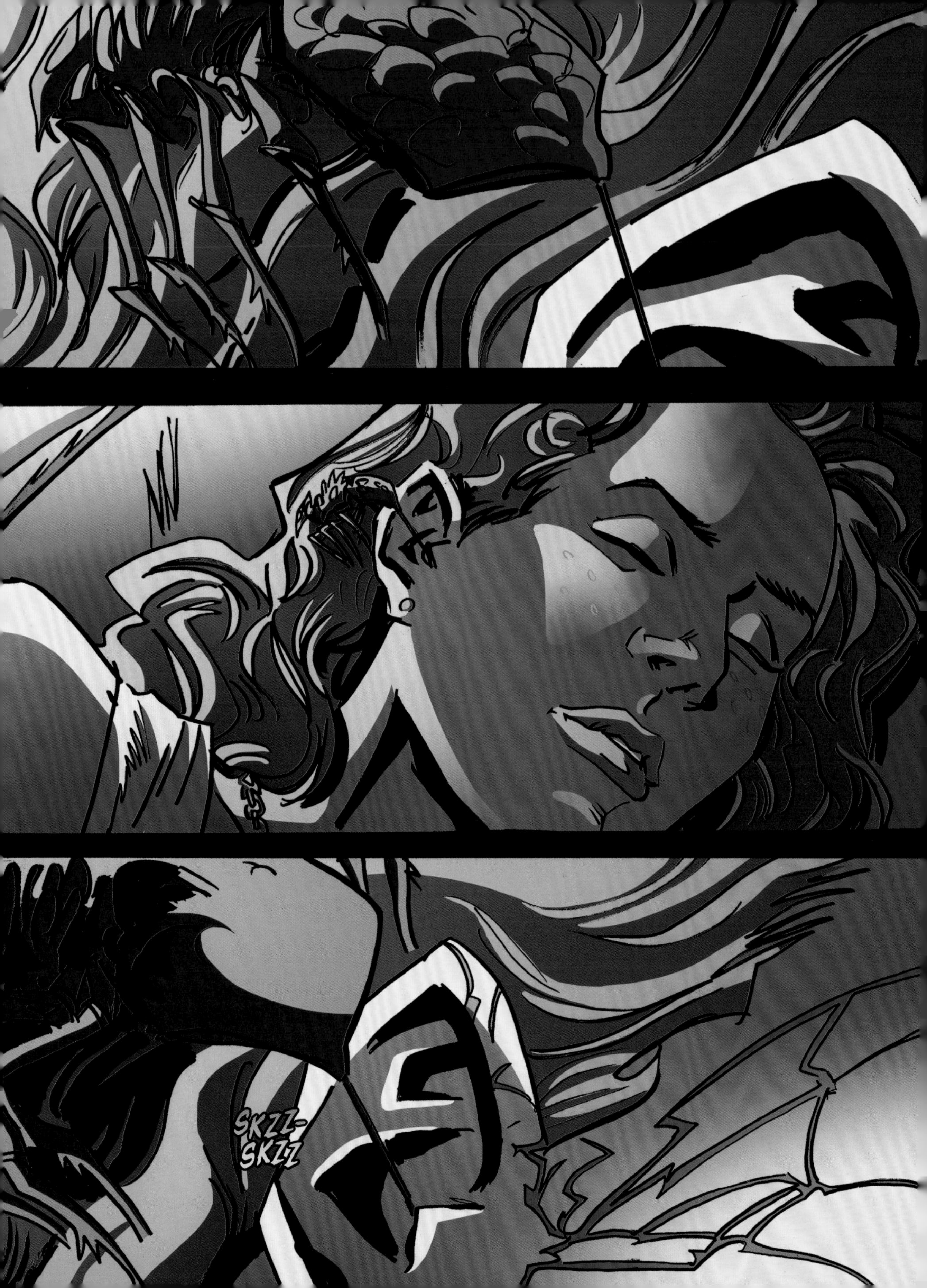
SKZZ-
SKZZ

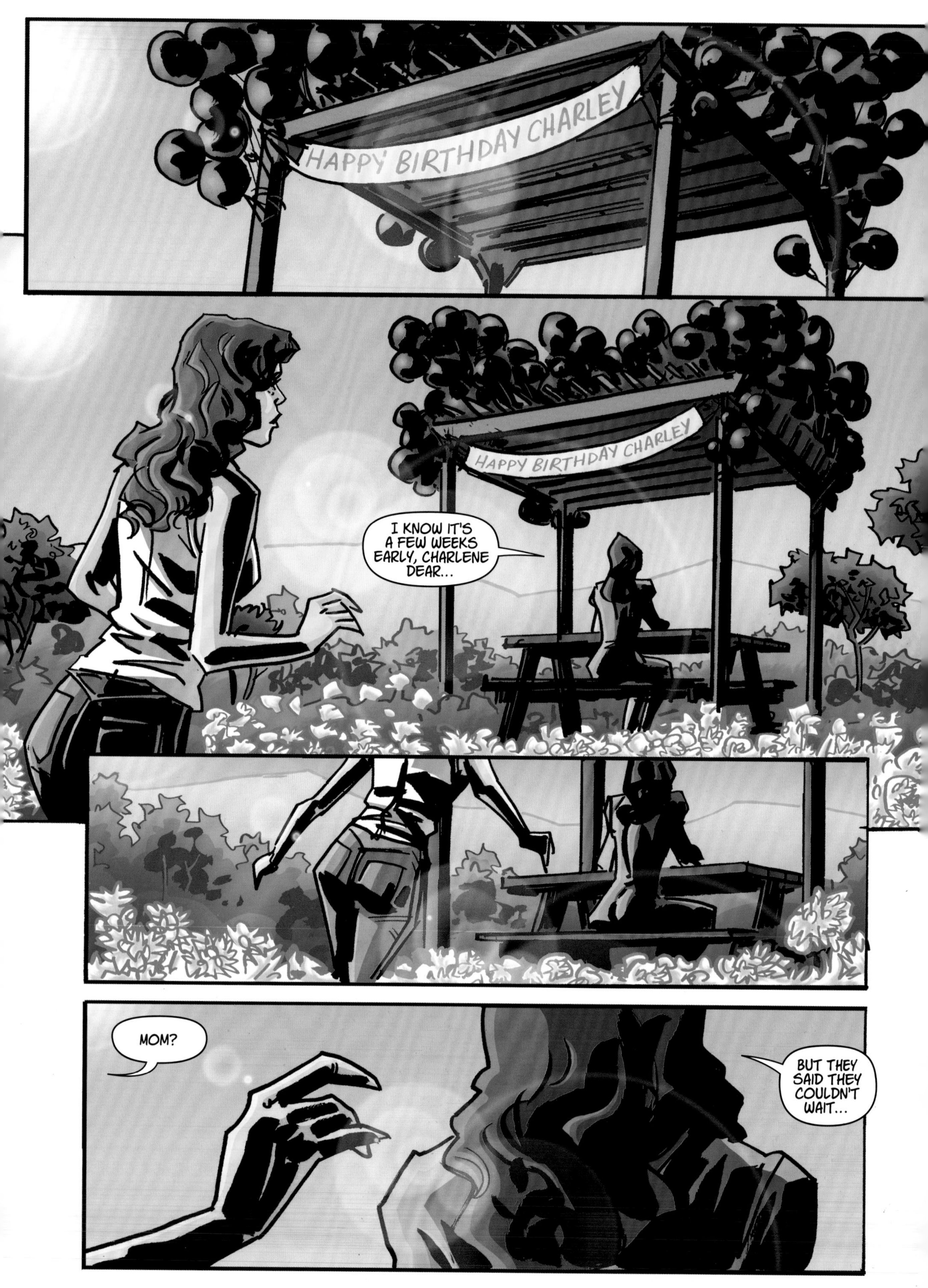
HAPPY BIRTHDAY CHARLEY
HAPPY BIRTHDAY CHARLEY
I KNOW IT'S A FEW WEEKS EARLY, CHARLENE DEAR...
MOM?
BUT THEY SAID THEY COULDN'T WAIT...

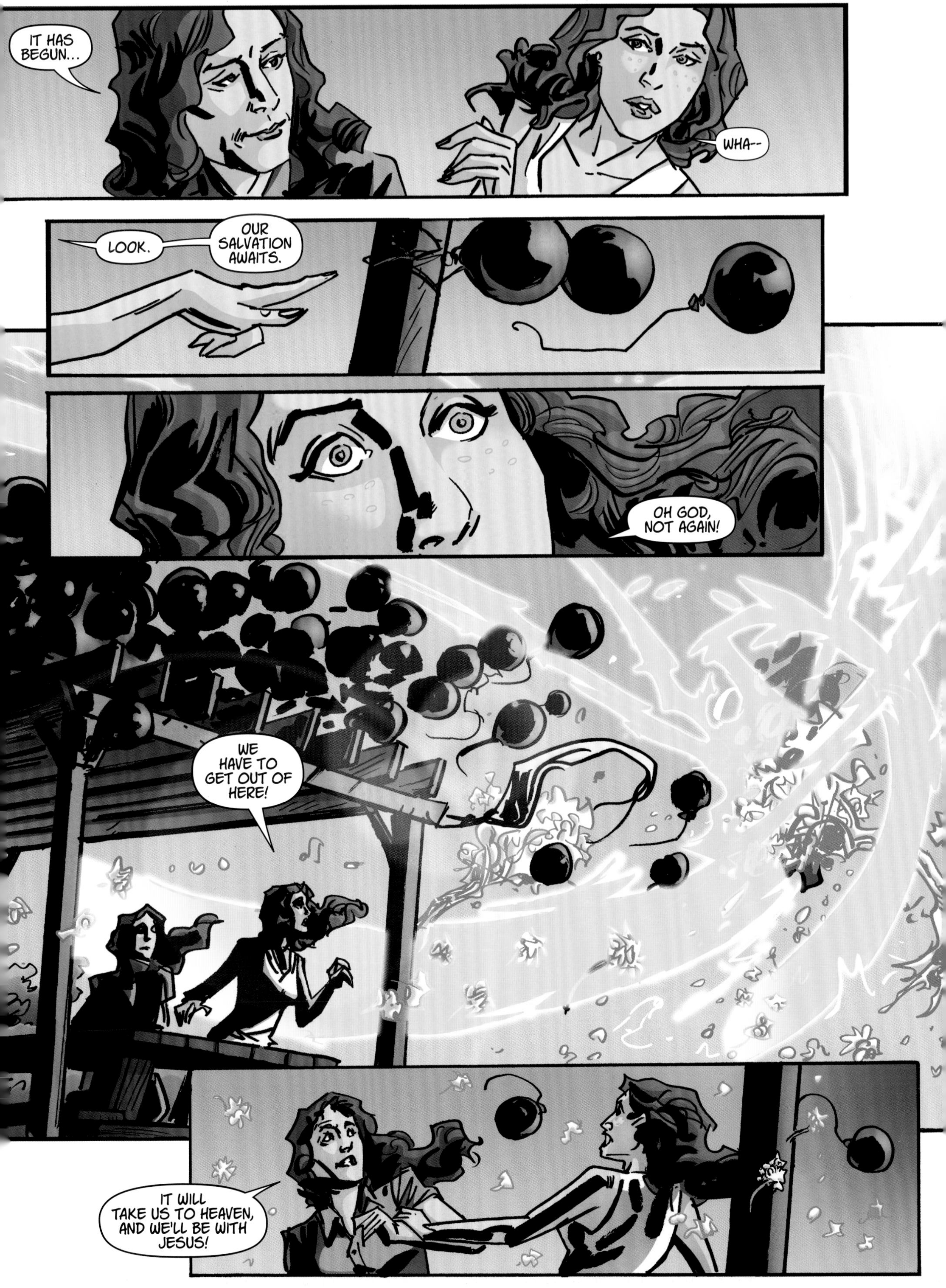
IT HAS BEGUN...
WHA--
LOOK.
OUR SALVATION AWAITS.
OH GOD, NOT AGAIN!
WE HAVE TO GET OUT OF HERE!
IT WILL TAKE US TO HEAVEN, AND WE'LL BE WITH JESUS!

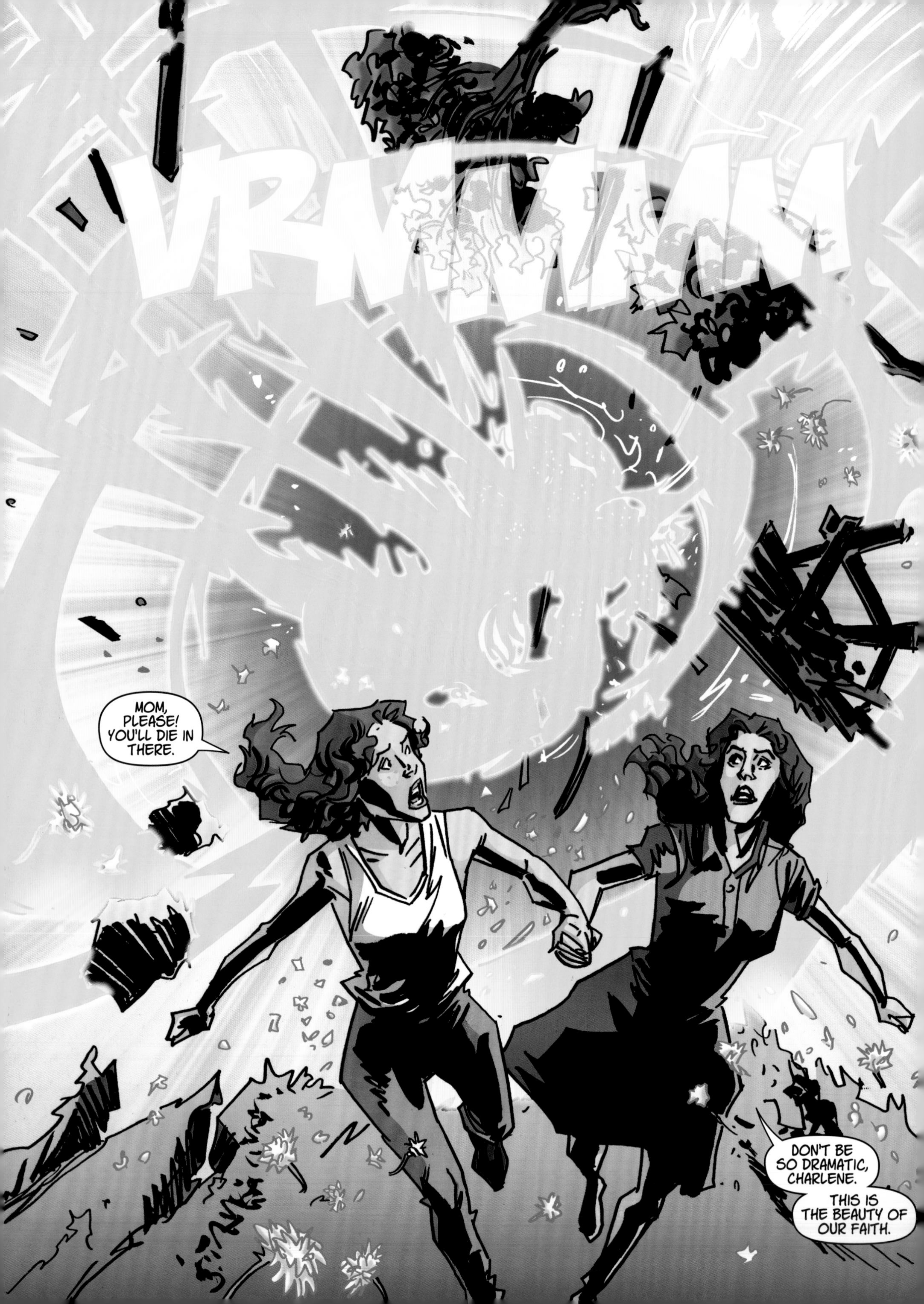
VRMMMM
MOM, PLEASE! YOU'LL DIE IN THERE.
DON'T BE SO DRAMATIC, CHARLENE.
THIS IS THE BEAUTY OF OUR FAITH.

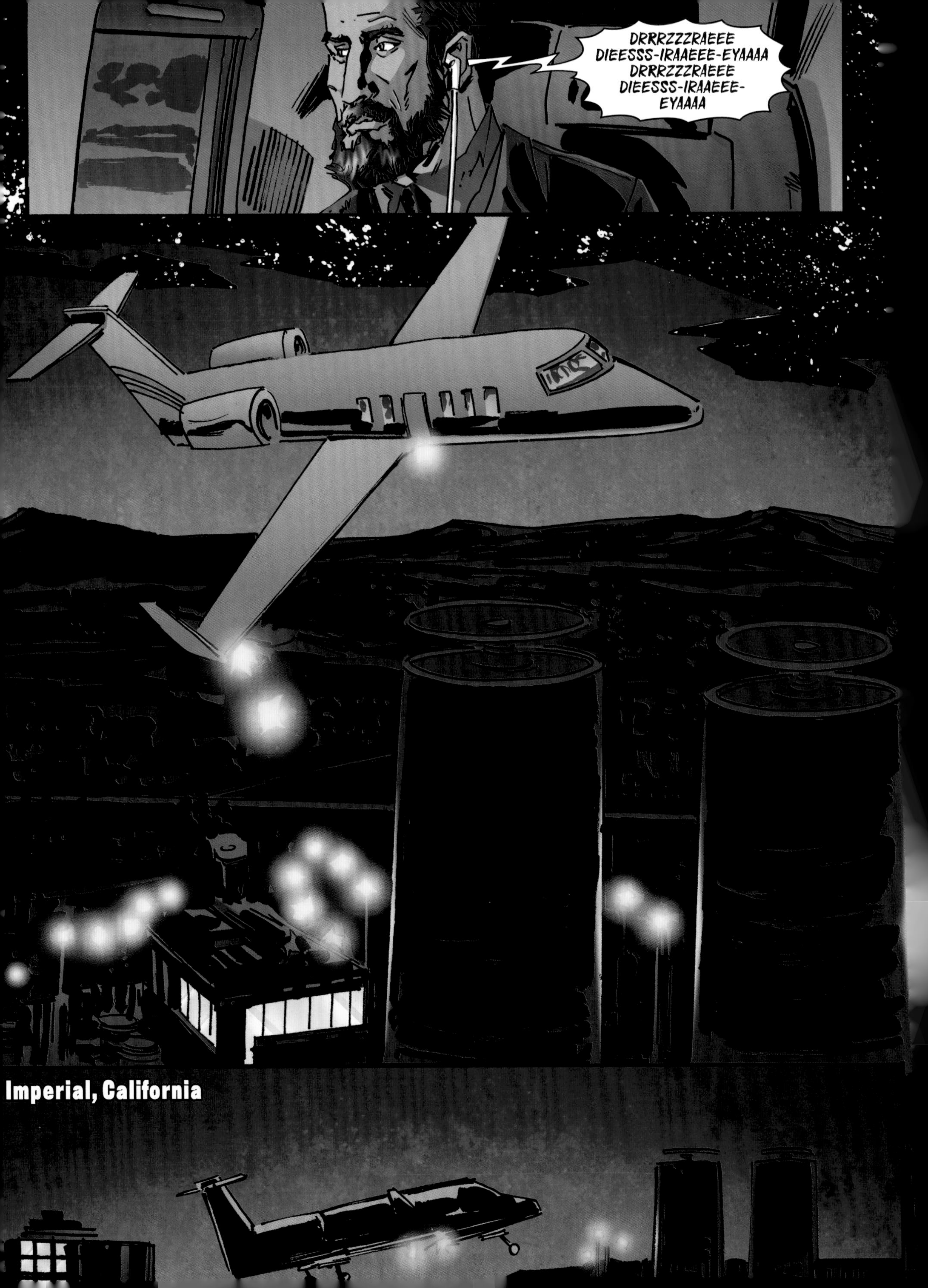
DRRRZZZRAEEE DIEESSS-IRAAEEE-EYAAAA DRRRZZZRAEEE DIEESSS-IRAAEEE-EYAAAA
Imperial, California

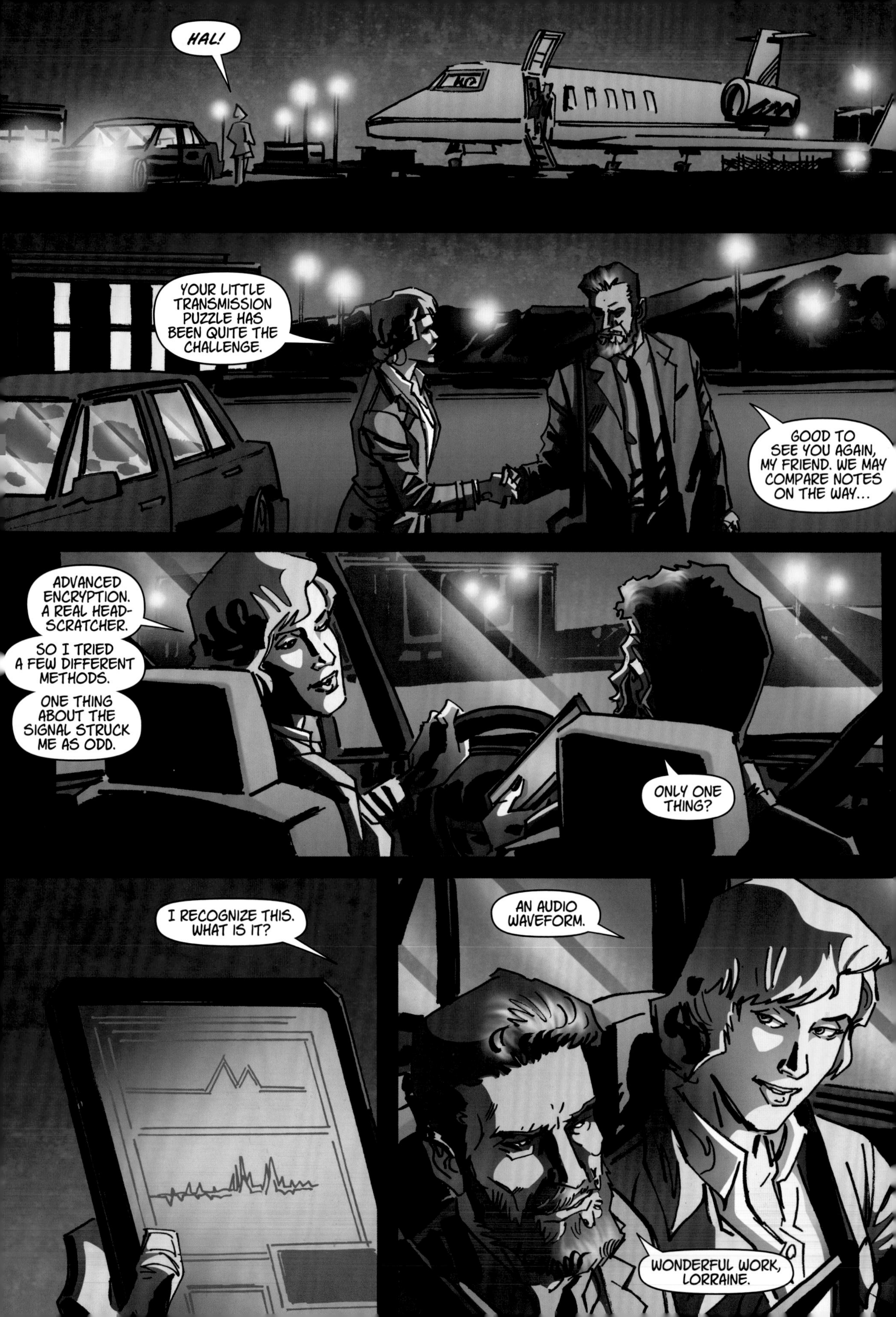
HAL!
YOUR LITTLE TRANSMISSION PUZZLE HAS BEEN QUITE THE CHALLENGE.
GOOD TO SEE YOU AGAIN, MY FRIEND. WE MAY COMPARE NOTES ON THE WAY...
ADVANCED ENCRYPTION. A REAL HEAD-SCRATCHER.
SO I TRIED A FEW DIFFERENT METHODS.
ONE THING ABOUT THE SIGNAL STRUCK ME AS ODD.
ONLY ONE THING?
I RECOGNIZE THIS. WHAT IS IT?
AN AUDIO WAVEFORM.
WONDERFUL WORK, LORRAINE.

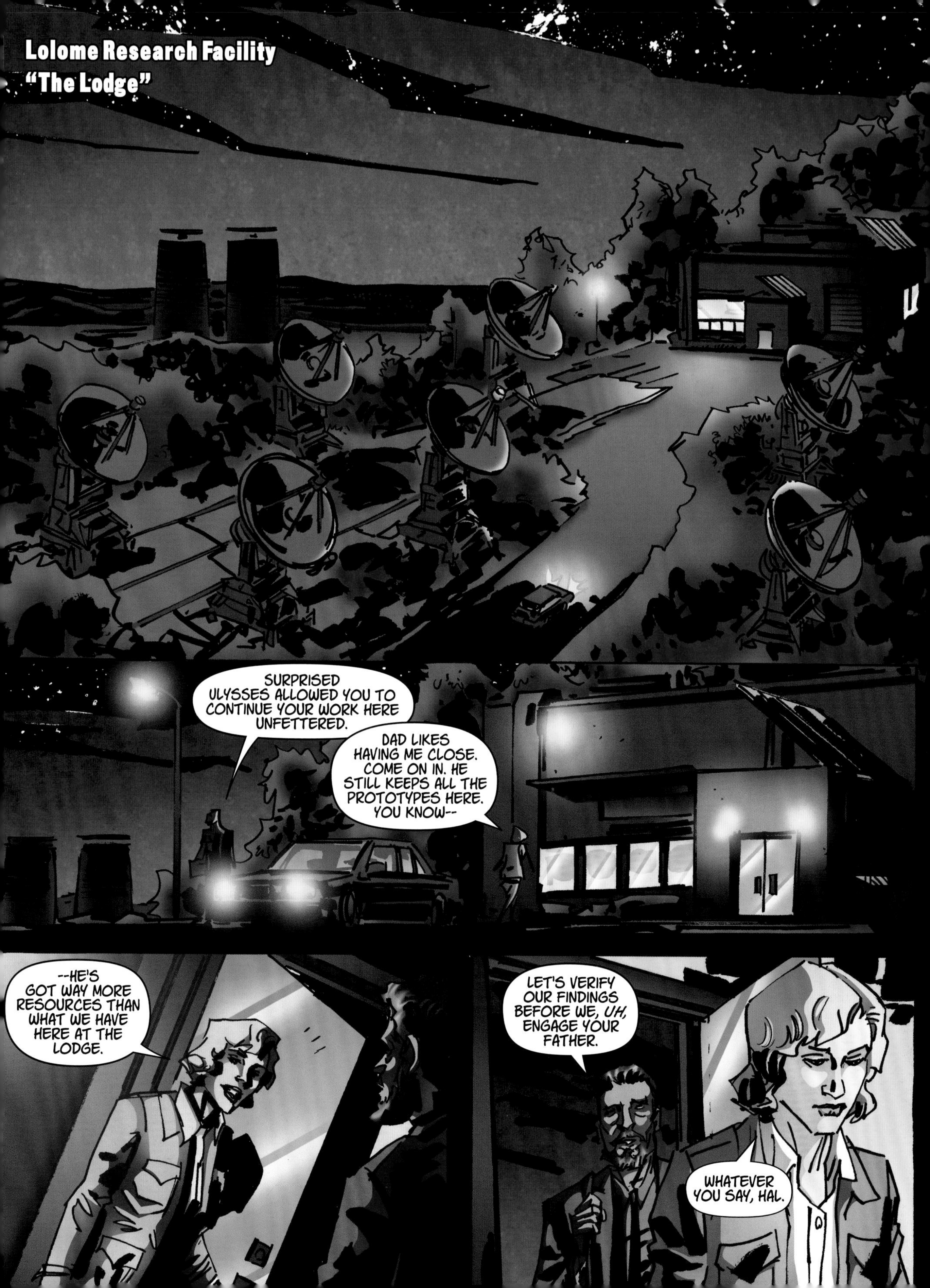
Lolome Research Facility
"The Lodge"
SURPRISED ULYSSES ALLOWED YOU TO CONTINUE YOUR WORK HERE UNFETTERED.
DAD LIKES HAVING ME CLOSE. COME ON IN. HE STILL KEEPS ALL THE PROTOTYPES HERE. YOU KNOW--
--HE'S GOT WAY MORE RESOURCES THAN WHAT WE HAVE HERE AT THE LODGE.
LET'S VERIFY OUR FINDINGS BEFORE WE, UH, ENGAGE YOUR FATHER.
WHATEVER YOU SAY, HAL.

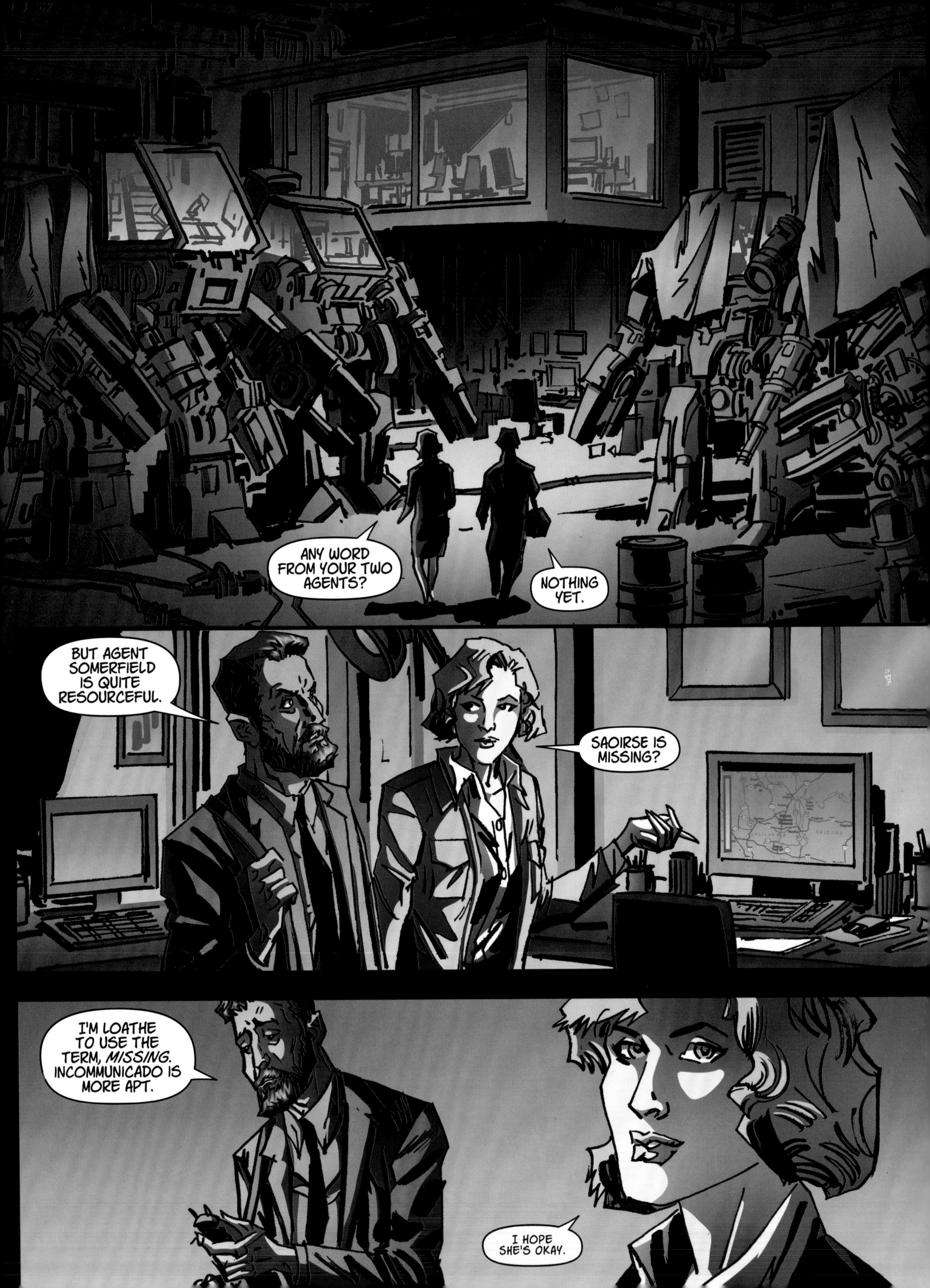
ANY WORD FROM YOUR TWO AGENTS?
NOTHING YET.
BUT AGENT SOMERFIELD IS QUITE RESOURCEFUL.
SAOIRSE IS MISSING?
I'M LOATHE TO USE THE TERM, *MISSING*. INCOMMUNICADO IS MORE APT.
I HOPE SHE'S OKAY.

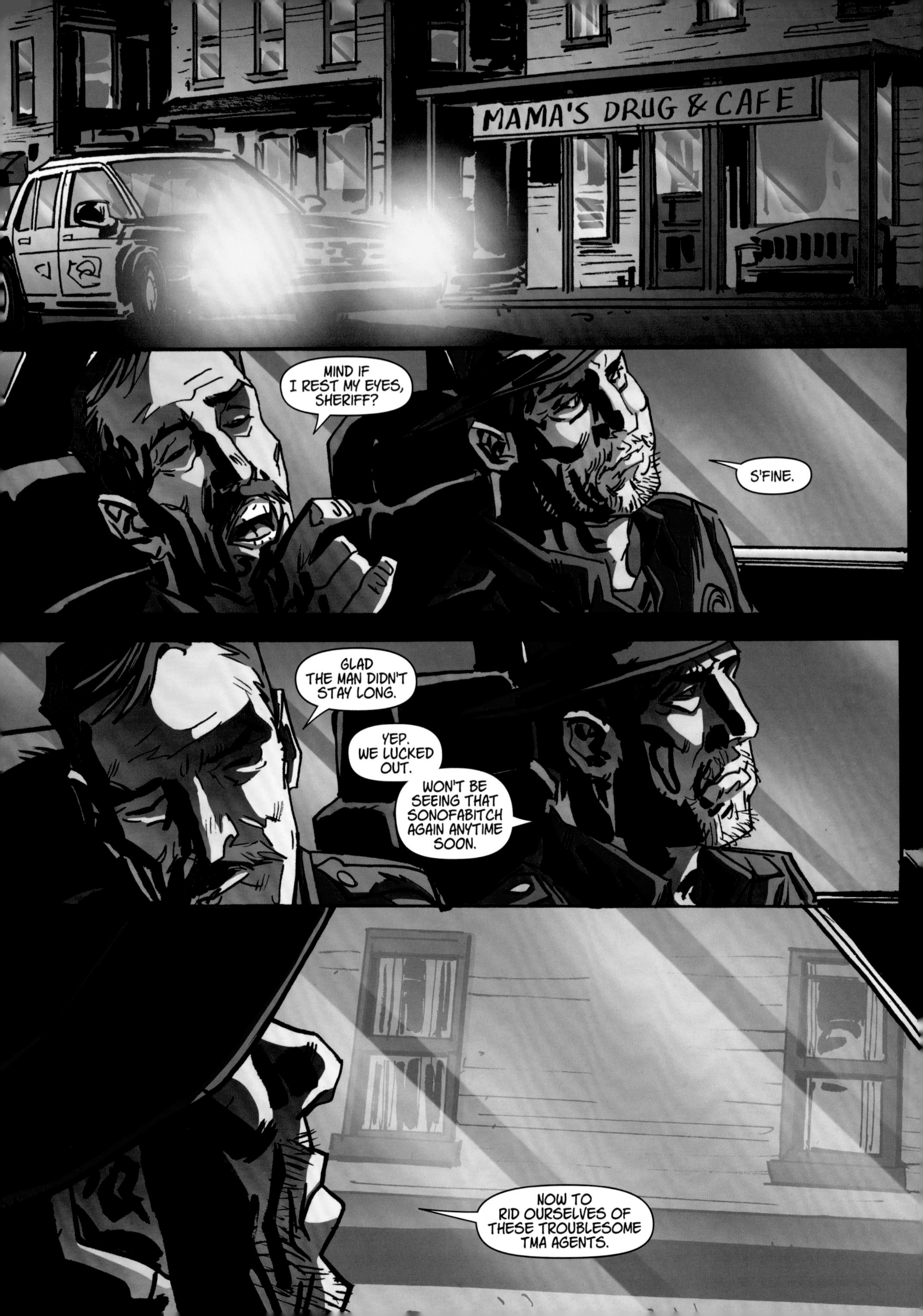
MAMA'S DRUG & CAFE
MIND IF I REST MY EYES, SHERIFF?
S'FINE.
GLAD THE MAN DIDN'T STAY LONG.
YEP. WE LUCKED OUT.
WON'T BE SEEING THAT SONOFABITCH AGAIN ANYTIME SOON.
NOW TO RID OURSELVES OF THESE TROUBLESOME TMA AGENTS.

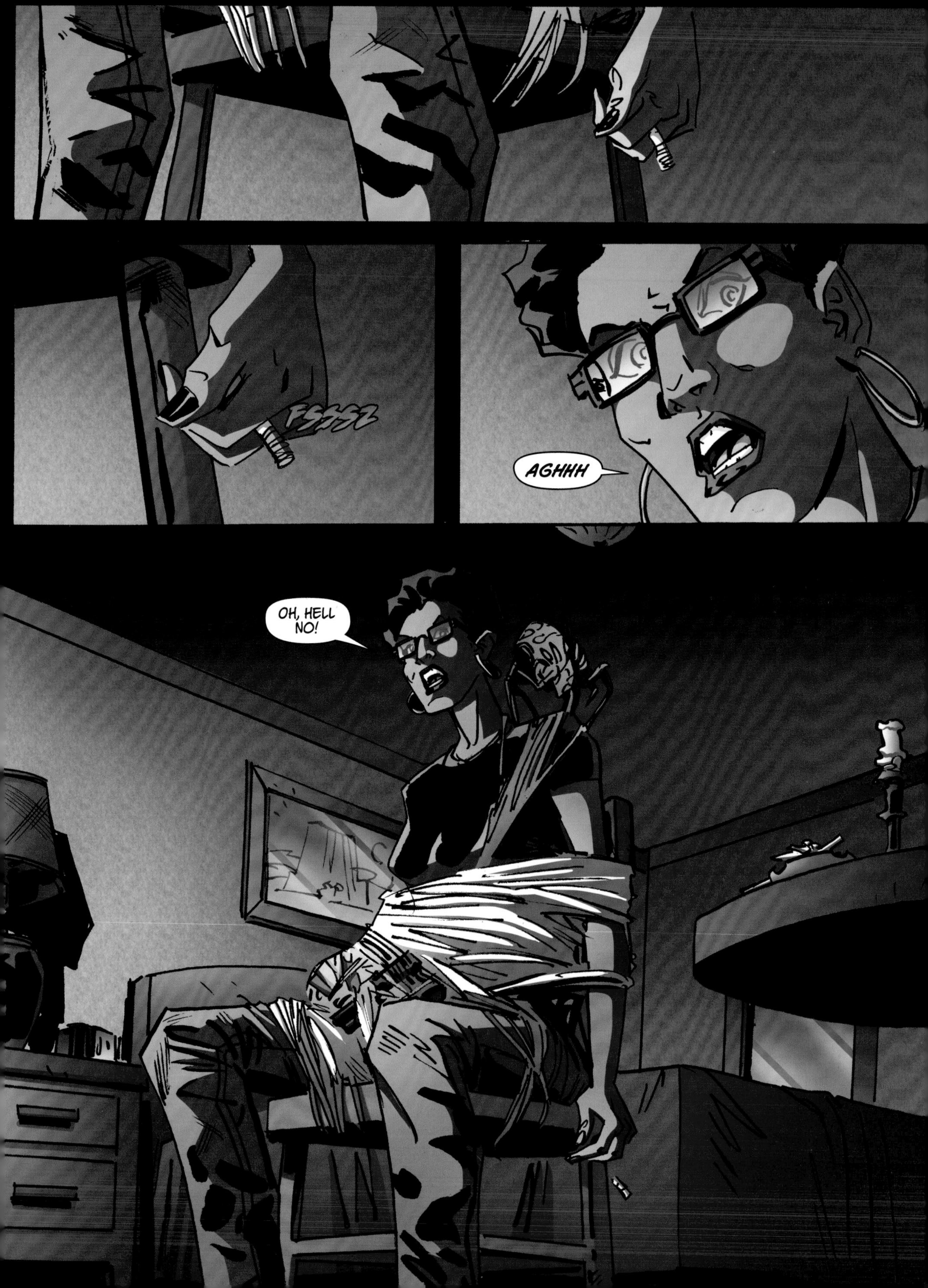
FSSSZ
AGHHH
OH, HELL NO!

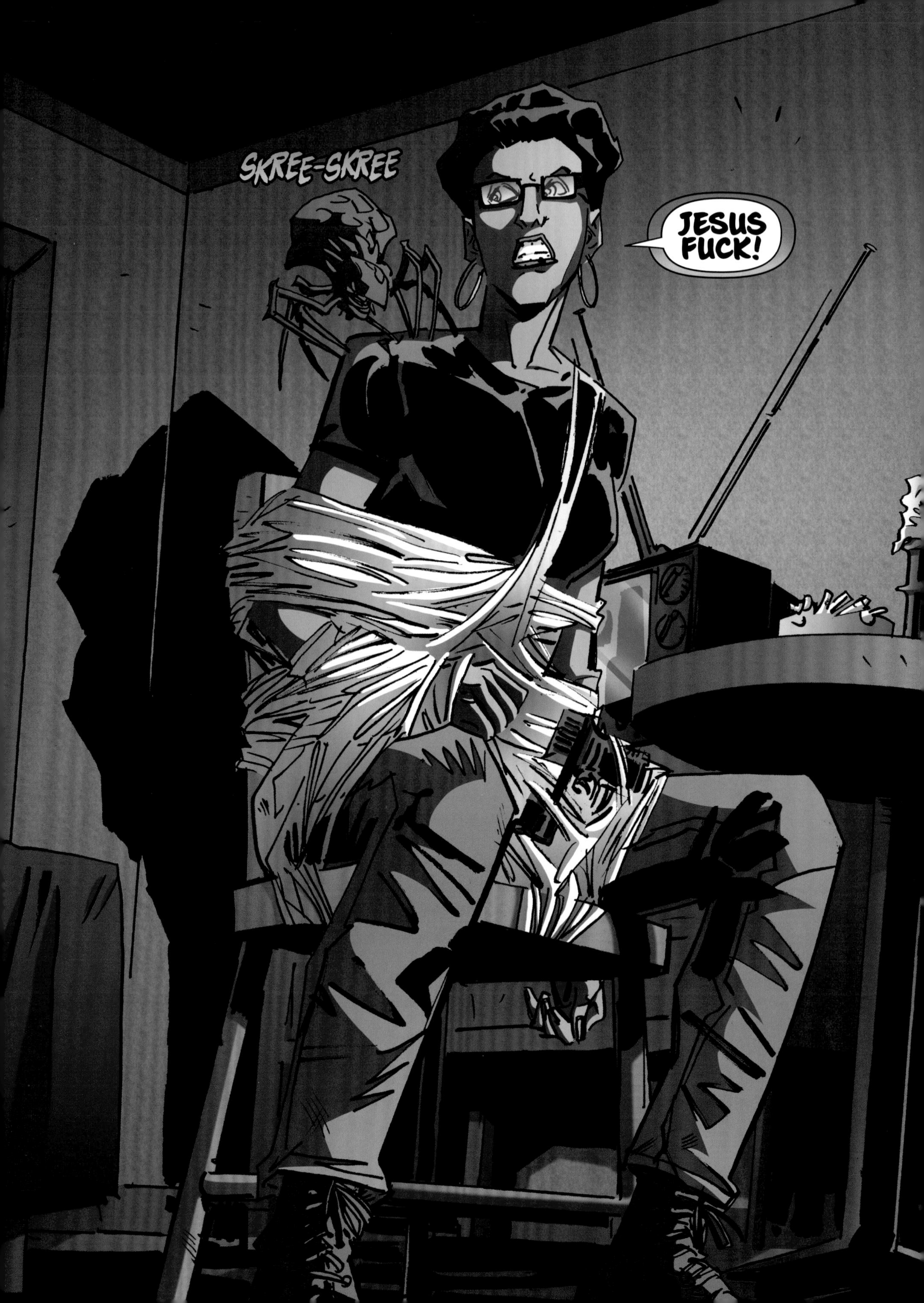
SKREE-SKREE
JESUS FUCK!

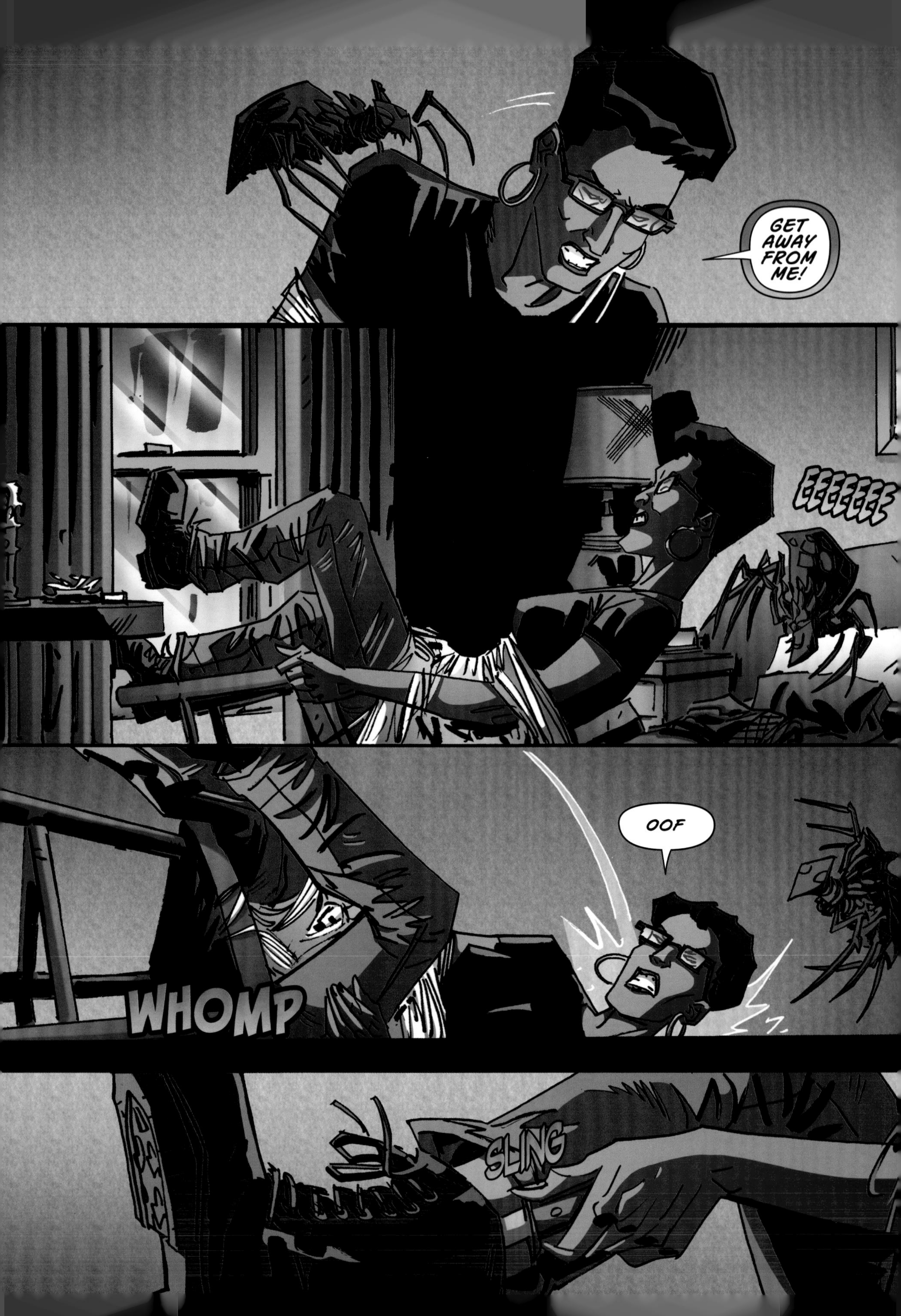
GET AWAY FROM ME!
EEEEEEE
OOF
WHOMP
SLING

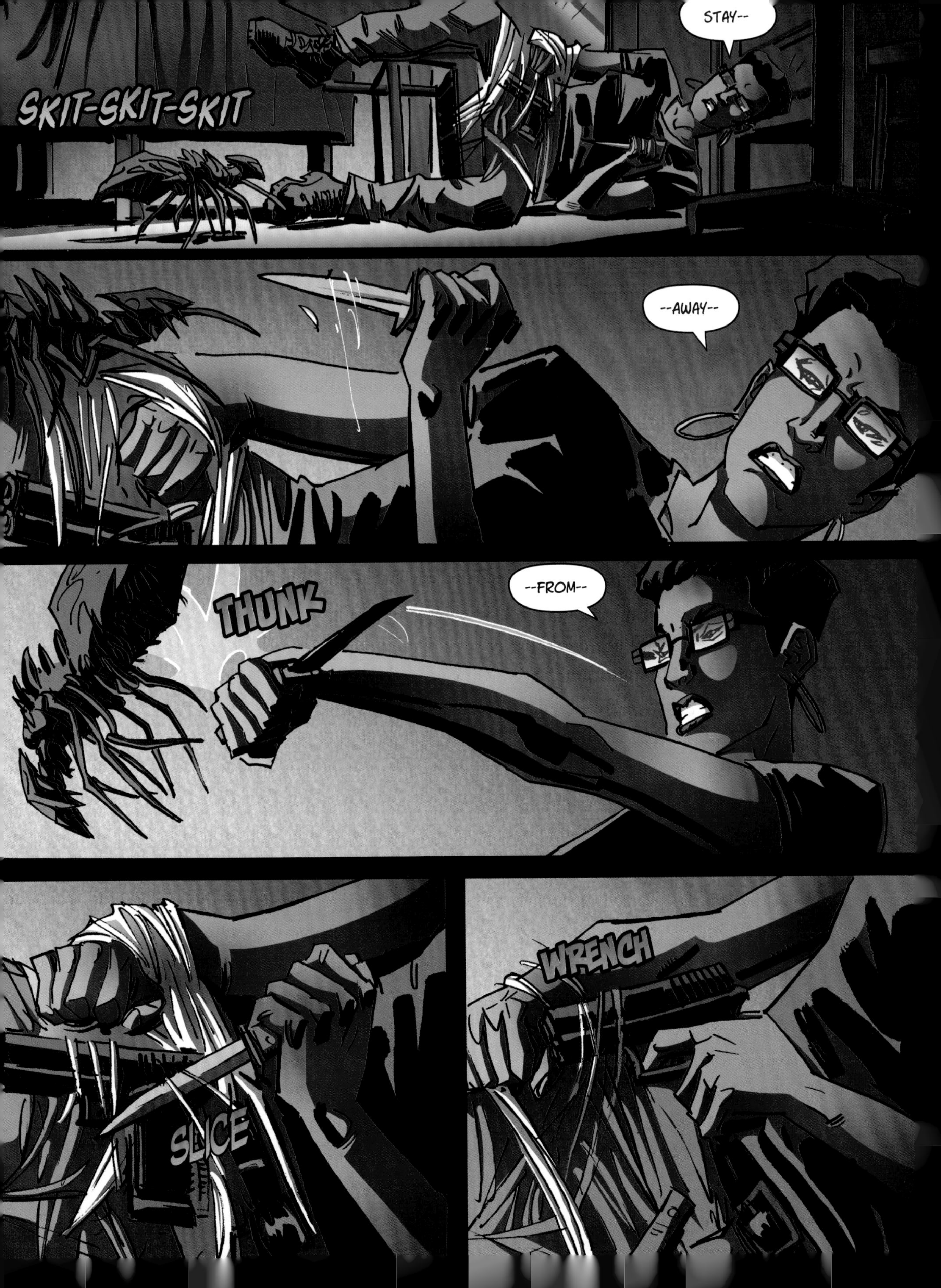
STAY--
SKIT-SKIT-SKIT
--AWAY--
--FROM--
THUNK
SLICE
WRENCH

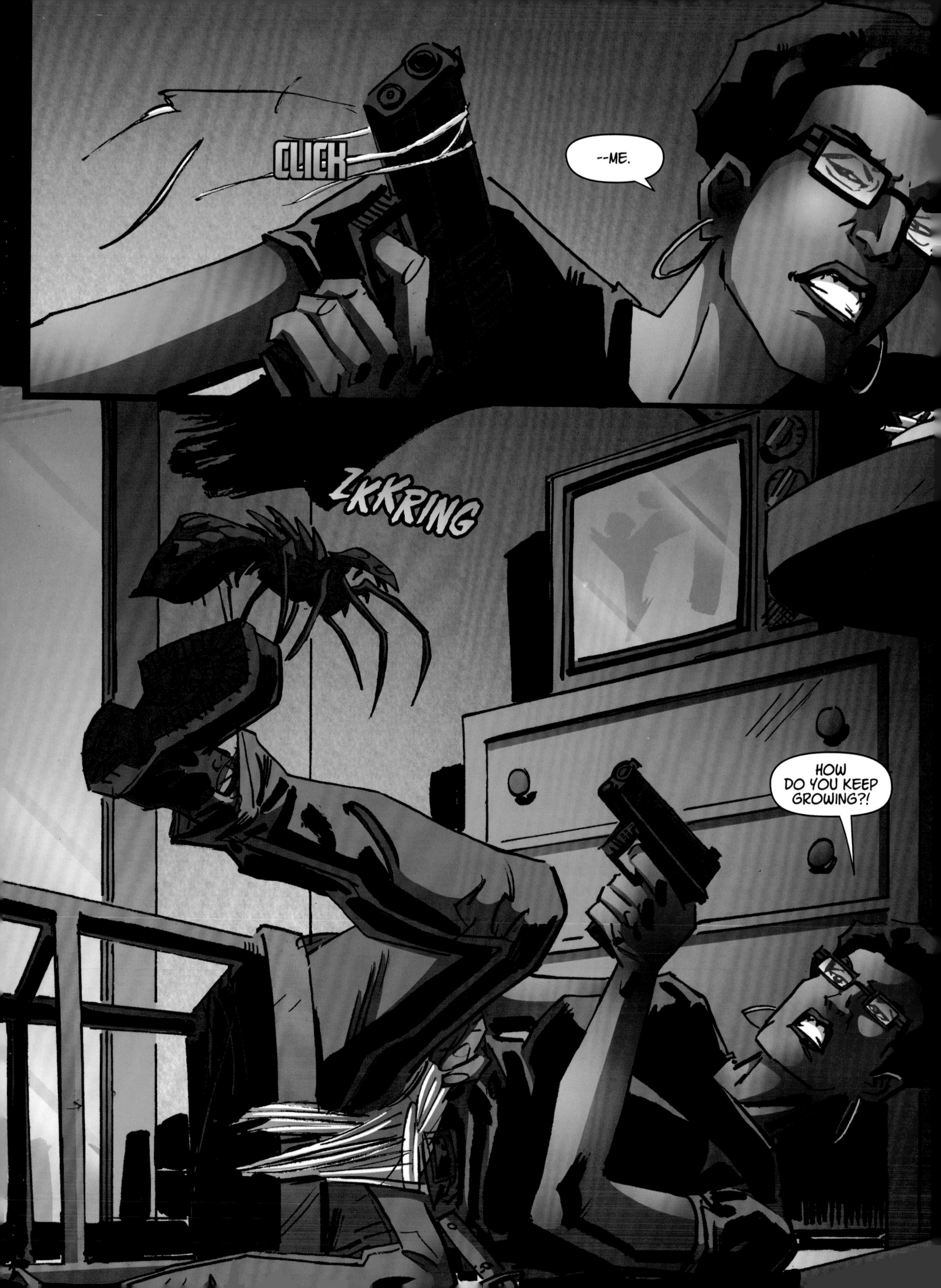
CLICK
--ME.
ZKKRING
HOW DO YOU KEEP GROWING?!

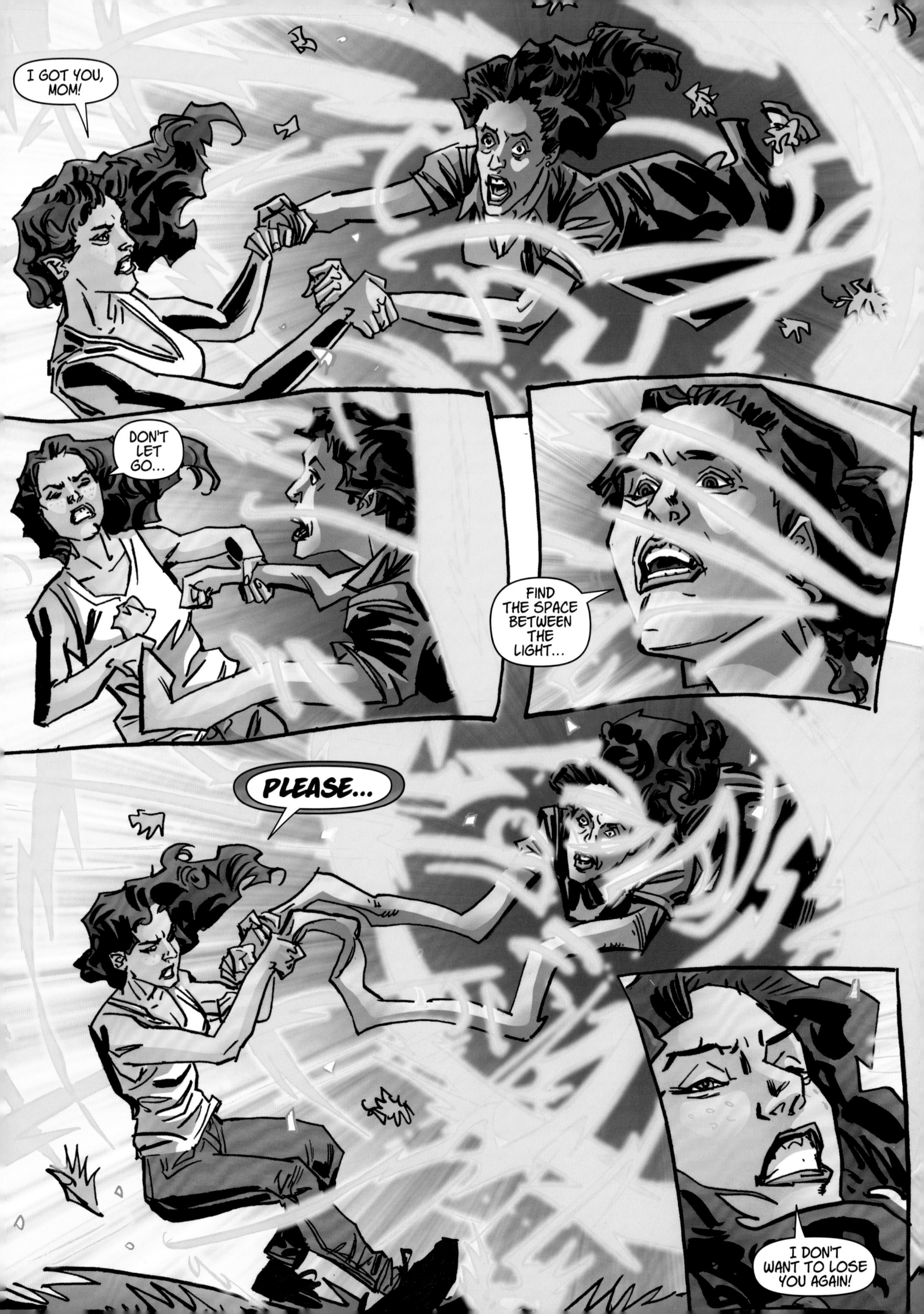
I GOT YOU, MOM!
DON'T LET GO...
FIND THE SPACE BETWEEN THE LIGHT...
PLEASE...
I DON'T WANT TO LOSE YOU AGAIN!

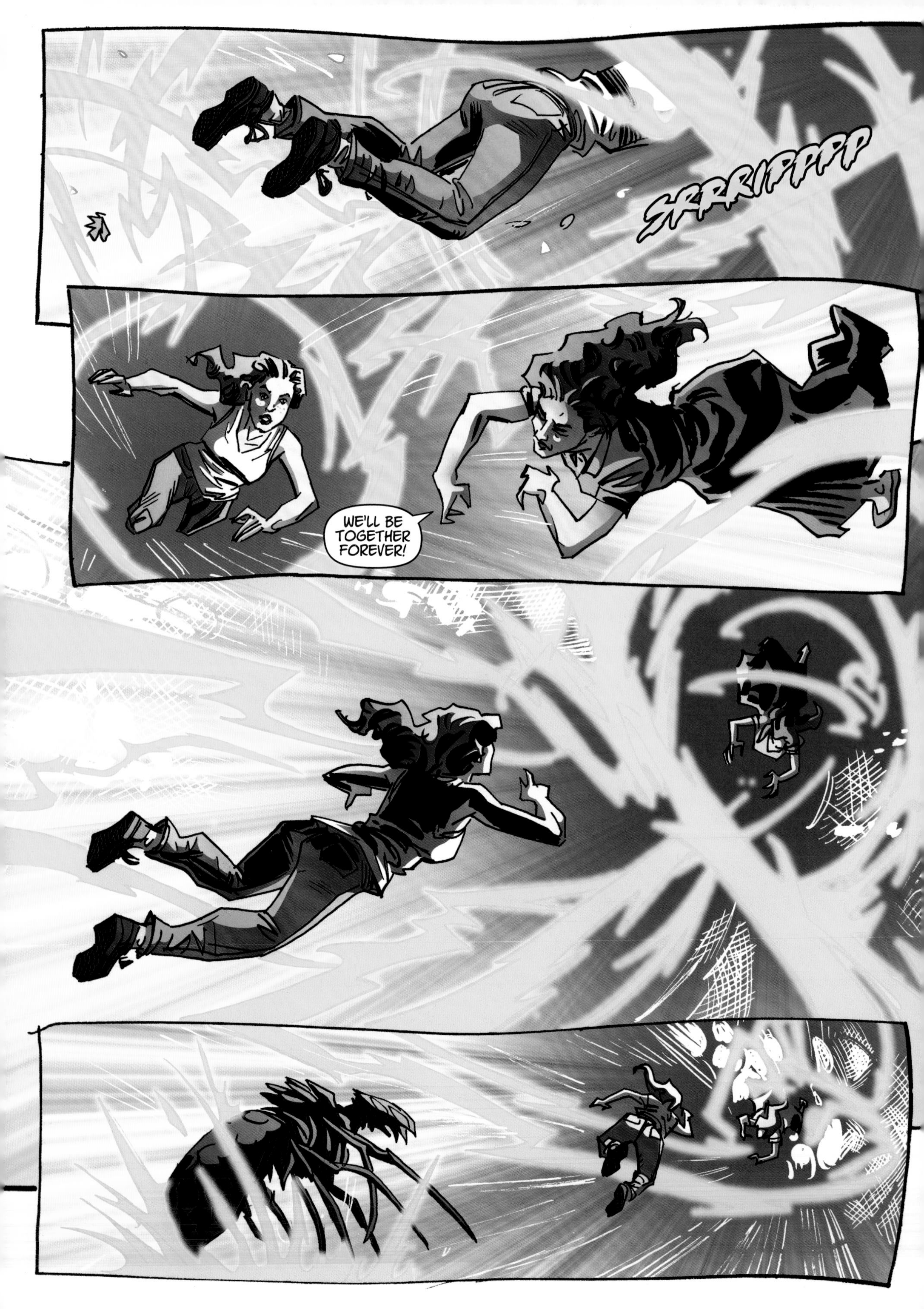
SRRRIPPPP
WE'LL BE TOGETHER FOREVER!

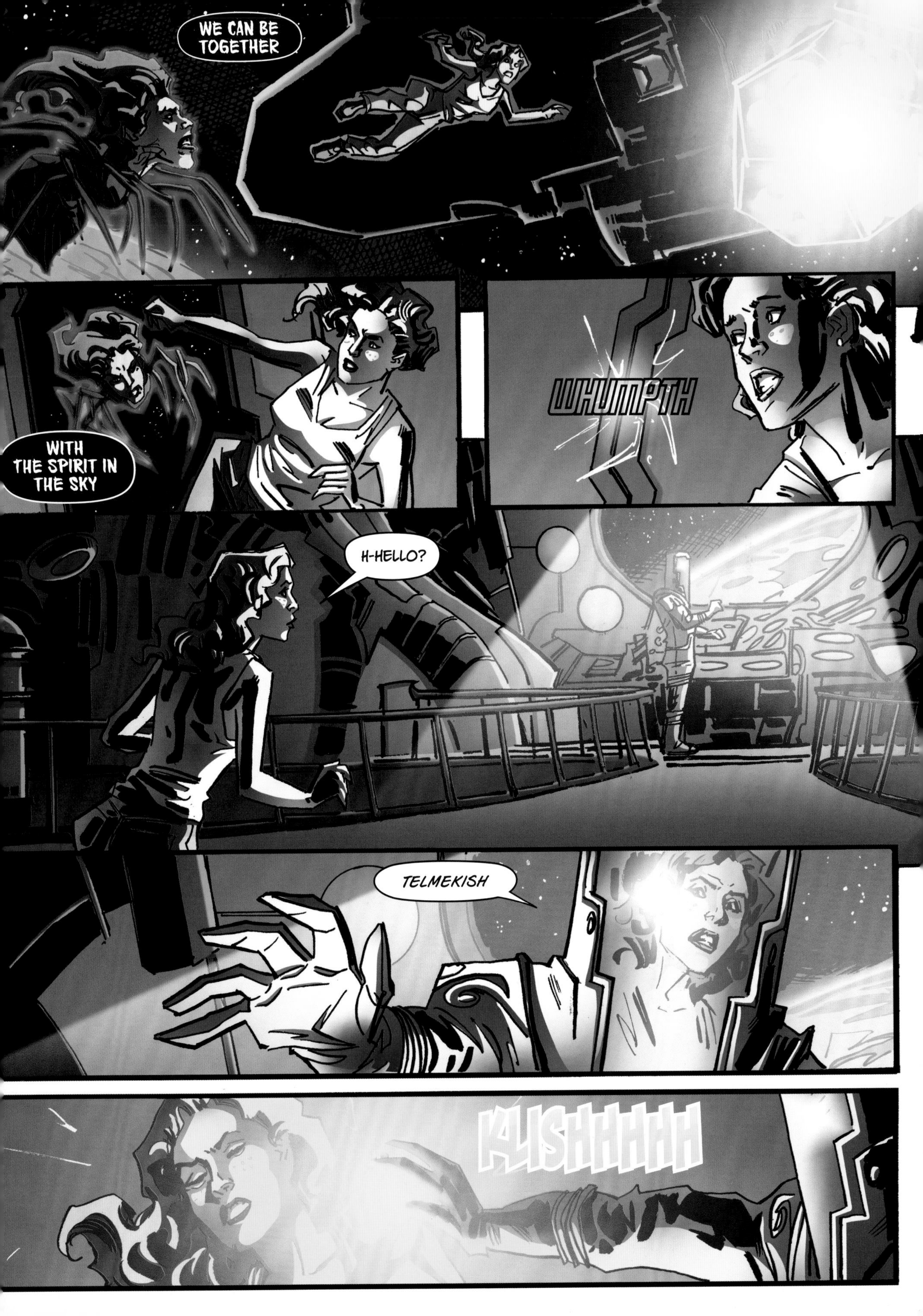
WE CAN BE TOGETHER
WITH THE SPIRIT IN THE SKY
WHUMPTH
H-HELLO?
TELMEKISH
KLISHHHHH

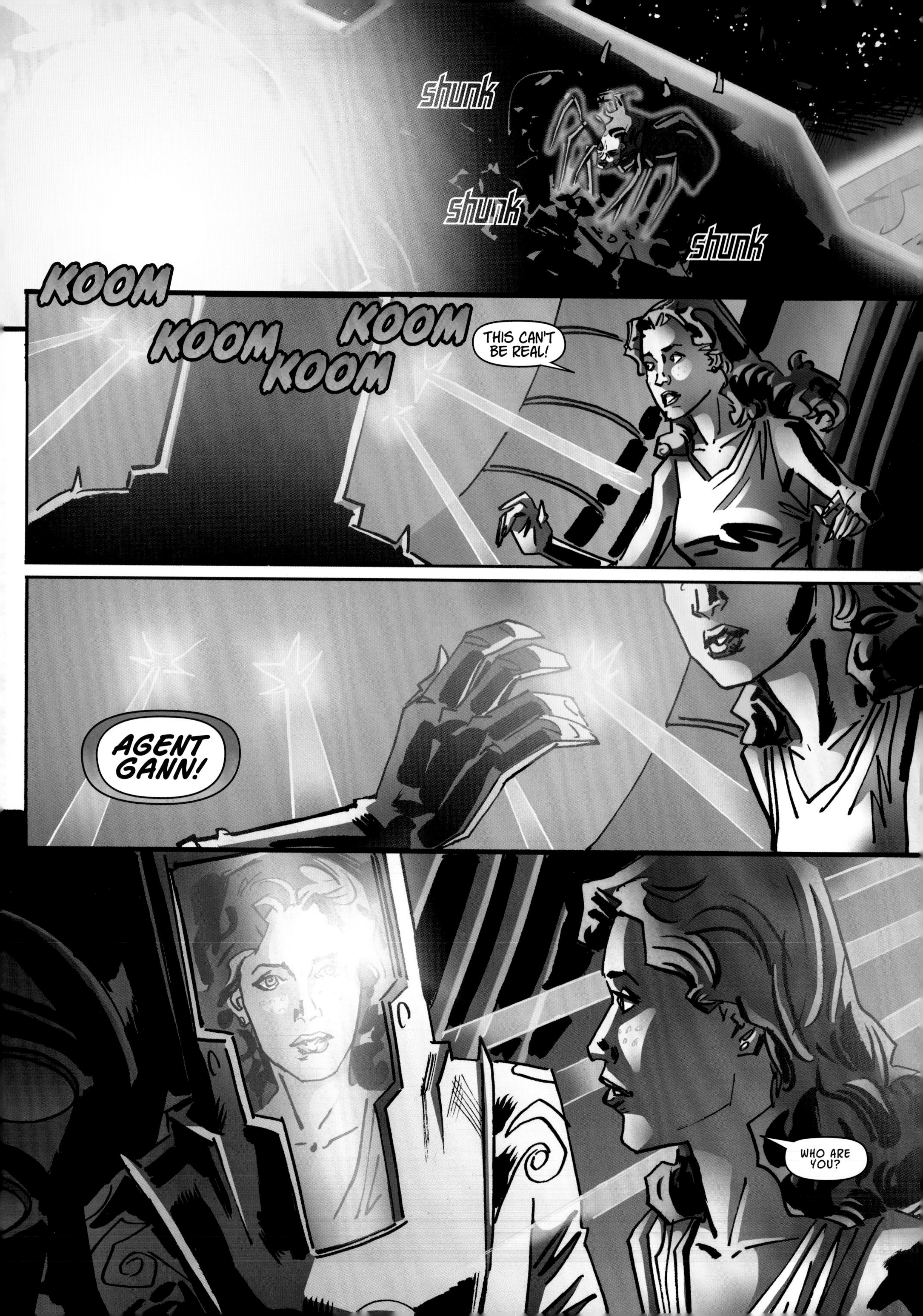
shunk
shunk
shunk
KOOM
KOOM
KOOM
KOOM
THIS CAN'T BE REAL!
AGENT GANN!
WHO ARE YOU?

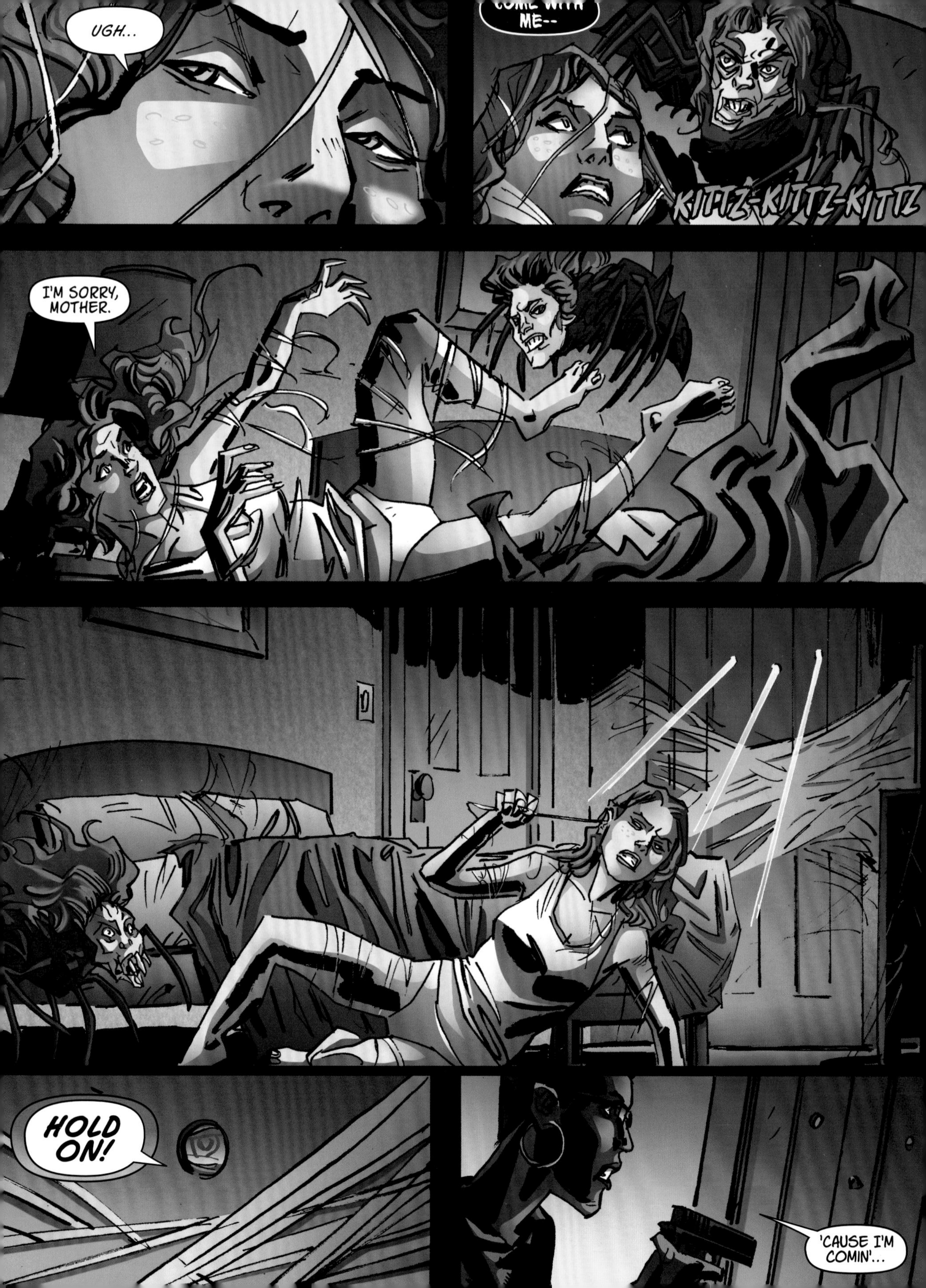
UGH...
COME WITH ME--
KITTZ-KITTZ-KITTZ
I'M SORRY, MOTHER.
HOLD ON!
'CAUSE I'M COMIN'...

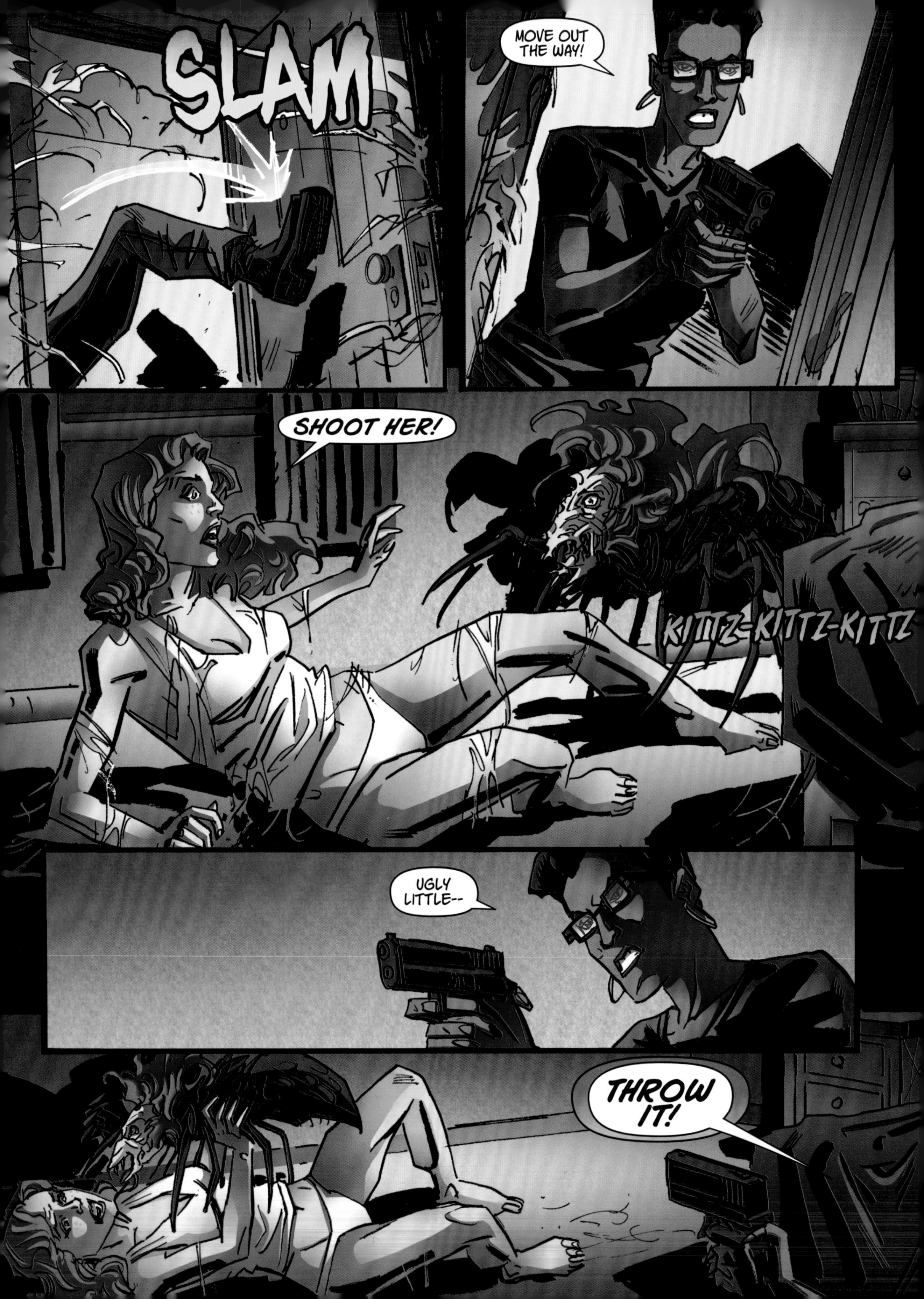
SLAM
MOVE OUT THE WAY!
SHOOT HER!
KITTZ-KITTZ-KITTZ
UGLY LITTLE--
THROW IT!

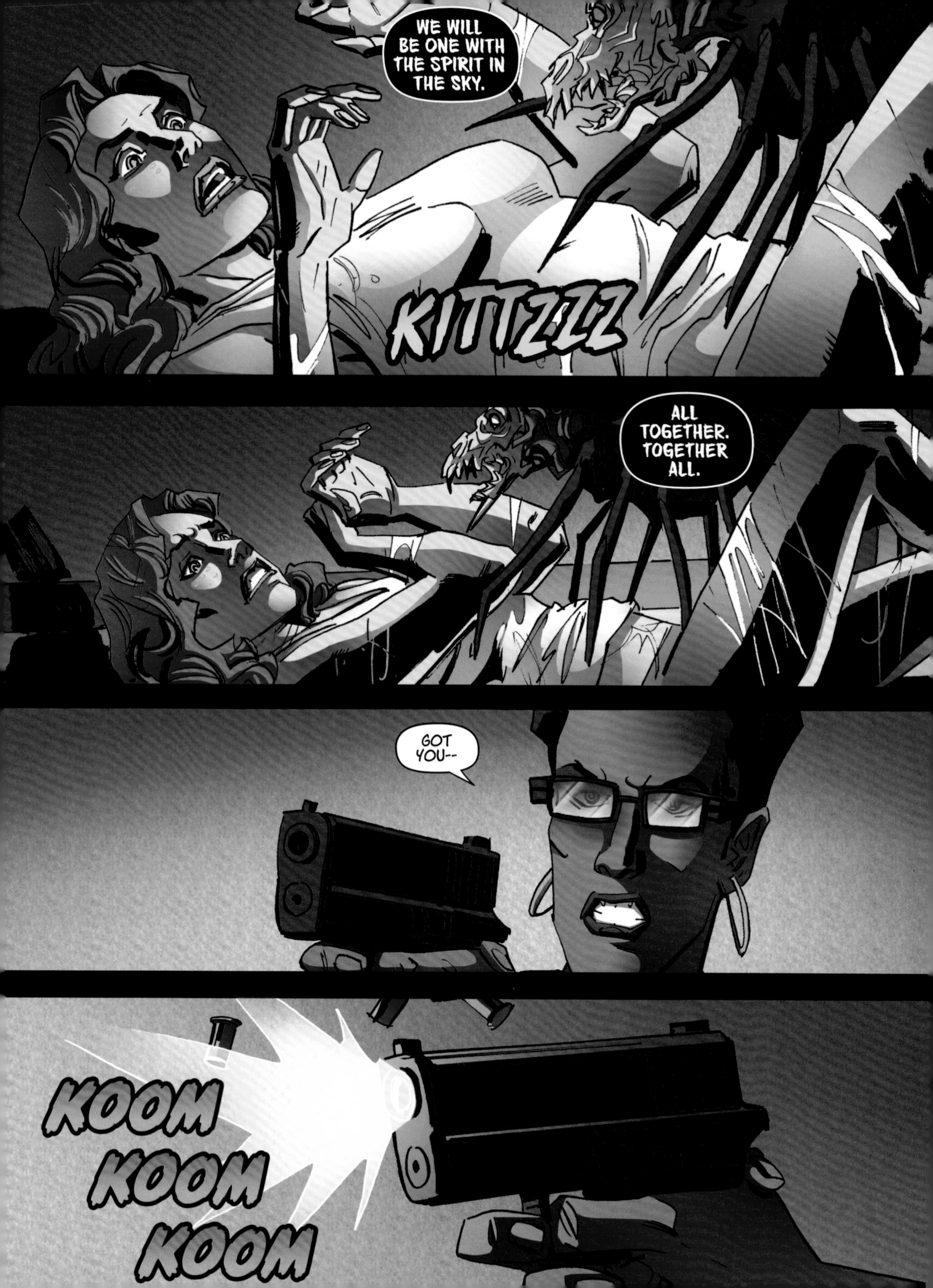
WE WILL BE ONE WITH THE SPIRIT IN THE SKY.
KITTZZZ
ALL TOGETHER. TOGETHER ALL.
GOT YOU--
KOOM
KOOM
KOOM

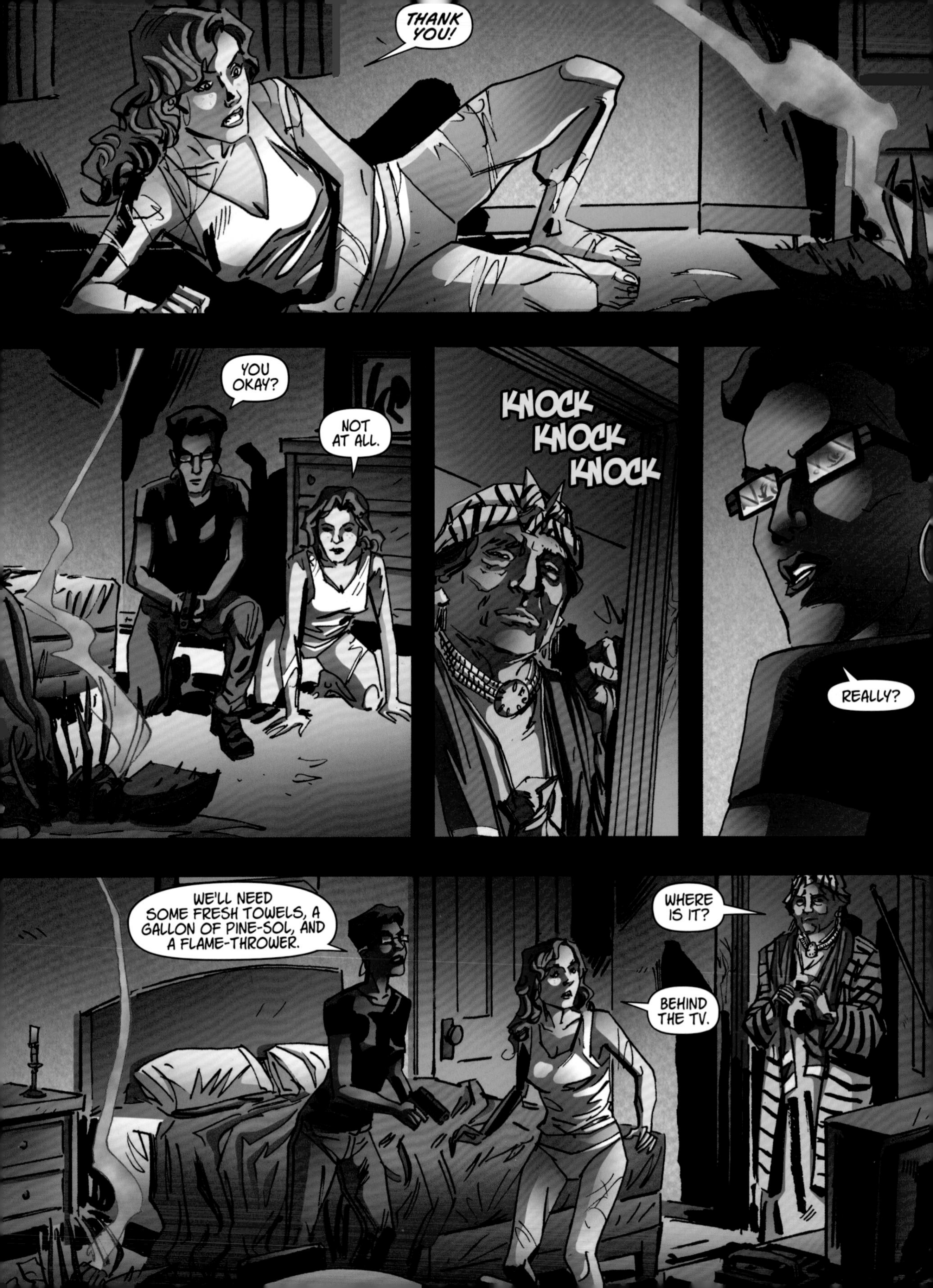
THANK YOU!
YOU OKAY?
NOT AT ALL.
KNOCK KNOCK KNOCK
REALLY?
WE'LL NEED SOME FRESH TOWELS, A GALLON OF PINE-SOL, AND A FLAME-THROWER.
WHERE IS IT?
BEHIND THE TV.

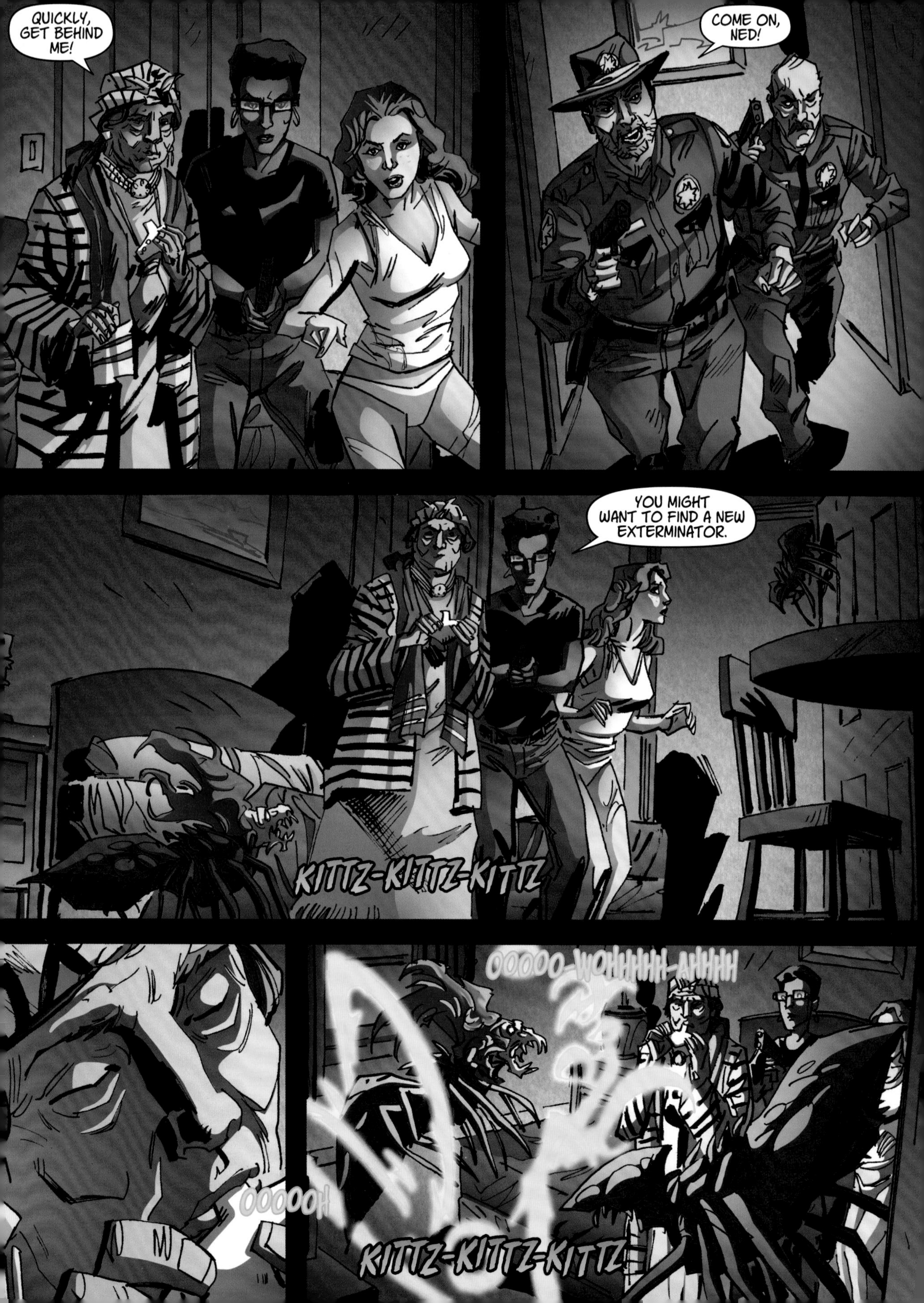
QUICKLY, GET BEHIND ME!
COME ON, NED!
YOU MIGHT WANT TO FIND A NEW EXTERMINATOR.
KITTZ-KITTZ-KITTZ
OOOOOH
OOOOO-WOHHHHH-AHHHH
KITTZ-KITTZ-KITTZ

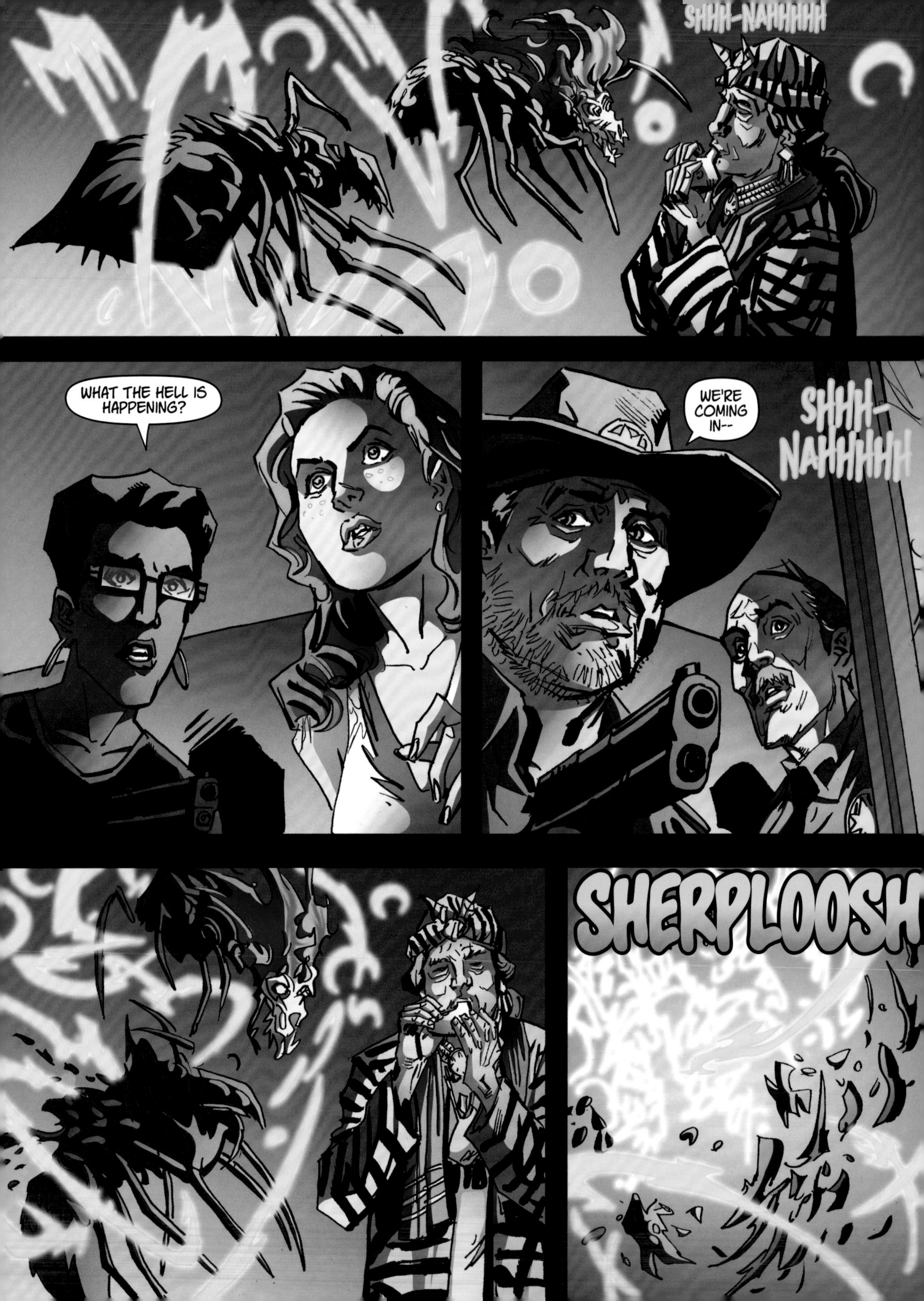
SHHH-NAHHHHH
WHAT THE HELL IS HAPPENING?
WE'RE COMING IN--
SHHH-NAHHHHH
SHERPLOOSH

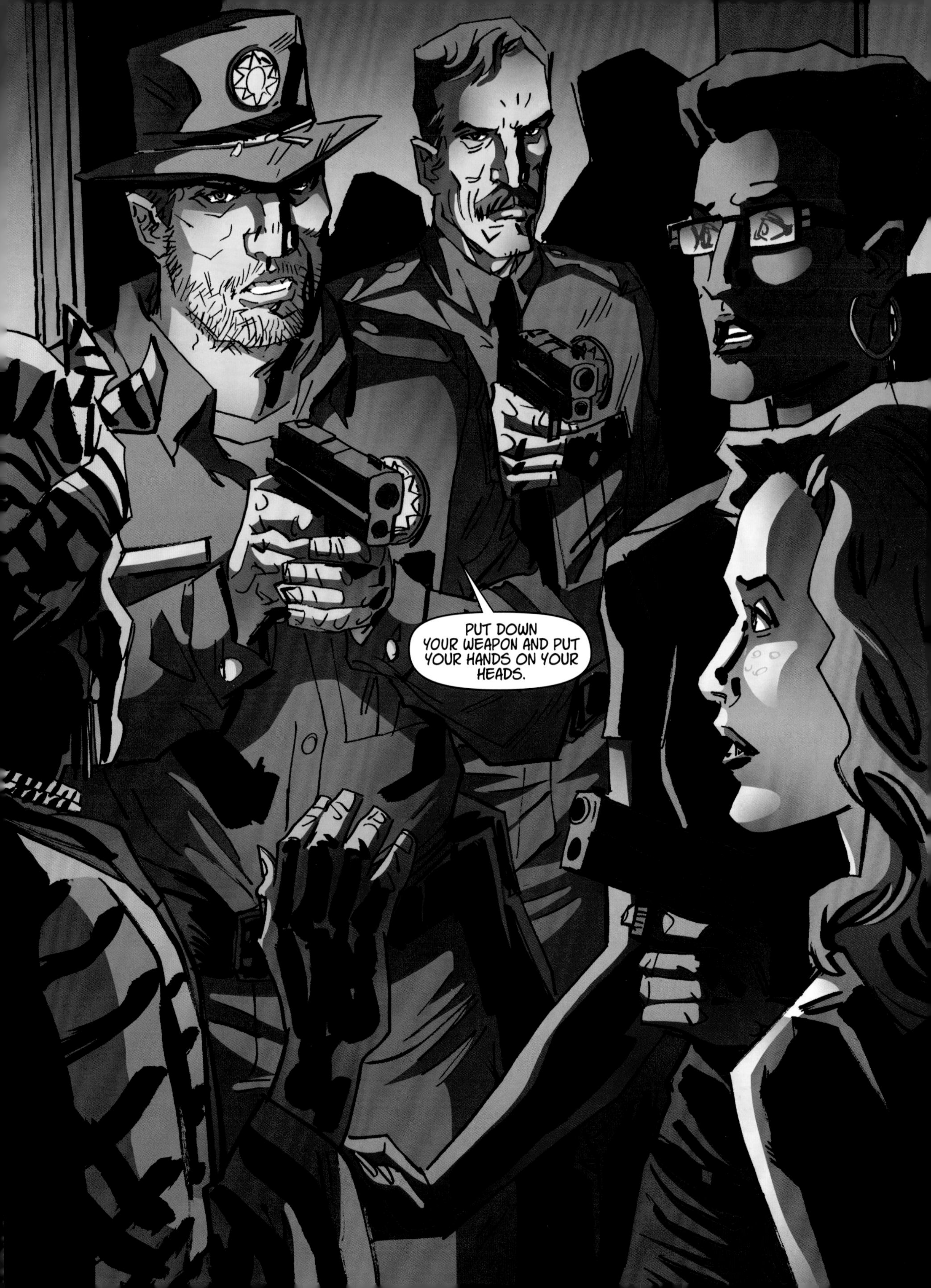
PUT DOWN YOUR WEAPON AND PUT YOUR HANDS ON YOUR HEADS.

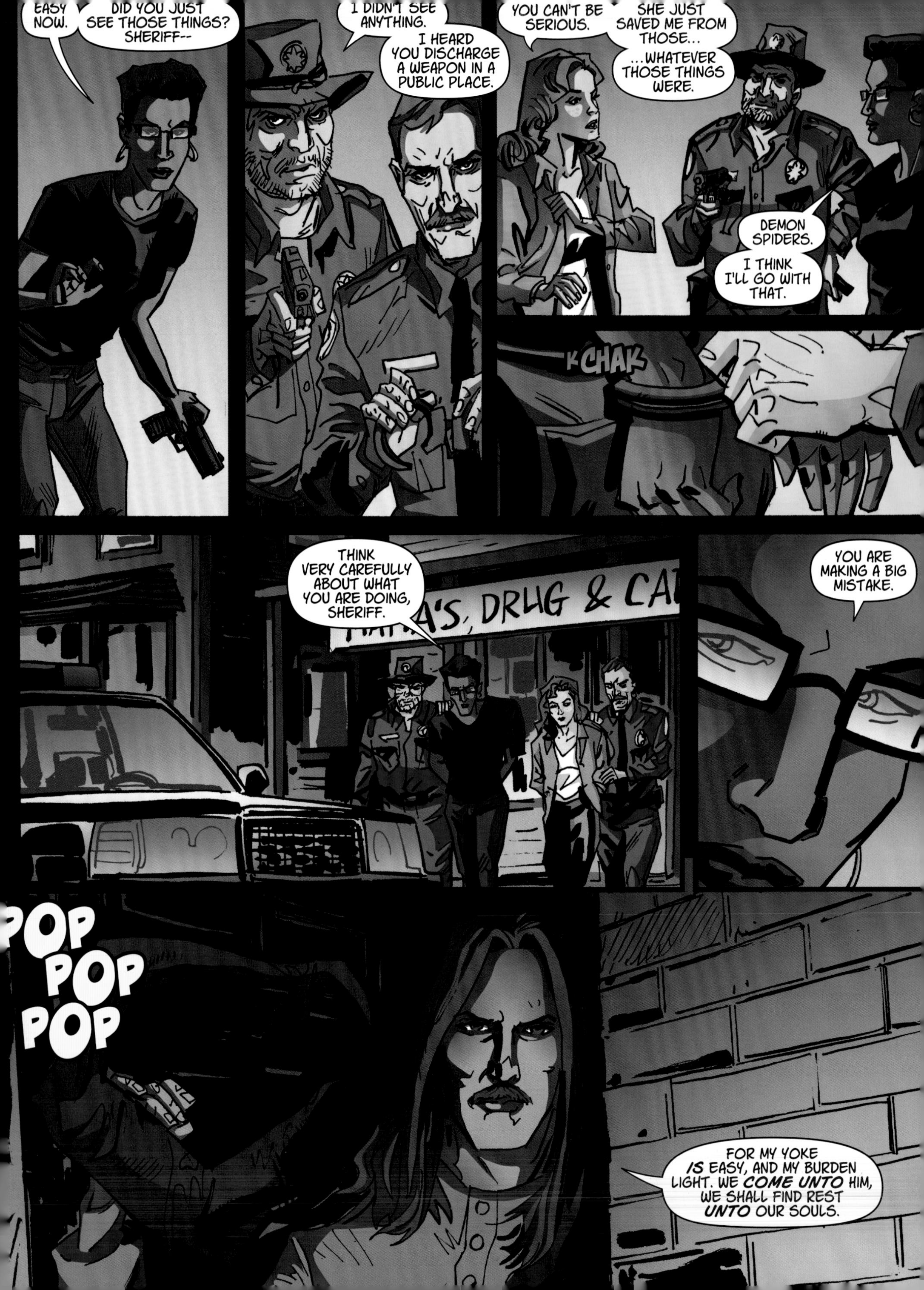
EASY NOW.
DID YOU JUST SEE THOSE THINGS? SHERIFF--
I DIDN'T SEE ANYTHING.
I HEARD YOU DISCHARGE A WEAPON IN A PUBLIC PLACE.
YOU CAN'T BE SERIOUS.
SHE JUST SAVED ME FROM THOSE...
...WHATEVER THOSE THINGS WERE.
DEMON SPIDERS.
I THINK I'LL GO WITH THAT.
KCHAK
THINK VERY CAREFULLY ABOUT WHAT YOU ARE DOING, SHERIFF.
DRUG & CA
YOU ARE MAKING A BIG MISTAKE.
POP POP POP
FOR MY YOKE IS EASY, AND MY BURDEN LIGHT. WE COME UNTO HIM, WE SHALL FIND REST UNTO OUR SOULS.

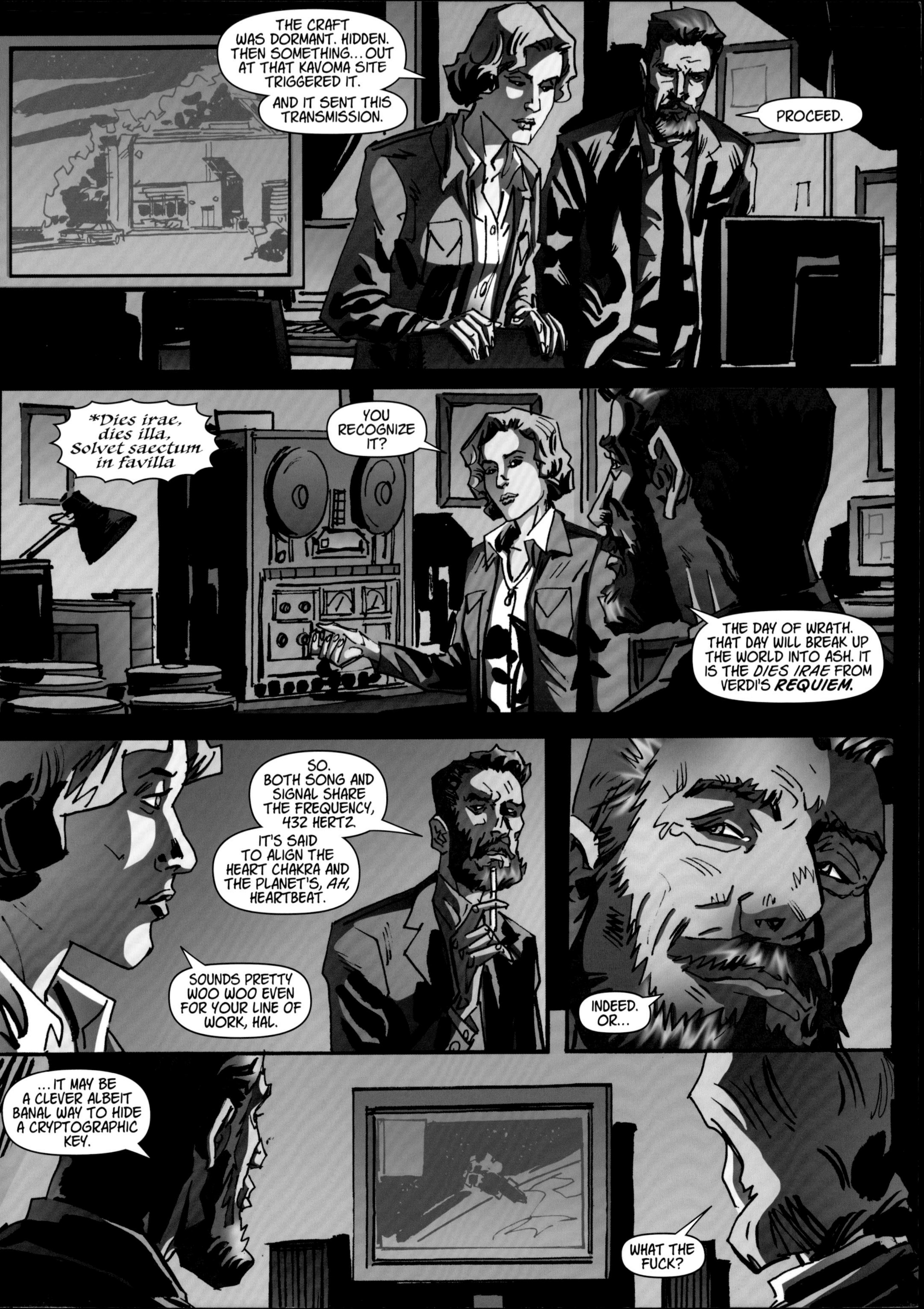
THE CRAFT WAS DORMANT. HIDDEN. THEN SOMETHING... OUT AT THAT KAVOMA SITE TRIGGERED IT.
AND IT SENT THIS TRANSMISSION.
PROCEED.
*Dies irae, dies illa, Solvet saectum in favilla
YOU RECOGNIZE IT?
THE DAY OF WRATH. THAT DAY WILL BREAK UP THE WORLD INTO ASH. IT IS THE DIES IRAE FROM VERDI'S REQUIEM.
SO. BOTH SONG AND SIGNAL SHARE THE FREQUENCY, 432 HERTZ.
IT'S SAID TO ALIGN THE HEART CHAKRA AND THE PLANET'S, AH, HEARTBEAT.
SOUNDS PRETTY WOO WOO EVEN FOR YOUR LINE OF WORK, HAL.
INDEED. OR...
...IT MAY BE A CLEVER ALBEIT BANAL WAY TO HIDE A CRYPTOGRAPHIC KEY.
WHAT THE FUCK?

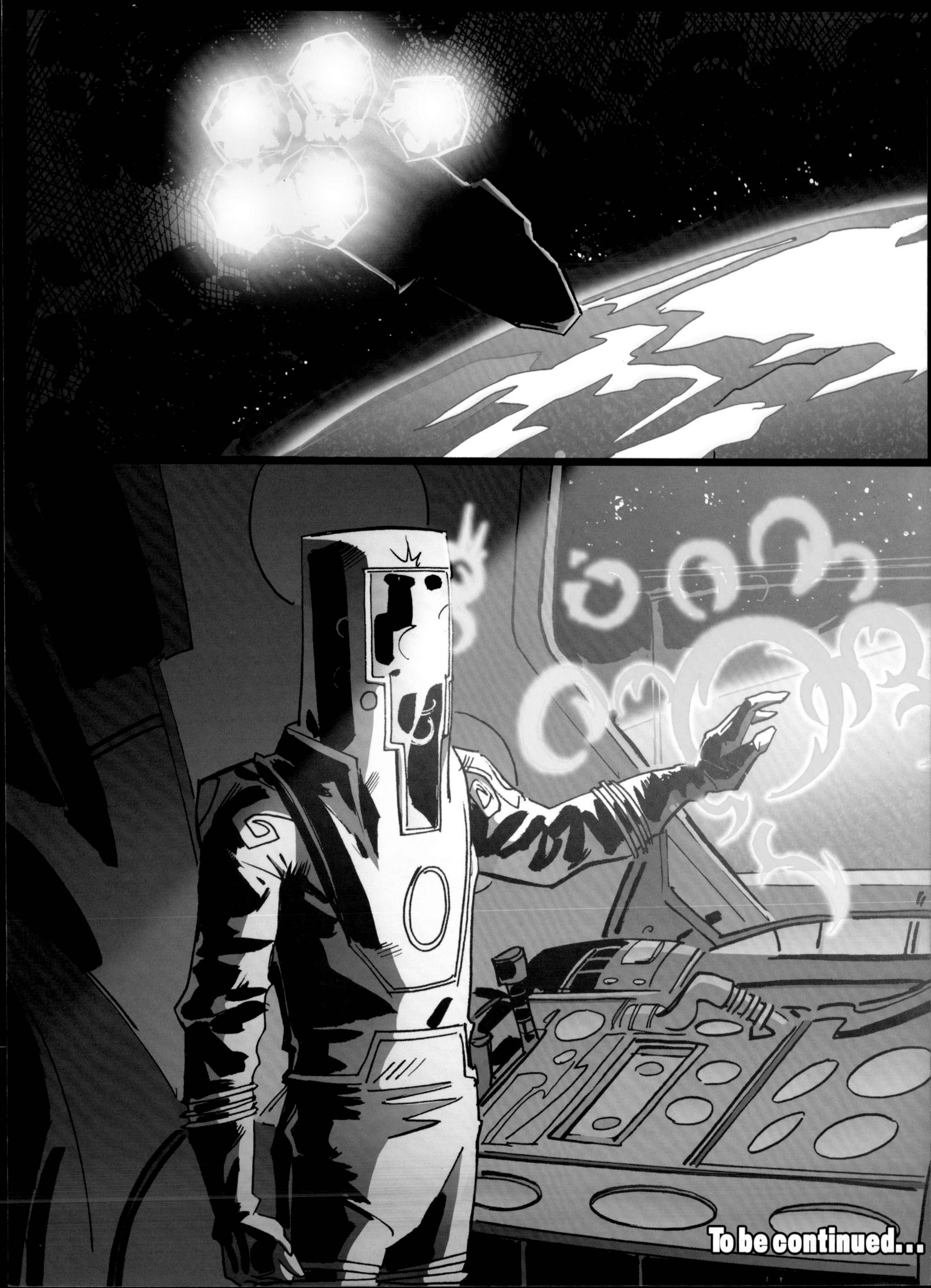
To be continued...

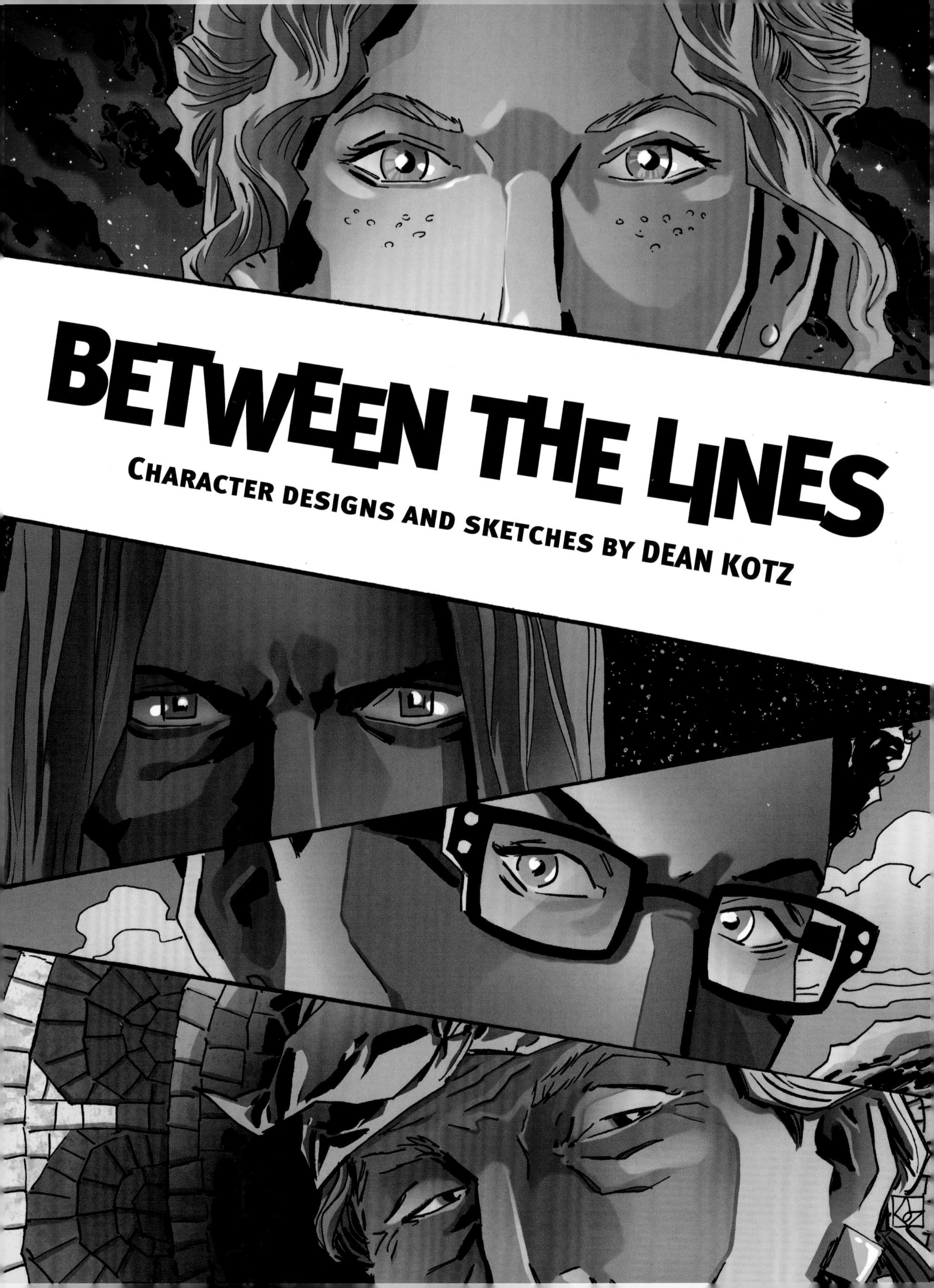
BETWEEN THE LINES
CHARACTER DESIGNS AND SKETCHES BY DEAN KOTZ

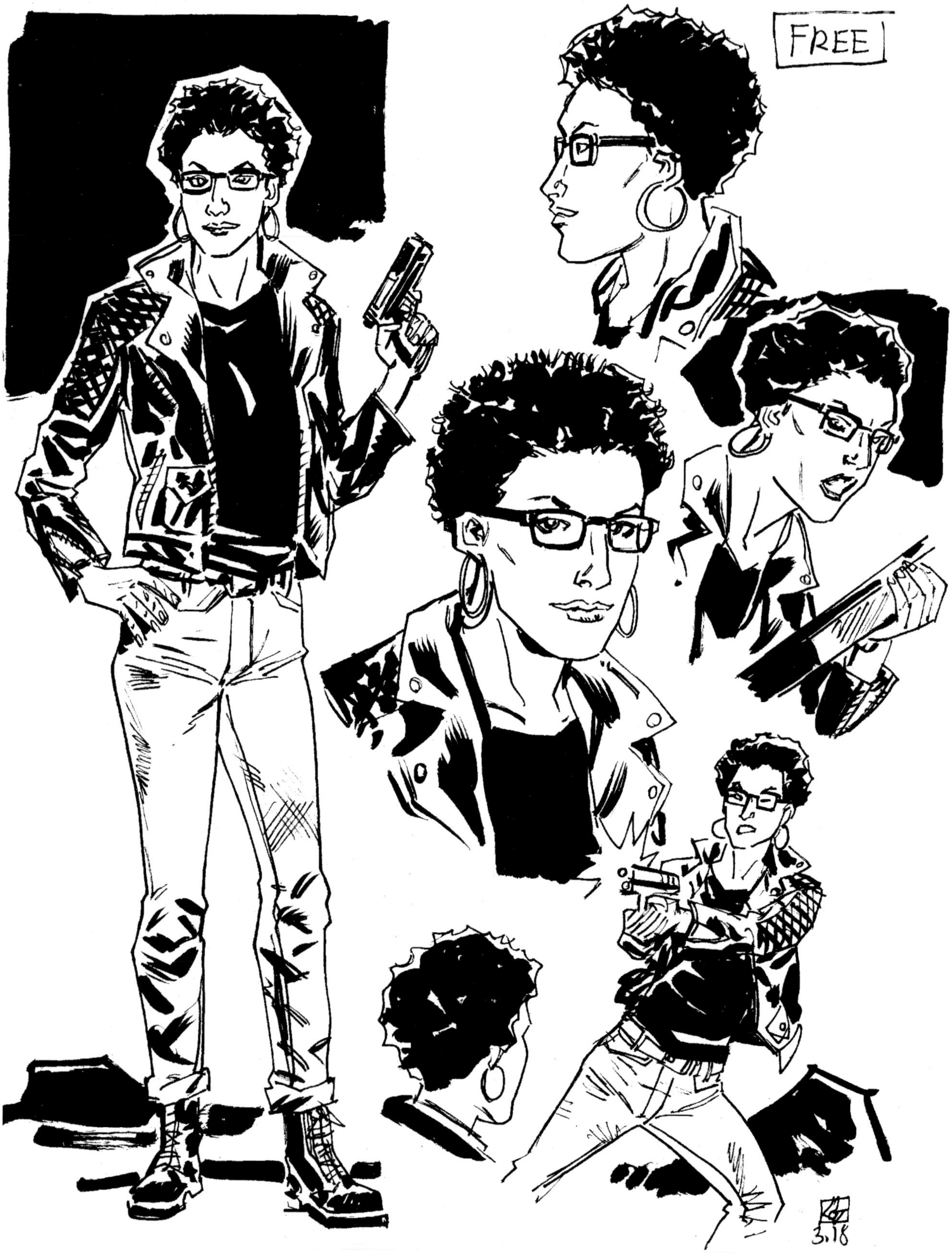
FREE

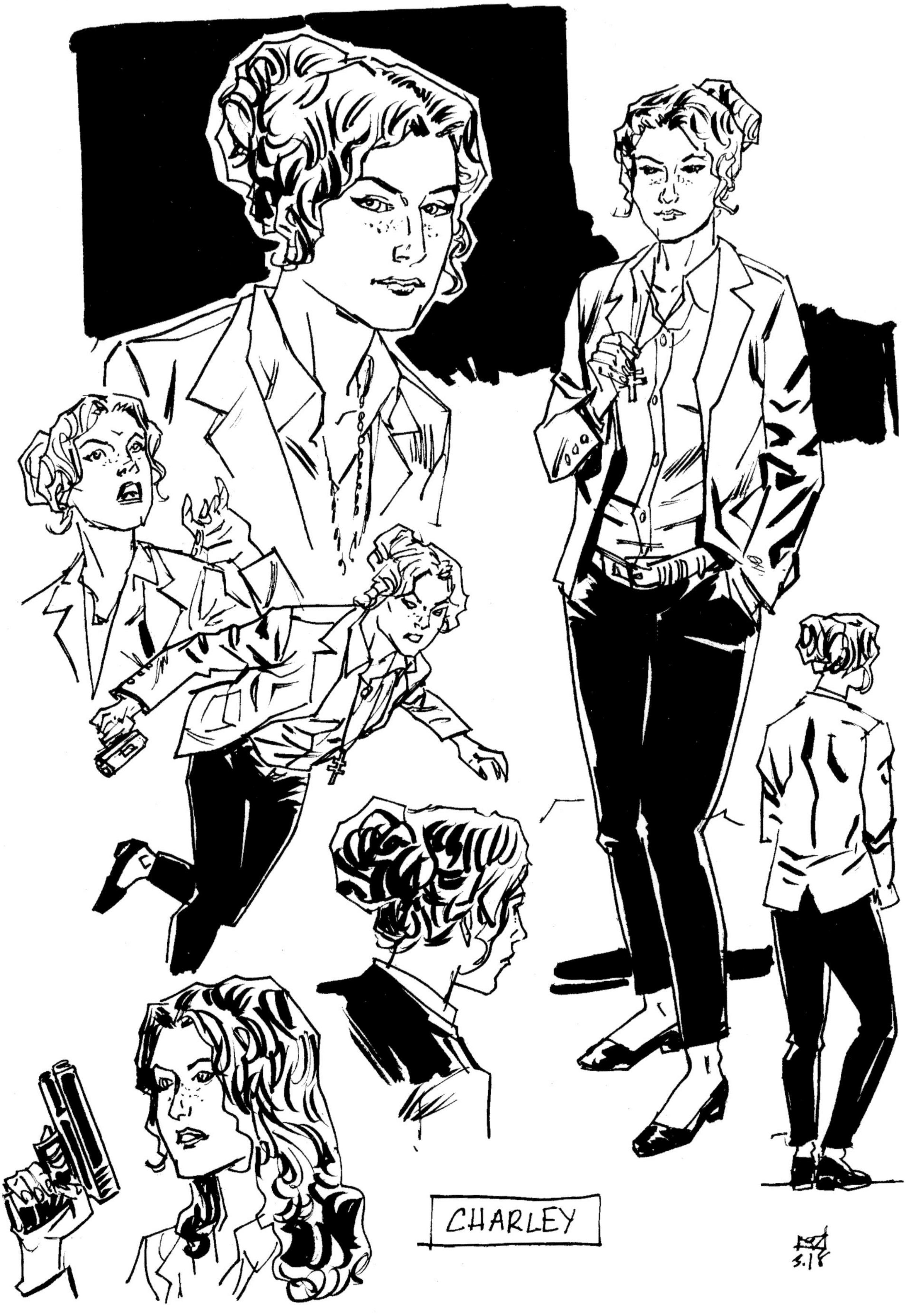
CHARLEY
3.18

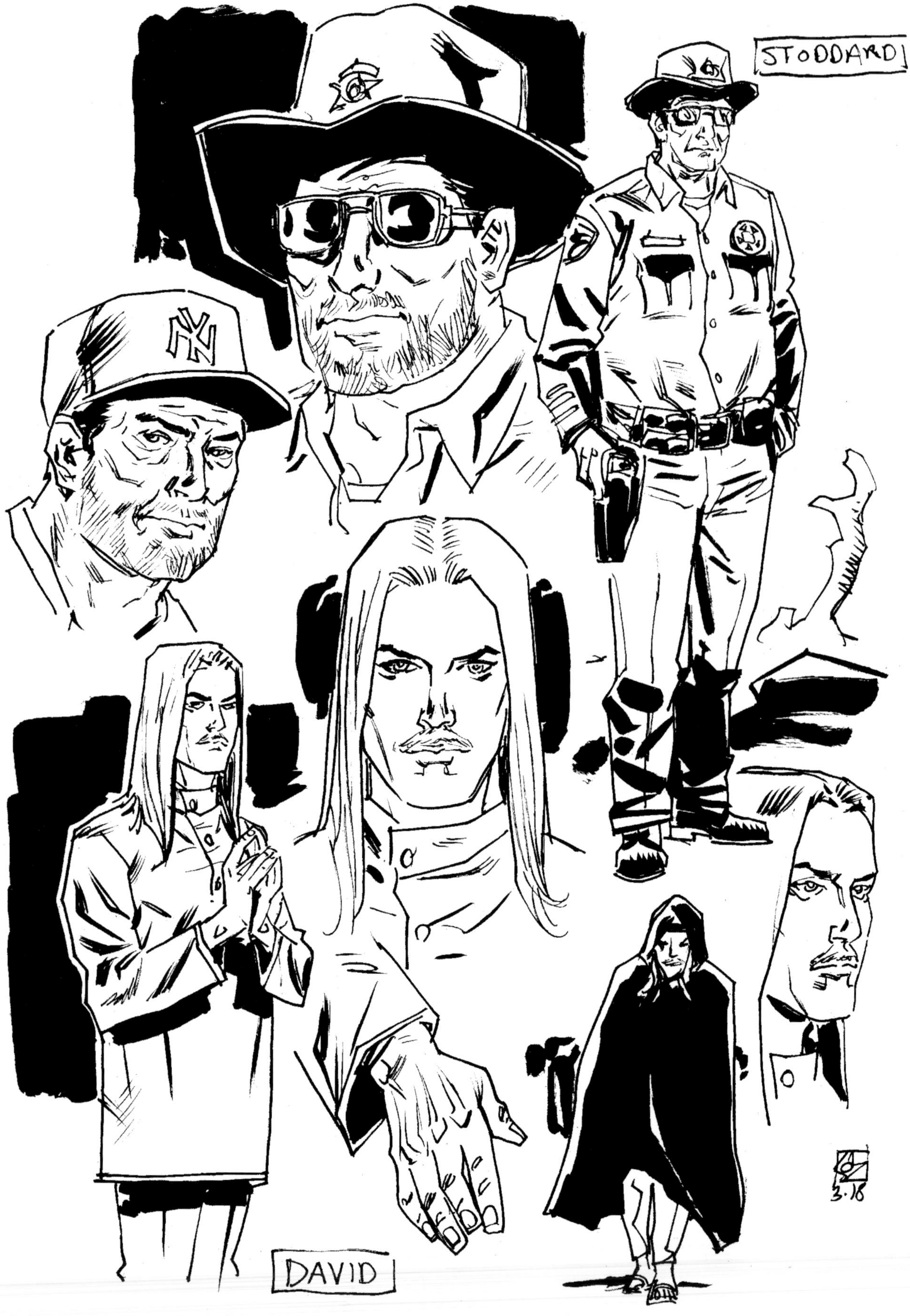
STODDARD
NY
DAVID
3.18

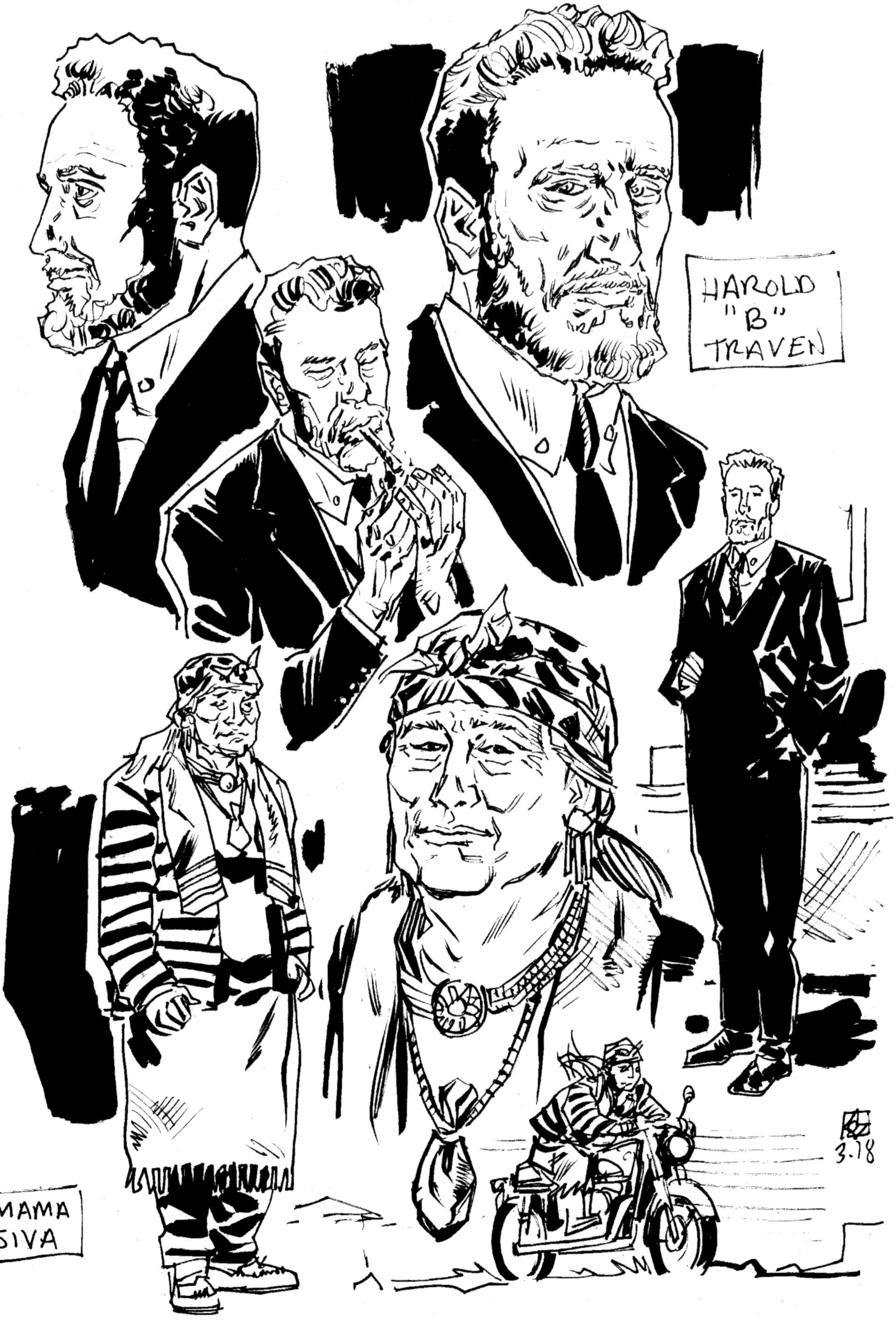
HAROLD "B" TRAVEN
3.18
MAMA SIVA

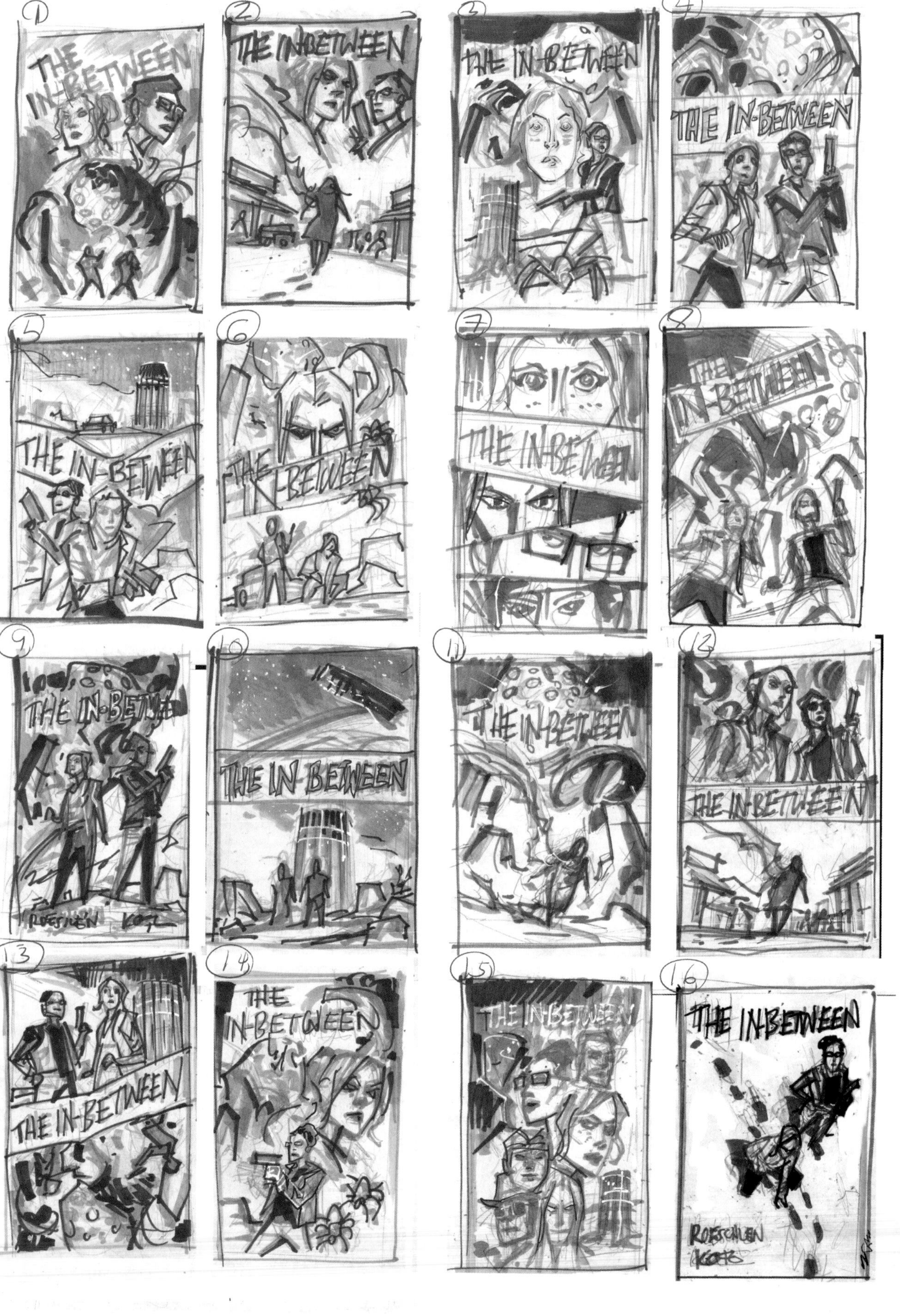
1
THE IN-BETWEEN
2
THE IN-BETWEEN
3
THE IN-BETWEEN
4
THE IN-BETWEEN
5
THE IN-BETWEEN
6
THE IN-BETWEEN
7
THE IN-BETWEEN
8
THE IN-BETWEEN
9
THE IN-BETWEEN
10
THE IN-BETWEEN
11
THE IN-BETWEEN
12
THE IN-BETWEEN
13
THE IN-BETWEEN
14
THE IN-BETWEEN
15
THE IN-BETWEEN
16
THE IN-BETWEEN

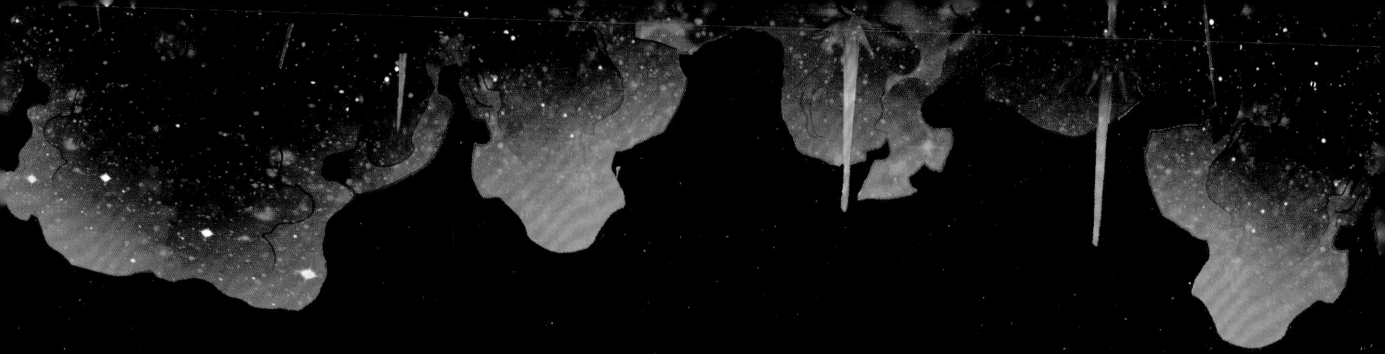

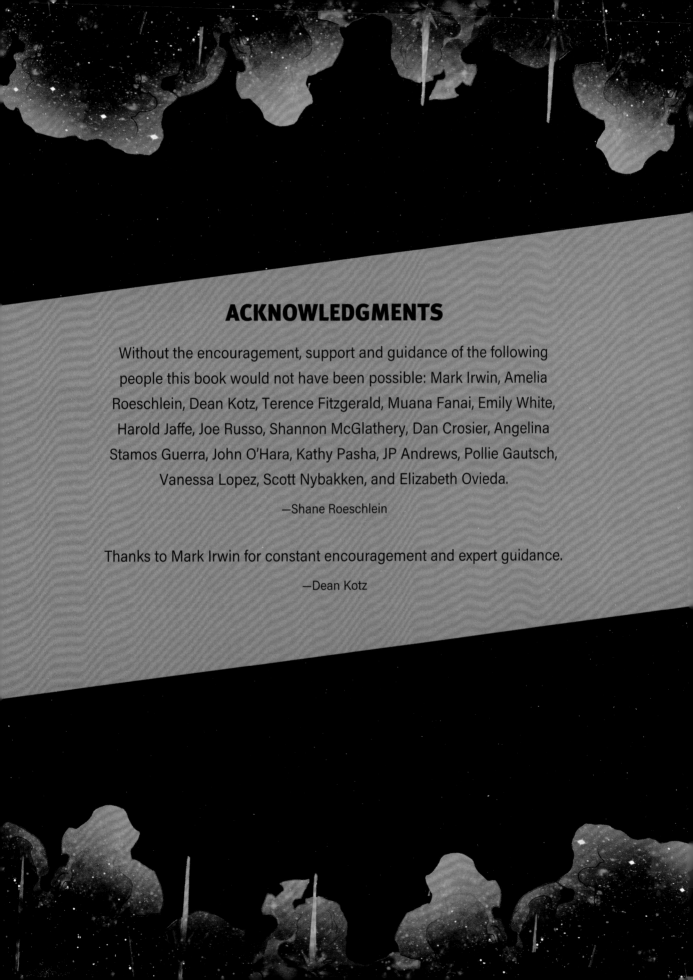

ACKNOWLEDGMENTS

Without the encouragement, support and guidance of the following people this book would not have been possible: Mark Irwin, Amelia Roeschlein, Dean Kotz, Terence Fitzgerald, Muana Fanai, Emily White, Harold Jaffe, Joe Russo, Shannon McGlathery, Dan Crosier, Angelina Stamos Guerra, John O'Hara, Kathy Pasha, JP Andrews, Pollie Gautsch, Vanessa Lopez, Scott Nybakken, and Elizabeth Ovieda.

—Shane Roeschlein

Thanks to Mark Irwin for constant encouragement and expert guidance.

—Dean Kotz

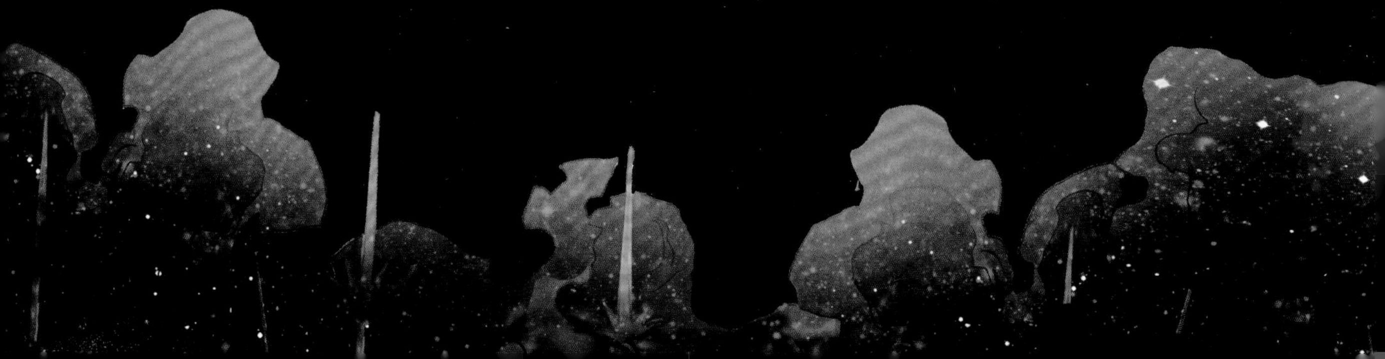

INSIGHT COMICS

An Imprint of Insight Editions
PO Box 3088
San Rafael, CA 94912
www.insighteditions.com

Find us on Facebook: www.facebook.com/InsightEditions

Follow us on Twitter: @insighteditions

Library of Congress Cataloging-in-Publication on Data available.

ISBN: 978-1-68383-462-5

Publisher: Raoul Goff
VP of Licensing and Partnerships: Vanessa Lopez
VP of Manufacturing: Alix Nicholaeff
Editorial Director: Vicki Jaeger
Designer: Brooke McCullum
Editor: Mark Irwin
Associate Editor: Holly Fisher
Editorial Assistant: Elizabeth Ovieda
Production Editor: Elaine Ou
Production Associate: Andy Harper
Senior Production Manager, Subsidiary Rights: Lina s Palma

ROOTS of PEACE   REPLANTED PAPER

Insight Editions, in association with Roots of Peace, will plant two trees for each tree used in the manufacturing of this book. Roots of Peace is an internationally renowned humanitarian organization dedicated to eradicating land mines worldwide and converting war-torn lands into productive farms and wildlife habitats. Roots of Peace will plant two million fruit and nut trees in Afghanistan and provide farmers there with the skills and support necessary for sustainable land use.

Manufactured in China by Insight Editions

10 9 8 7 6 5 4 3 2 1